THE
BELOVED
PRISON

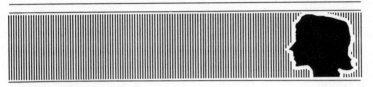

THE BELOVED PRISON

A Journey into the Unknown Self

Lucy Freeman

ST. MARTIN'S PRESS
NEW YORK

Grateful acknowledgment to Random House, Inc., for permission to quote from The Selected Poems of W. H. Auden.

Design by H. Roberts

Library of Congress Cataloging-in-Publication Data

Freeman, Lucy.
    The beloved prison : a journey into the unknown self / Lucy
Freeman.
        p.   cm.
    ISBN 0-312-02866-0
    1. Freeman, Lucy—Mental health. 2. Psychotherapy patients—
United States—Biography. 3. Psychoanalysis—United States—
Biography.   I. Title.
RC464.F73A33   1989
616.89′19′0924—dc19
[B]   89-4077

First Edition

10 9 8 7 6 5 4 3 2 1

This book is dedicated to Dale Schroedel, my niece, and Mollie Theodores, my dear friend, who have been the nearest thing to daughters.

Contents

Acknowledgments

I wish to thank, first and foremost, Robert Weil, Senior Editor, for his many valuable suggestions, his expert editing and his sensitivity to and knowledge of psychoanalytic thought. My thanks to Sandra McCormack for suggesting the title and for her support of the book.

I also thank Bill Thomas, Assistant Editor, for important contributions; Sharyn Rosenblum, publicist at St. Martin's Press, for her enthusiastic spirit; Carol Edwards for her thoughtful copy-editing; and Raquel Jaramillo for her visual interpretation of the search for understanding of the self as portrayed on the cover.

My thanks, too, to Ruth Wreschner, literary agent, who believed in the book's theme. And to my brother, Edward Greenbaum, and two sisters, Sally Rosenberg and Sue Polera, who told of their feelings toward our mother and father. Last, but not least, I am grateful to my final psychoanalyst for encouraging me to write this book.

THE
BELOVED
PRISON

1

The Attack

The man who only eight months before had vowed undying love in front of a minister stared at me. Suddenly he lurched toward me, third glass of scotch in hand.

"You bitch! You dumb bitch!" he shouted.

He slammed the glass down on his onyx coffee table. The furniture as well as the apartment belonged to him. I had sold all my possessions except for a few clothes and treasured books when I left Manhattan to join him in the Windy City. Supposedly to live happily ever after. Raise children, become a wife and mother at long last.

Suddenly, without warning, he drew back his fist, struck me in the right breast. He raised his fist again, then hurled it into my right eye. I fell across the coffee table, slowly sank to the floor. I did not care what came next. I felt too powerless to struggle.

I thought, He wants to destroy me, he is going to

kill me. Then, This has happened before, humiliation at the hands of an angry man. The earlier brutality lost in the haze of memory, though not the ferocity of the attack. The wild look of formidable fury on the man's face.

The little girl within, who once believed in Prince Charming and Sir Galahad, silently cried, Mother, Mother, why aren't you here to protect me from this madman? A cry from the depths of long ago.

And another question, this aimed at my psychoanalyst sitting in safety in his comfortable apartment high in the sky in the center of New York City.

Why didn't the six years I spent on your couch three days a week bring enough inner awareness so I could sense the emotional storms in this man before I raced like a woman possessed into a terrifying marriage?

2

The Thoughtless Act

The night as I tried in vain to fall asleep on the couch in his living room, banished from the double bed in his room, I asked, Why, why, why? What have I done to deserve such brutal assaults?

I met Thomas Johnson (not his real name) when I was sent to Chicago in July 1952, part of *The New York Times* reportorial team covering the double political conventions. Both Democrats and Republicans were choosing candidates for the Presidency.

The city editor, David Joseph, asked me to take the assignment. The past four years I had reported only on mental health after asking the publisher one day, "You have a ship news editor and a real estate editor, don't you think news about the human mind is just as important?" and heard his reply, as he smiled, "Take it, it's yours."

I pointed out to Mr. Joseph, an always amiable editor, "I haven't covered anything but psychoanalytic, psychiatric and psychological news for years."

His voice held a plea. "We need you for the woman's angle. To interview wives of the Presidential candidates. Do some features on women's roles at the convention. No other woman on the city staff has as complete a general news background as you. Please help us out."

"Of course," I said. "It'll be like taking a vacation."

He grimaced. "Vacation? You'll find you never worked so hard in your life."

Twenty-six *Times* reporters, editors and columnists headed west. All men except for three women— Anne O'Hare McCormick, our revered lady political columnist, Ruth Adler, who took photographs and wrote of our tasks for *Times Talk,* of which she was editor, and myself. I roomed with Ruth. Anne had a room of her own, as did the male pundits, including Arthur Krock and James Reston.

The GOP convention came first. Most of us traveled in taxi pools from the Blackstone Hotel to Convention Hall, five miles east of Chicago, an unfragrant spot in the midst of abattoirs. I learned a political convention was part circus, part cerebration. The atmosphere was one of pressured abandon, with excessive drinking by a number of delegates and members of the press after each day's nonstop work. Yet also holding an undercurrent of extreme concern as the choice for the nation's next President got under way.

The Republican convention held drama, what with General Dwight Eisenhower recently home from Paris and NATO. My one moment of Brobdingnagian bedlam occurred as I fought my way through waves of reporters meeting the train that brought in Mame and the general. Republicans seemed to sense he would garner them the first Presidential victory in twenty-four years as he had helped gain victory in Europe.

There were times I thought I would be trampled to death by the exuberant, maniacally aroused mob. Especially in Chicago, the stormy as well as wind-driven city, mobs seem to have a way, as they would again in 1968, of inciting violence in the police.

Mr. Joseph proved right, I never worked harder in my life. I covered three and four assignments a day, whereas in Manhattan it would normally be one. But I also enjoyed a camaraderie I had never experienced. Born of sharing both excitement and fatigue.

My big assignment came during the Democratic convention as I sat in Convention Hall, horns blasting, the delegates cheering loudly, following the evening speech delivered by Mrs. Franklin D. Roosevelt as she welcomed Governor Adlai Stevenson, shortly to be nominated for President. My story made the front page of the *Times*, along with several other accounts of the evening, including Governor Stevenson's moving acceptance speech. I thought, This is the first statesman I have ever seen running for the Presidency.

Ruth later reported in *Times Talk* that "deadline after deadline was met with split-second timing." I wrote speedily, knowing the final New York deadline was near. I was not conscious of one word, the unconscious part of my mind must have taken over. I felt happy that as a result of my first analysis, about to end, I trusted my unconscious somewhat.

The high point for me of both conventions was Governor Stevenson's thoughtful speech. His wife was not present (she was divorcing him, it had just been announced in the newspapers). But he had three stalwart sons by his side, all smiling. His sense of dignity, his graceful language, his humor, endeared him to most reporters. Except the recalcitrant Republicans of the Chicago *Tribune.*

Stevenson also had great personal charm as I learned when I met him at a reception. He clasped my hand, his expressive brown eyes looked straight into mine, he made me feel we were alone on a desert island rather than in the midst of a babbling crowd. He asked, "Have you been enjoying yourself?"

"Yes, ever since you were nominated," I replied.

I knew little about Chicago except it was the home of Carl Sandburg, Nelson Algren, Saul Bellow and Studs Terkel, the Chicago Cubs, the White Sox and the meat-packing industry. Also the exciting jazz of the Bud Freeman, Dave Tough variety. I had one friend there, he worked at the American Hospital Association, whose annual meetings I covered. He invited me to dinner the night the Democrats closed their convention.

This invitation changed the course of my life, perhaps for the better, though there were times when it seemed for the worse.

After we met at the Drake Hotel overlooking Lake Michigan, finished an exotic meal of lobster, shrimp and chocolate mousse, my friend pleaded, "I know how exhausted you are but I've been invited to a party here at the hotel. I'd love it if you'd drop in for a few minutes. The host has read your book and is dying to meet you. Just say hello and run."

The book was *Fight Against Fears.* It had been on *The New York Times* best-seller list almost three months the year before, was bringing in royalties. It described how psychoanalysis helped me to a happier life.

"I'll come for just a few minutes," I said.

We took the elevator to the sixth floor. I was introduced at once to Thomas Johnson, a leading authority in the hospital field. As tired as I felt, I sensed deep charm—in his smile, his manner, his open, handsome face reminiscent of Kirk Douglas, just achieving movie fame. Tom's eyes, the blue-gray of slate, held strength but also a strange, intriguing vulnerability. Lines of laughter were etched from the sides of his nose to his mouth.

"I want to know you better." His voice was warm, husky.

I said apologetically, "I'm sorry but I have to leave almost at once to pack. A few of us are catching a late train home."

He put his hand on my shoulder, the touch felt intimate, I wanted him to keep caressing me. Then he said, "I'll be in New York next week. May I take you to dinner Friday night?"

"Fine. If I don't get an assignment that takes me out of town," I said. "Will you call me at the *Times* when you get in? Just to check."

"Of course." He kissed my cheek, announced to several men and women standing near, "This is my girl from now on."

I sailed out onto Michigan Avenue thinking, Governor Stevenson must be happy tonight, I hope it works out well for him. When I reached the hotel Ruth was already packed. I threw my few clothes into the suitcase. We joined several of the men reporters in the lobby, embarked for the railroad station. Arrangements had been made for us to go and return via the leisure of a train.

The following Friday evening I sat opposite Tom in the Starlight Room of the Waldorf-Astoria. After a scotch he asked, "Will you come to work for my hospital study group in Chicago? I'll pay twice what you're getting at the *Times*."

I was surprised, pleased but thought, Nothing could take me away from my prized work. Said, "Thank you for your generous offer. But I'm happy where I am." Added, "I don't believe I could leave New York to live any place on the globe."

"Not even if you fell in love with someone who lived in a distant city?" Serious tone.

I laughed. "I'm afraid I'm what they call a permanent Manhattanite. I can't think of anything that would blast me out of this city."

During our steak dinner Tom said, "I'll have to think of another reason to persuade you to come to Chicago. Permanently."

I did not dare draw conclusions from that remark. Asked, "Do you find it an exciting city?"

"No place is exciting if you don't have someone you love." Honesty in those expressive eyes. "I haven't found anyone since I was divorced ten years ago."

"Do you have children?"

"A son and daughter who live with my ex-wife in Boston. I see them every so often."

We kept the conversation casual from then on. As he dropped me home in a cab, he said, "I'll be back in two weeks doing research at Mount Sinai Hospital. May I take you to dinner then?"

I agreed, again asked him to call the city room to make sure I was not dispatched to Washington, D. C., or Los Angeles, where a few mental health meetings were scheduled. As I undressed, I wondered how serious his remark he wanted me to live permanently in Chicago. I felt a strong sexual attraction to this man of charm.

After our second Manhattan supper he asked if he could see my ground-floor apartment, part of a large town house just off Madison Avenue on Sixty-third Street. We strolled there from the Waldorf, up Park Avenue, holding hands. Clouds chased each other across a full moon. Every so often as the moon emerged I studied his strong face during the seconds of light.

Suddenly he stopped, turned to me, said, "Let's get married and grow up together."

What a mature thing to say, I thought, he knows we both are not perfect, we have conflicts, as my analyst would be the first to acknowledge about me. But Tom seemed to wish to mature, as did I. That word *mature* as contrasted to *childish* arose at times in my analysis.

My heart pounded the way romantic novels say it should when you fall in love. Is this my chance to be a woman, raise a family? I thought. Dare I make a commitment without knowing this man more intimately?

I asked him into the apartment, he studied my paintings, looked at the two walls of books as I poured scotch. He seemed deep in thought, said little, kissed me tenderly on the lips as he left. Announced he would return in three weeks, asked, "Will you please think over my proposal of marriage?"

"I will," I promised, half-seriously.

My head spun from the scotch. I had racked up one unhappy marriage, did not want to embark on a second disaster. But also did not wish to remain a woman alone.

This offer of love enduring coincided with the last month of my psychoanalysis with Dr. John Thurrott. It would end the final week of October at his request, after six years. I had visited his office three times a week, often absent, however, when sent out of town. He never charged, aware my work would occasionally call for excursions to the far reaches of the country.

At my next session, one of the few times left to discuss anything, I told him of Tom's proposal. As though to say in disdain, See, I don't need *you* anymore. John, as I called him from the start with his approval, had become exceptionally important in my life. I felt accepted as a person for the first time. He never sounded hateful, critical, demanding, didactic but sympathized with my fears and agonies.

I told him once, "I love you very much."

He said gently, "That was the way you felt about your father."

I felt rejected, asked sharply, "Why haven't you ever married?" He had told me he had never taken the marriage vows.

"Because I have a greater need to remain single." Quietly.

Now I said, referring to Tom, "I love him. I need him. And he needs me."

"You felt that way once before."

Reminding me of my first failed marriage. I protested, "I'm more adult now. It's almost three years after the divorce."

"Why don't you take time to make up your mind?" Almost a plea. "Get to know him better?"

"I will," I agreed.

I decided that before I accepted Tom's proposal I would try to learn more about him. I asked Robert Garst, city editor, for a month's leave of absence to work on a second book. He had granted a leave when I wrote the first. Bob, a gentlemanly, aesthetic, slim Virginian, was admired and respected by reporters because he trusted us to get the facts, always backed us up in arguments involving either the general public or the higher-ups. He promptly agreed to the leave, wished me luck.

Telling no one, I flew to Chicago for two weeks to live with Tom. To decide whether we might stand a chance of making a success of that esoteric, highly difficult relationship that so often ends in misery for both man and woman. Tom was nine years older, that seemed a reasonable gap. He appeared to hold high respect for me, as I did for him.

Before I left, I went through the agony of my last session with John. I pleaded, "Do you really think I should stop analysis? I feel so confused. I think I need more help."

"Don't you believe it's about time you were on your own for a while?" That ever gentle voice.

My mother had just left New York to live in Hollywood, Florida, with my married sister Sue. My father had died the previous year after two severe strokes. Three days before he died I decided to take a few days vacation. Usually I scorned vacations, drowned myself in work.

I set off with a friend who had rented a house at Ocean Bay Park. This is the largest community on Fire Island, which lies in the Atlantic Ocean, extending northeast almost half the length of Long Island. Each year Fire Island turns into vacation paradise for sun-starved New Yorkers. At the end of three days I planned to return to New York, then fly to Chicago to cover the annual meeting of the American Psychological Association. It always convenes just before Labor Day.

The second day of vacation, missing the daily decibel of typewriters, telephones and reporter gossip—my adult nursery song—I walked the quarter mile from my friend's phoneless house to the lone phone booth at the ferry slip. I called Frank Adams, assistant city editor, a man whose laughter often boomed contagiously across the city room. I wanted to check on the Chicago assignment.

I reached the *Times* on its special reporters-to-city-desk number, asked for Frank, a former outstanding newspaperman. Hearing his cheerful, "Hello," I responded just as cheerfully, "How are you, Frank? This is Lucy."

Dead silence. Then a worried voice, "Lucy, where *are* you?"

"On Fire Island, Frank." I joked, "Is it against the rules to take a three-day vacation? I got permission from Bob Garst."

"It's not that, Lucy dear," he said. "Your family has been frantically trying to reach you for two days. So have I."

"There's no phone in the house where I'm staying so I couldn't leave a number." I wondered what could be so urgent. "I'm calling you from a booth at the ferry slip."

Frank said slowly, "I hate to be the one to tell you this, Lucy. Your father is dead."

My father had suffered a first stroke two years before at fifty-nine, then a year later a second stroke left him paralyzed on his right side. Through rehabilitation he regained almost the full use of his limbs. He even managed to drive a car with a special shift to his office in New York three days a week. He could move quite freely, we thought he would eventually regain full use of his right arm and leg.

I could not believe the tragic words traveling over the phone to Fire Island from the city desk. I insisted, "My father *can't* be dead. I saw him last week and he was fine."

I had visited his home for an outdoor picnic. While waiting for a steak to broil on his charcoal grill he had searched for and found a four-leaf clover, handed it to me for luck.

"I'm very sorry, Lucy dear, but your father died the night before last," Frank was saying.

"Oh, Frank!" A little girl with a shaft through her heart.

"I know what he meant to you. You don't have to go on that Chicago assignment. Take a few days off."

"Of course I'll go!" Nothing, not even the death of my adored father (perhaps especially the death of my adored father because of its intense pain from which I needed to flee) would interfere with work. *He* had taught me work comes first. Nor did I desire empty hours in which to grieve, feel even sorrier for myself.

"I'm coming right home," I said. Added gratefully, "I'm glad you were the one to tell me." I cherished his friendship more than ever.

I ran like one demented out of that phone booth, no Kleenex, no handkerchief to dry the tears streaming down my face. I flew over the boardwalk as if pursued by rapists, as in my nightmares. I thought, Why did I have to be on vacation when my father died, why didn't I tell someone where I would be, maybe they were holding his funeral that very moment.

I rushed into my friend's house, sobbed, "My father just died." He took me in his arms, held me close. I dried my tears on paper napkins, threw toothbrush, nightgown, bathing suit and beach robe into my suitcase. He walked me to the dock, a ferry was pulling in. He offered to ride to Bay Shore but I told him I wished to be alone, not wanting him to see me awash in tears.

On the half-hour ride across the Great South Bay, the warm breeze stirred memories of days on my father's boat as we headed up Long Island Sound, once even to Martha's Vineyard to see his younger brother, my Uncle Ed. I thought, I did not even get the chance to kiss my father goodbye, I will never again feel his cheek against my lips or his arms around me.

What was the use of living, now there would be no one who loved me. Who would call me "sweetheart" as though he meant it? Or taunt me for dressing as though bound for a ragpickers' ball?

When I reached the mainland I dashed for a phone booth. First I called my father's second wife, Donna, to find out when the funeral would be held. She said worriedly, "Lucy, where on earth are you? We've tried so hard to reach you."

I explained, she told me the funeral would take place the following morning, invited me to stay the night at her home. I said I would go directly to my apartment, change into a black faille suit, take an evening train to Mamaroneck.

Then I made a second important call. To my mother, living alone at the Hotel Lombardy at 111 East Fifty-sixth Street. I expected to find her in hysterics.

"Hello." Her voice was sweet as always when answering the phone, as though expecting Cary Grant.

"Mother?" I shrieked. "Are you all right?"

"I'm fine." Not the tone of utter desolation but calm. "Where have you been?"

"On Fire Island for two days. My first vacation in three years." Bitterly, "That'll teach me to take one."

"I'm sorry your vacation has such a sad ending, Lucy."

"How do you *really* feel, Mother?" I did not believe she was "fine," she was putting on a show, trying to keep up her spirit, restrain from wailing and weeping.

"I'm really all right, Lucy," she said.

"Don't you feel like crying?" She *must* have felt a loss even though she had not lived with him for sixteen years.

"I cried yesterday when I first heard."

What a short spell of sorrow, I thought, did she really hate him so much because of his abandonment of her and the children? Had she perhaps not even shed a tear, glad he was dead, punished without the chance of pardon?

"We'll go to the funeral together." I would change plans, call my father's wife, tell her I was with my mother and we would appear at the funeral service.

"I'm not going," Mother announced.

"Not going?"

This was heresy. She could not hold that intense a hate.

"No." Firmly.

"Why not?" Confusedly.

"Because I don't want to."

I did not believe she would refuse to attend my father's funeral. Even if she felt uncomfortable in the presence of his second wife, Mother was, after all, the honored first wife who bore him four children.

"Mother, please come with me to the funeral," I begged. My last attempt.

"Call me when you get back, Lucy." A voice that informed me no one could persuade her.

Funeral services were held in a wooded area of White Plains at the synagogue on Soundview Avenue. Herbert Wolff, one of my father's law partners, delivered the eulogy. I sat between my sister Sue and my sister Sally, the litany on my lips, Don't cry, don't cry, don't make a fool of yourself. It worked until we reached Mount Hope Cemetery in Ardsley. Watching the coffin lowered into the grave, thinking of my father's spirited mind consigned to oblivion, I walked away, turned my back to the other mourners to hide the stream of tears.

My brother, stricken as the rest of us, tried to comfort his sisters and stepsisters, Nancy and Alice, now suddenly the sole man in my father's two families. As we followed the hearse bearing my father's coffin to the cemetery, my brother remarked wryly, "Laurie would have liked riding in this latest model Cadillac." We children called him Laurie, at his request, the short version of Lawrence. The Cadillac was his favorite car, he owned several during his lifetime.

Sue said sadly, "It was a crime Laurie died so

young. He wanted so very much to live. I never saw anyone who wanted to live more."

And now there would be no one to help me decide what to do when I felt confused, as I did about Tom. I was alone, adrift on a ship at sea, without compass, waves threatening high. I wanted to leave New York yet did not want to leave the city of my birth and work. Wanted to marry Tom yet did not want to marry him. Unsure I could be a "proper" wife, whatever that meant.

Perhaps two weeks of living with him would provide the answer. As yet we were not sexually involved and this was a risk, I knew. He kissed me passionately but made no overtures beyond that. The third time he visited New York I asked if he wanted to stay overnight. He said, "Let's wait until we are married. The old-fashioned way." I felt rejected but admired his gallantry.

When I told John what Tom said, he commented, "This may be a way of telling you he is unsure of himself sexually." Then added a warning, "He may be hiding the violence of those unable to perform sexually."

And then asked, "Do you want to risk getting killed?"

I was shocked. "What do you mean?" Tom had spoken of love, not death.

"When men cannot perform sexually with a woman, they blame the woman. She becomes in fantasy the mother of infancy who has made them impotent. Castrated them. They may become violent with a wife. Want to kill her."

This was beyond my sexual ken. I thought Tom gallant and caring in not wanting sex before marriage. Unlike the promiscuous men who had wandered my way at times.

I sighed, said to John, "I'll find out in Chicago if he is able to have sex." Added sarcastically, "He had two children so we know he performed at least twice."

Ending the last session, John shook my hand warmly. I held back tears until I reached the street, then shed a few. I felt I had come a long emotional distance in analysis.

Tom met me at Midway Airport, hugged me close, kissed me ardently. We drove to his apartment, a one-bedroom in a high-rise overlooking Lake Michigan, at 1350 Lake Shore Drive, just north of the Drake Hotel. He had bought dramatic Bird of Paradise flowers to fill a huge vase.

That night in his double bed we made love. I felt his passion and my own, no longer doubted his sexual ability or our compatability. I intended to work on my book but during the two weeks neither of us completed much work. He showed me the Art Institute, the University of Chicago on the South Side, the elegant shops of Michigan Avenue.

The last day he urged, as we stood bundled in winter wear at the airport, "Marry me as soon as you can. Resign your job. Come back for a Christmas Eve ceremony."

As the plane rose above the snowdrifts I thought, I respect his dedication to better care for the poor and needy in the nation's hospitals, I love him, yearn to be close to him, wish to know him better, he seems to love me, he is able to express himself sexually. He is no murderer as John suggested he might be. Why not try to be a wife, have children? I can write books as easily in Chicago as New York. And without that dreaded daily deadline.

He called later that week. I told him I would resign from the *Times*. We set the date of our wedding for the evening of December 24. I wondered how I would break the news to my friends on the paper.

The next day I walked slowly over to the city desk.

Frank had been promoted from assistant day city editor to day city editor while I was gone.

I sat down on the chair reserved for reporters as they briefly described their assignment before writing it, were told how many pages their copy should cover.

Frank smiled, asked, "How was your leave? We missed you."

I said, not daring to look into the eyes of one of my closest friends, "I'm resigning to get married and live in Chicago, Frank."

He stared at me in disbelief, as though I had just told him I was growing another head. Then he said sadly, "What a way to start my first week as day city editor. Your resignation."

I said nothing, thought, Am I doing the right thing? Will I regret this?

As if reading my mind, Frank asked, "Are you sure this is what you want to do, Lucy?"

"*Want* to do. And *have* to do." I sighed. "I know you'll understand. I want to be like other women. Raise a family."

"I do understand." Grimly, "It's just that I hate to lose you. So will the other men. You've made a lot of friends here."

"I feel sad at leaving," I admitted. "But the job is no longer enough, Frank." He was happily married, the father of two delightful daughters. I had often visited his home in Rye. He had been my bridge teacher during the hours after stories were handed in and we were required to remain in case copy editors had questions.

He put out his hand. "Good luck, dear. I hope you raise a large and happy family."

I promised, "After the marriage in Chicago on Christmas Eve, we'll come back and Tom can meet all my friends. We'll give a party at Sardi's."

"*We'll* give the party," Frank said.

I faced renting my spacious apartment, placed a sublet ad in the paper. Following the financial success of my first book I had been able to quit the cell on East Forty-ninth Street, where crosstown buses roared past day and night, though fewer at night.

Two dashing gentlemen responded to the ad. They offered to take over the lease, buy the purple sofa, the gray carpet. As well as the flowered green drapes that pulled across windows overlooking a small garden. My blooming begonias quickly wilted in a dirt destitute of whatever richness plants need to grow in this city of soot.

We haggled over prices. They wanted me to give away furniture, carpet and drapes. We finally agreed on what to me was a pittance. I did not feel guilty at neglecting to inform them a covey of pigeons had set up house directly over the bedroom and would be a 6 A.M. menace to sleep. As they left, one told me he was Huntington Hartford, heir to the A & P Tea Company fortune. The other said he had just been divorced from Gypsy Rose Lee, the famous stripteaser. He was the one who would occupy the apartment.

I packed to ship westward a few of my cherished books, including every girl's classics: *Little Women, Little Men, Heidi, Back of the North Wind* and *Alice's Adventures in Wonderland.* Also several leather-bound sets from my girlhood home in Larchmont, including the entire works of Edgar Allan Poe and Washington Irving.

I also included several paintings, chiefly of the sea, but only a few dresses and lingerie, knowing closet space in Chicago was limited. I gave away to relatives and friends other paintings and bric-a-brac I treasured.

On the flight to Midway, carrying a suitcase, I felt I had acted from the heart. I truly believed a far happier life lay ahead with this charming, intelligent, loving man. I had been rescued from the daily grind, from the pressure of the fast-moving world of the reporter, from a slavey-like existence of being ordered about by editors. I would now be my own boss, leisurely finish books I chose to write. Not assignments others commanded me to cover.

I could also, joyous thought, look at a scene and not have to produce words to describe it for newspaper readers. I was free to take pleasure in seeing without working for my daily bread. Escape from bondage to the everyday chore of using words in an original way to attract readers. Unless you have done this day after day, year after year, your eye on the clock, you cannot know the surge of joy at such release.

Tom and I were married Christmas Eve in the chapel of a Presbyterian church (he was Presbyterian) near the University of Chicago. Unlike my first marriage, where the ceremony was jammed with relatives and friends from the newspaper, no member of my family, nor anyone I knew, was present. Just Tom's few friends, the minister, Tom and I.

The best man was one of Tom's hospital colleagues. This man's wife, whom I met the very moment before the ceremony, served as my matron of honor. We stood in the quiet of the darkened, empty church and I felt my first moment of alarm. Told myself, Lucy, you are committing a wild, abandoned act in marrying a relatively unknown man. Yet knowing too, nothing could have restrained me at this time of my life from embarking on the marriage.

As the minister read the sacred words of the marital vow I thought, My father who art in heaven, my hallowed, brilliant, awesome, beloved father, who loved me dearly even though you twice slapped me viciously and sometimes cut me down with sarcastic words, I miss you acutely at this strange moment in an unknown city, by my side a man who might be saint or monster. You stood next to me during my first marriage as you gave me away, now I stand alone in sudden sadness.

I wanted with all my heart to believe Tom and I would live happily ever after. I thought my years on the couch would enable me to go forth and find love and fulfillment as a woman. And if this meant throwing away my career, fine. I was tired of belonging nowhere. To nobody.

The years of glamour and excitement, chasing all over the city, the nation, held a certain allure, though at times terror, too. They were now part of the punitive past. I was ready to give up the glory of the by-line and the chase for news, for which I had been rewarded financially and earned a certain prestige but for which I also paid a price as the work took me further and further from feeling a complete woman.

I was ready to live in a city where I knew no one, start anew. Become the perfect wife for my perfect husband. Little did I know within a few months I would feel like Cinderella led to the slaughterhouse. Like all those Chicago cows.

3

The Difficult Decision

With all the strength I could call forth from brain and body I tried to be a complete wife. I shopped for food, cooked dinner each night, something I had never done before because my first husband enjoyed cooking and I did not. I cleaned up after each meal, took care of the laundry, both Tom's and my own, using the washer and dryer on the top floor. This was also something I had never done before, I had always sent laundry out.

I enjoyed the freedom of a day without a deadline for the first time in my working life. I had been on a newspaper at least eight hours a day, often longer, five days a week since graduating from Bennington College.

While on the *Times* I spent seven days a week at work, on my two days off writing articles for the Sunday magazine section or book review. Interviewed actors and actresses for the drama section. I once told Lester

Markel, editor of the Sunday *Times*, "Thank you, Mr. Markel, for contributing money to my analysis."

He smiled, said, "Glad to help out such a worthy cause."

No longer did I wish to fulfill one of my strongest childhood wishes—to meet every person in the world and shake his hand, become his friend. From the age of five I thought everyone I met was fascinating.

I now felt respectable, less the rebel. More feminine, no longer the golf or baseball player of high school days. I wanted to take care of Tom, learn the dishes he desired, be the world's finest laundress.

Those first months were romantic storybook days of intimate closeness. Then Tom started to spend weekends away from Chicago, busy with his survey of the nation's hospitals. He had started his career as a social worker, then became a national authority on hospital care.

While he was gone I finished writing my second book, *Hope for the Troubled*. It described how unhappy men and women could cleanse themselves through therapy of "that perilous stuff which weighs upon the heart."

Then slowly, so slowly I was not aware of its developing deadly impact, a cloud of darkness closed in on us. The apartment turned into an enemy. Our clothes and other possessions were jammed in disorder into three closets. My paintings and books remained in storage on Division Street because of lack of space. Tom's art, mostly Klee reproductions, graced the living room, a room I found depressing with its somber shades of browns, grays and beiges. My taste ran to colorful lush blues, purples and greens.

The same muted colors in abstract patterns adorned the curtains. A wire mobile swung from the living room ceiling over the brown couch. Our bedroom, doubling as Tom's study, was black and white. The whole seemed sterile, though in good taste.

We had few interests in common, he liked Mozart and Beethoven, played classical music constantly on the radio. I preferred Goodman and Basie but never got the chance to hear them. I loved to dance, he did not know how. I liked bridge and poker, he thought playing cards or any other game frivolous, a waste of time. His idea of athletics was to wash his red Dodge on Sunday morning. He scorned my choice of golf or tennis as puerile.

Feelings of the magical intimacy we once shared slowly vanished. One night after I had been unable to sleep for hours, when I realized he was still awake I reached for him, caressed his hair with my lips. He did not move. I whispered, "Don't you want me?"

"I really don't care," he said.

I huddled on the far side of the bed. I would not beg for sex. A man was supposed to feel pleasure from a woman's touch, not grudgingly endure a mechanical act without affection or tenderness. I felt as though struck across the face. He called me "wife" in front of visitors but it was the mouthing of a word, no tone of love. I realized I did not think of myself as "Mrs. Johnson" but still used "Freeman" as though it were my married name.

He stopped making sexual overtures, lost all interest in my body and mind. I wondered if he felt smothered in that small apartment, wanted his space back.

When he left for work in downtown Chicago each weekday morning, I roamed the apartment like a fish out of water, gasping for breath. I started to detest the chores of housework, shopping and laundry. I thought sex the reward for these odious jobs and if sex ceased, why carry them out? I stared dazedly at the small patch of Lake Michigan available as our eastward view. Daydreamed of the phone ringing on my desk in the city room, someone calling to alert me to an important news story in the mental health field.

Anne Targ, wife of William Targ, editor at World Publishing Company, both of whom had become friends in New York, sent me a cartoon from *The New Yorker*. It showed a middle-aged, balding and plump man standing at the open door of his apartment, home from work, watching his unhappy wife scrub the floor. He announces, "Cinderella! Your Prince Charming is home!" Anne wrote, "When I saw the enclosed cartoon I knew only you would feel as I do about housework. How goes it?"

I deeply resented falling to my knees, soaping bathroom and kitchen floors or vacuuming rugs. Tom believed we should not hire a cleaning woman but save money for a larger apartment. I wondered if we would ever look for one, if the desire to save the marriage was now that strong.

One day I rebelled, thought, I will no longer do this foul menial work. My mother once told me, "Dust a little if you must but never scrub a floor." She never did, we always had a maid, cook and usually a chauffeur. I thought it demeaning to swish around brush and soap just because Tom thought this the image of "woman." It was debasing to a wife if she did not wish to do this work. I had deluded myself that becoming a full-time housewife would make me feel feminine. It made me feel a savagely angry slave.

My greatest shock was realizing how much Tom depended on alcohol. He had concealed this perfectly before we married. He now consumed three or four scotches each night before dinner as I sipped one. I watched him metamorphose either into depression, where he said not a word, or anger, when he would attack with words.

At first only unspoken fury arose between us like a crimson fog. No angry charges hurled but each silently accusing the other of failure in love.

Tom walked in the door each evening, acted as though I were an intruder in his crowded quarters. One night, after his usual scotches, he accused, "You don't know how to set the right climate for marriage. Or for sex."

I did not know what he meant. No other man had referred to "climate for sex" or accused me of lacking a quality because he was emotionally or physically unable to make love.

Tom would sometimes keep me up into the early hours of the morning arguing the senseless, "Why can't you change?" An accusation those not in tune emotionally and sexually hurl at each other.

Because sleep was cut short with quarrel, we both consumed Benzedrine during the day, sleeping pills at night. I had never downed more than an occasional aspirin, this medical regime with which Tom seemed well acquainted was new and, I thought, destructive to both. He explained he had resorted to it before I came on the scene because he had difficulty sleeping soundly.

One evening he loosed a verbally violent attack. He sneered, "You've changed! You're not the woman I fell in love with. You can be quite a bitch."

No man or woman had ever accused me of bitchlike qualities, I had tried all my life to please everybody. John had suggested many times, "Please try to be more assertive. Stand up for yourself when you believe you are right. People take advantage of you."

I asked Tom, pleading, "How have I changed?"

"You don't understand me," he stormed. "You never did. I was blind. You lied to me. You married me under false pretenses."

I was stunned, managed to ask, "What did I promise you? Tell me. I'll try to change."

He shook his head. "You can't. You couldn't possibly understand me. You haven't got the capacity. How could I have been so blind?"

I was to hear this assaultive litany over and over the next few months, except the nights he would not speak a word, even when I served his favorite dinner, pot roast with mashed potatoes and peas. Part of me thought I might be able to change enough so his love would return but a larger part knew the marriage had struck the rocks of incompatibility.

I thought of John's warning against marrying without knowing the man. Realized I had plunged full speed ahead into disaster. Blind, deaf and dumb, unaware of signs that told of emotional danger. I could not blame Tom. I could have said no when he proposed. I had only myself to charge with responsibility.

I realized the utter hopelessness of it when Anne and Bill Targ visited their hometown. I invited them to dinner and Tom promised to leave work early. I concocted a delicious prune whip, one of my first desserts not imported from local bakeries. I laughed, thinking of Anne's reply when I wrote asking for recipes: "I put everything in the meat as seasoning with the exception of *Je Reviens,* my new imported Worth perfume."

Tom knew this was an important evening to me, both personally and professionally, for Bill wanted to publish my next book. But Tom never appeared nor telephoned. Sadly I served dinner with his place empty. The three of us gallantly ate the prune whip. To me it savored of sawdust.

I apologized, "I don't know what happened to Tom or why he didn't call. It must have been an emergency."

Anne, often brutally frank with herself and friends, asked, "Are you having trouble, Lucy?"

"Oh, Annie!" Tears in my eyes, I confessed, "We don't get along at all. We're both miserable."

"What are you going to do about it?" she asked.

"I don't know." Hopelessly.

As they left, Bill hugged me, advised, "If it gets too bad, come back to New York, Lucy. It's your city. You belong there."

When Tom walked in at midnight I asked worriedly, "Are you all right?"

"I'm fine." Arrogantly, "Did *your* guests have fun?" Emphasizing the "your."

"They felt sorry they didn't meet you. Did you forget you said you would show up for dinner?" I thought, He does not miss dinner as a rule, wondered if he were afraid he would get drunk and start berating me in front of the Targs.

He stared at me, shrugged his shoulders, said angrily, "What the hell do you care whether I show up or not? You don't give a damn for me or my feelings."

He was obviously drunk, I said no more. But it was that night, after several more scotches, that he slammed his fist into my right breast, then my right eye and I fell to the floor thinking, He is truly mad and I must somehow get out of this sudden hell.

And it was that night I slept for the first time on the sofa in the living room, never to return to the bedroom. I was now afraid of him, all I asked was that he stop striking me. I would have left on the spot except every morning following the nights he had thrown words of hate, he would apologize. Say he had not realized what he was doing, beg me to remain, promise he would change.

Part of me wanted to stay with Tom, prove we could restore the love we felt the first months of marriage. I could not understand how such ardent feelings could so swiftly turn into fury. A fury I had never before seen in a man with whom I had a sexual relationship.

There were moments I thought of giving up. Flying back to Manhattan and the *Times*. But to slink back meant I had failed as a woman. I could hear my reportorial friends sneer, "She couldn't make it twice at marriage." I also thought failure meant I had failed in analysis, I should now know myself well enough to make a man happy.

In an attempt to keep up morale I sought assignments from Harry Reutlinger, managing editor of the *Chicago American*, owned by Hearst. He asked me one day to visit Joliet Prison in Statesville, Illinois, thirty miles west of Chicago, to interview a young man of twenty-eight serving a life sentence for murdering a little girl and a woman. I was to report on his life in prison.

After interviewing William Heirens, I wrote the story, then thought, What a book this would make if I could explore what in his life caused him to become a murderer. I took a second trip to Statesville. I had met the warden during my coverage of prison association conventions and he gave me access to Heirens. I then asked Heirens if he would cooperate in my writing a book showing how early emotional trauma might have caused his wish to kill. He consented, even as he protested he was innocent. Perhaps he wants to understand his past, I thought. Perhaps, too, he is lonely and wants a visitor to comfort him. He told me no member of his family came to see him, he had no friends.

On the wall of the victim's home, thirty-six-year-old Frances Brown, a former Wave, he had written in lipstick:

> For heavens sake catch me
> Before I kill more
> I cannot control myself

These words intrigued me, an open plea for help. His conscience was screaming to the world to save him from the murderous impulses that drove him to destroy and tear apart the female body. He had been caught after months of work by an astute detective. He matched the fingerprints of Heirens found at the scene of a daylight robbery, where the police had arrested him, with those in Brown's apartment. They were also discovered in the room of seven-year-old Susan Degnan. He had crept one evening through an open window into her bedroom on the ground floor, killed her, then dismembered her body, scattering the parts in Chicago sewers. At that time he was a freshman at the University of Chicago.

He had murdered Susan in January 1946, Frances Brown on December 9, 1945, and was suspected of other murders involving young women. After his capture he confessed under truth serum. He told doctors "George did it," an alter ego but also the name of his father. He received consecutive life sentences for three crimes, also confessing to the murder of a third woman.

I asked him to read the finished manuscript, he made few changes, still insisted he was innocent. I had visited him a number of times over a period of eight months, taken copious notes, also interviewed his mother, father, attorney and others who had known him.

One Sunday morning Tom walked into the living room, which had become both my sleep and work room. I sat at the typewriter trying to finish the book, which I sold to Crown Publishers under the title *Catch Me Before I Kill More.*

One hundred neatly typed pages were piled on a small table beside me as I worked on the second hundred. Tom sauntered over to the table, grabbed the one hundred pages, snarled, "I'm going to burn these in the incinerator."

I felt petrified. They were my only copies. It was like destroying a newborn baby. He threatened my remaining strength, I thought, If he destroys those pages, this is the end.

Quietly, as though to a tantrum-ridden boy, I said, "Please put those pages down, Tom."

He stared at me as though deciding whether to defy me or defer to me. Then he raised his right arm, hurled the one hundred pages in my direction. They floated in the air like small white kites, slowly settled to the carpet in haphazard pattern.

He also hurled the sarcastic words, "I only wanted to see what you'd do. You care more for that book than for me."

At that moment his charge became true. As I slowly picked up the pages, I thought, This is the last indignity. I have stayed through assaults on body and mind. But when my work is threatened it is like a knife to the heart.

For the first time I dared oppose him, he sensed my rage and possibly the depth of his own destructiveness. His threat to annihilate the one satisfaction left, drove me to defy him.

The following midweek he flew to Los Angeles to gather material on hospitals there. I heard the slam of the door as he went his way westward without a word of farewell. It sounded like a drumbeat of doom.

I quickly packed an overnight bag, headed for Midway. I knew I had reached the end of my psychic rope, living in an alien city alone and depressed. I realized I was so enmeshed in fantasies that when at long last I tried to be a wife, I automatically failed. I had plunged from my walking act across the daily high-wire of reportorial life into a neurotic net of childhood dreams about the nature of love.

I caught a plane to New York, felt the elation of

heading home. I was ready to face the enemy—the enemy within. I would somehow free myself from the quagmire of violence and hatred into which I plunged when a man proposed. I would no longer tolerate being hissed at as a "slut," "impostor," "cheat."

I had brought this disaster on myself and had to find out the "why." John had sensed I was headed for terror as I raced into Tom's arms without knowing him, or he, me.

The plane zeroed in on La Guardia Airport, a swift taxi took me to the Barclay Hotel on Lexington Avenue. Since my father's death my substitute adviser was his brother, my Uncle Ed. The two of them, with Morris Ernst and Herbert Wolff, had founded the respectable law firm of Greenbaum, Wolff and Ernst.

I telephoned Uncle Ed, asked if he had time to meet me the next day, explained I had flown east unexpectedly. He caught the urgency in my voice and busy though he always was, suggested we meet at noon at the Williams Club. He had given Tom and me a wedding reception there a month after our marriage, substituting for my mother who was in Florida.

When we met for lunch, not wanting to waste a second, I confessed, "My marriage is on the rocks. Tom and I are miserable." Added sadly, "I feel crucified. Like Joan of Arc. And Sacco and Vanzetti." Uncle Ed often cited the fate of the latter as cruel and unfair, the accusations without proof.

"You left out Dreyfus!" Biting, just like my father. Their brilliant mother had taught them this vocal weapon, not their kindly, gentle father, the judge.

This did not mean Uncle Ed was unsympathetic toward my suffering. Only that he wished I would stop feeling sorry for myself, take constructive action.

I confessed, "I don't know what to do."

His next words, in scathing sincerity, "You, the mental health expert of America, don't know what to do?"

I winced, bore the cruel blow. One that labeled me "coward."

He smiled. "Go back into analysis, of course."

"Won't everyone think I'm a failure after writing a book about how successful analysis is?" A wail. Though he had said what I desperately wanted him to say.

"What do you care what people think?" A challenge.

I knew *he* did not care what people thought. He possessed a magnificent kind of courage, compounded of indifference to the slings and arrows of those who sought to denigrate him plus deep faith in his own judgment. He had fought in World War I as a colonel. During World War II, on leave from the law firm, he served as brigadier general at the Pentagon, executive officer to Undersecretary of War Robert P. Patterson. Uncle Ed claimed to be the only Jewish general in the Pentagon. He was awarded the Distinguished Service Medal in 1945.

"Do you want to leave your husband, come back to New York and find an analyst here?" he asked.

"I'm not sure," I said.

"Are there good analysts in Chicago?"

"The Chicago Institute for Psychoanalysis is well known." I knew the director, Dr. Franz Alexander. His daughter Kiki had become one of my few friends, I had asked her to take photographs for the Heirens book. I was also acquainted with some of the Institute faculty, met them over the years at annual psychoanalytic meetings.

As we parted Uncle Ed gave me a peck on the cheek, an ardent gesture for him, ordered, "Find someone who can help you."

"Thank you for helping me decide what to do." I gave him a solid kiss on the cheek.

I had received from my relative-mentor what I needed—sanction to continue analysis. Uncle Ed did not make me feel ashamed either because I failed at the marriage or wished to return to analysis.

In his book *A Lawyer's Job,* a personal history of his career in the law, in the army and in private groups such as the Anti-Defamation League, Uncle Ed painted this picture of my father: "Laurie readily absorbed any subject with the greatest of ease. He did not know what profession he would follow when he graduated in 1909 from Williams College with a Phi Beta Kappa key. He was intrigued by physics, mathematics and engineering. He knew a great deal about them without ever seeming to study and always carried a slide rule in his pocket. Ever since he was a boy he could fix toys and clocks.

"There were only fifteen months between my brother and me, and while we were always very close, we were as different as we could be. He was blond; I was dark. He was mechanical; I was clumsy. But the prime difference lay in our social lives. Laurie was a ladies' man. He danced beautifully, was in great demand at parties, and lovesick girls rang him up from morning till night. I was the shy type. His intimates included the garageman, a business tycoon, a notorious public character, an outstanding judge, and a little nobody. Any two or three of them might spend the day together, fishing with Laurie on his boat. He treated them all alike, with affectionate abuse.

"He was thoroughly involved in the law, but he came to the office and left whenever he liked, and somehow found the time to manage a local law office in White Plains as well as helping to organize the Quaker Ridge Golf Club and to create the Beach Point Club, serving as president of both, while being active in local Demo-

cratic politics and chairman of the State Board of Social
Welfare under both Governors Lehman and Dewey. He
was a 'character'—and one of the most gifted people I
ever met. It was not until after I went overseas in World
War I that I emerged from the impact of his towering
personality."

Reading of Uncle Ed's feelings, I felt relieved I was
not the only one to fall under my father's spell. Just out
of law school, he worked at the firm of Cardozo & Na-
than. Michael H. Cardozo, Sr., was the cousin of United
States Supreme Court Justice Benjamin Cardozo. For
a time my father shared a desk with Franklin D. Roosevelt, told me he enjoyed working with him, he was affable and brilliant. In later years my father occasionally
drove me to President Roosevelt's home at Hyde Park
to discuss a legal matter in which they both held an
interest. My father asked me to sit in the car and wait,
sometimes an hour or more (I took along books to read).
If I could not go he asked Sue. Once in the dead of
winter, she nearly froze to death.

My father was known as a brilliant lawyer, special-
izing in constitutional law. He worked hard, was erudite,
often used words that impressed me as a child. Like
perspicacious and *amanuensis*. He inspired in me a
love of and reverence for the "word."

He also inspired another kind of love, one perhaps
not quite so laudable. He was the first to take me to the
racetrack when I was fifteen. We drove for his usual
three-week winter vacation to Hollywood, Florida, a few
miles north of the Hialeah Racetrack. One sunny day he,
Donna, the woman he would later marry, and I set out
for the track. Thus I learned of the lure of betting on
horses. I believe my original fascination for this way of
spending a day suspended between fantasy and reality
stemmed from my father's delight at the track.

One more call in New York and I could fly back to

Chicago. I telephoned John, asked if I could see him. He did not have the time on such short notice, apologized, then suggested, "Call me at seven. It's my supper hour and we can talk." He saw patients late into the evening.

I telephoned from the airport and knowing his time was limited, plunged right in. Announced, "My marriage is a failure. I should have listened to you."

"I'm sorry." Sincerity in the gentle voice.

I asked quickly, hoping he would say no, "Do you think I should go back into analysis in Chicago?" I wanted him to reply, "Come back to me."

"I think that's a good idea." Voice cheerful, as though he wished me well.

"Do you know anyone in Chicago?" Perhaps he would give me a name.

"Sorry, I don't. But you must know analysts there."

"I'll ask Dr. Herman Serota. I know him casually. He's on the faculty of the Chicago Institute for Psychoanalysis."

"Let me know what you do," John said.

"I will. And thank you for giving me your sanction to return to analysis."

"You didn't need it," he said. "But I'm glad you called."

As I flew westward—not to my home, for it never had become a home but to me a concentration camp—I thought of Dr. Serota, "Mike" as his friends called him. He and another friend of mine, Helen Douglas, daughter of Senator Paul Douglas of Illinois, were then a twosome, though they never married. I had met Mike through Dr. Milton Wexler, a psychoanalyst at the Menninger Clinic, today practicing in Beverly Hills. He shared an office with the late Dr. Ralph Greenson, the analyst who tried to help Marilyn Monroe during the last tragic months of her life. Milton introduced me to Mike in Atlantic City the year *Fight Against Fears* was published. Many of the analysts were curious to see what this woman looked like who dared write about her analysis. I could trust serious, thoughtful Mike to find me the proper analyst in Chicago.

I reached the apartment the day before Tom flew in from Los Angeles. The first thing I did after taking off my raccoon coat and hat was to call Mike, make an appointment to see him in his skyscraper office.

I sat in a chair facing the Chicago lakefront, lovely when the icy winds that slit into you like frozen blades bloweth not—roughly the month of August. I smiled at Mike, he always seemed delighted to talk when we met at analytic conventions.

I explained, "My marriage is blowing up in my face. I want to find an analyst who will help me save it."

"Man or woman?" he asked.

I thought for a moment, said, "I guess I would like to try a woman. See if it's any different from going to a man."

He wrote down the names of four women, later told me he weighted his words in favor of the one he thought best for me. Her name was Dr. Minna Emch.

He said of her, "She is a fine analyst and on the faculty of our Institute." Then added, knowing this would appeal to my reportorial bent, "Her brother-in-law is Ben Hecht."

He was one of my idols, I thought *The Front Page*, which he wrote with his close friend Charles MacArthur, a classic, a brilliant satire of newspaper life. On a par with Evelyn Waugh's *Scoop*, the story of a fatuous garden editor sent by mistake from a London newspaper to cover the war in Ethiopia.

Mike also told me, "Dr. Emch's husband, Arnold, is a member of a large firm of management consultants and on the editorial board of the journal *Psychiatry*, published by the William Alanson White Institute." This was a link, Mike knew, to John. I had told Mike that Clara Thompson, one of the founders of the White Institute, had been John's favorite personal analyst. He had gone to three, the first two were Freudians. He told me he hated one so much that when he suddenly died, "I was sure my death wishes killed him."

I dialed Dr. Emch's phone number. A maid answered, I gave my name, waited.

In a moment a soft, melodious voice said, "This is Dr. Emch."

I introduced myself nervously, explained, "I'm a former reporter on *The New York Times*. I quit my job a year ago to marry a man who lives in Chicago. The marriage isn't working and I'd like to talk to you about further therapy. I had six years, three times a week in New York."

I found out later the brightest thing I could have done was to mention newspaper work. She loved her brother-in-law, who had been a reporter in Chicago. His wife Rose, Dr. Emch's sister, also had been a reporter.

"Why don't you come to the house Thursday afternoon at three?" The gracious voice.

"I'll be there. Thank you very much." I suddenly felt a calm I had never known in Chicago. Perhaps New York, too.

She gave directions, she lived a mile north on Lake Shore Drive. I could drive there in five minutes in our new Oldsmobile, which I shared with Tom. My mother had sent us a belated wedding present of one thousand dollars, which helped buy it. I used it during the day, Tom took the bus directly to and from work, a five-minute ride.

From the first analysis I gained awareness there was a way different from my driven life. With John I was not able to go enough of the way but I made a fair start.

It takes one kind of courage to explore a new land or achieve a scientific discovery, another to explore feelings and fantasies of the mind believed wicked and forbidden. My failure in marriage meant, I knew, that the depression I suffered was an amorphous, icy blanket covering buried feelings, freezing them further.

I was starting to accept there was no way to rush the knowing of the inner self, against which powerful defenses have been erected, then strengthed over the unhappy years. Fear, rage, greed, jealousy, envy do not rise swiftly out of the depths of denial.

An old Chinese proverb holds, "The longest journey starts with but a single step." I had taken the first few steps with the analyst in New York on my journey into the unknown self. Now, in this city of cruel winters, I was about to embark on the next few steps.

A kind of psychic tale in two cities, I thought.

4

The Past Becomes
the Present

I was prepared to continue the psychic trip into the
unknown part of my mind. I looked forward to the
initial hour with Dr. Emch but first I had to tell Tom.
I was afraid he might object but if he did, I would move
out of the apartment.

When he returned I reported on my flight to New
York, the advice from Uncle Ed and calling Dr. Emch.
To my surprise, Tom did not object. He even said he
thought he might try analysis, had thought of calling
the Institute for the name of a suitable male therapist.

But there was no offer from him for my return to
the sharing of the double bed. I continued nights on the
couch. I thought, A couch where I live and a couch at my
new analyst's home.

During the days I waited nervously to meet Dr.
Emch I thought of what I would say to her. How I would
explain my marriage, my work on the *Times*, which I
had discarded so swiftly and thoughtlessly.

I now knew I had been reckless, impetuous, to give up reporting. At least in such an impulsive way. Like a child intent on getting something he wants desperately that turns out to be horrifying. At the cost of abandoning something stable, even though routine.

As if to prepare for what I would tell Dr. Emch, I recalled the excitement of the first moment I entered *The New York Times* city room on the third floor of the fourteen-story building on Forty-third Street, just off Broadway beyond the Paramount Theater. A lofty office on the top floor held the owner and publisher, Arthur Hays Sulzberger, a close friend of my father and Uncle Ed. They had grown up together in adjacent town houses in Manhattan. Uncle Ed was the personal lawyer for Mr. Sulzberger and his family.

The city room lay in front of me as I entered a masculine domain. I found myself the lone woman in a sea of male reporters. I was part of an experiment as World War II was soon to deplete the ranks of male reporters.

I hardly dared savor the glory. All those men. I had always looked up to a man as far more valuable than my inferior self. Suddenly I was placed in equal position with a man in a profession I believed hallowed. I also dared the fleeting thought that among all these masculine forms perhaps I would find a husband.

Before me stretched a sea of steel desks. Mounted on their tops, like small cannons, typewriters in action sounded like muted machine-gun fire. My two-inch heels clicked loudly as I walked nervously down the aisle, led by the city editor's clerk.

"Here we are." He stopped in front of a desk on the aisle. "This belonged to a reporter just sent to Australia. He wanted to be a foreign correspondent."

God bless him, I thought, for leaving a vacant desk that is now mine. A shrine I set my mind on occupying ever since I first wrote an essay. Writing was the way of survival, if I could not write I would perish.

"If you need anything just ask another reporter." The clerk waved at the vast city room. Added, "Good luck."

He started to walk away, turned, a thoughtful look on his face. "The ladies' room is back there." He pointed westward to the Eighth Avenue side of the city room. "The secretaries use it," as though to explain why a ladies' room would exist when there were no lady reporters. There had been a few. I was not the first but when I was taken on there was no sign of another female reporter. Nancy Hale had left to write novels and short stories for *The New Yorker.* Kathleen McLaughlin worked on a top floor as editor, planning a "woman's section" for the paper.

My first assignment, a feature story, was to cover a tea party where a pedigreed dog served as host. His wealthy owners dreamed up this unusual social affair to raise money to benefit the American-French War Relief, which purchased milk for starving French children. My words, I hoped, would help through publicity to bring in the money. The story appeared on the first page of the second section, guaranteeing a fair readership. The headlines and first two paragraphs read:

DOGS HOLD A TEA
TO HONOR POODLE

Cairn Terrier Owned by Mr.
and Mrs. H. O. Milliken
Is the Growling Host

Doggy decorum reached new heights yesterday
afternoon when several of the most prominent

dogs in New York attended a tea given by Ginger, a Cairn terrier, at his home, 137 East Seventy-third Street, also the residence of his owners, Mr. and Mrs. H. O. Milliken.

Although the guests were greeted by growls as they entered the door, they made themselves at home when they saw that the host was held safely on a leash. Then they settled down to await the arrival of the guest of honor, Mister, a French poodle owned by Mr. and Mrs. William Bird. Mr. Bird, a foreign correspondent for *The New York Sun*, returned here from Paris in October. In the usual tradition of guests of honor, Mister was abominably late.

From then on, it was all upward as I learned the ropes of reportorial skills in the biggest city of them all. Mrs. Franklin D. Roosevelt, wife of the President, became my regular assignment whenever she, as First Lady, arrived in the city. I covered her for the first time when she appeared on March 22, 1941, at the headquarters of the British War Relief Society.

She called Colonel Charles A. Lindbergh's latest statement against American intervention in the war "wishful thinking." She expressed hope that eventually one group would be set up to take care of all relief aid for Great Britain. In this way, she said, aid would be put on an efficient and businesslike basis.

Two months later she appeared at the Greek War Relief headquarters to inspect a model Athenian air raid shelter and trench. I quoted her as saying, "Everyone in the world is filled with admiration for what the Greeks are doing." She posed for a photo that appeared in the *Times* with Judy Garland, described as "a young screen actress" attending the inspection.

A month later I described Mrs. Roosevelt's visit to the third floor of Arnold Constable's. She wrote a note to Madame Chiang Kai-shek, enclosed in a box that contained a Chinese print dress she had selected as a gift for Madame Chiang. "I've sent dozens of thank-you notes to her," Mrs. Roosevelt explained, "and now I'm glad to be able to send her something." She said though she had never met Madame Chiang, she talked to her several times on the phone.

In a different type of story at Town Hall later in the year, Mrs. Roosevelt called for the establishment of a ceiling on commodities "since there is no other way to keep prices on a reasonable level." She warned there might be a ceiling on wages in these war years.

I approved of her ideas and way of expressing them, though I never really became close enough to know what she was like as a person. But I enjoyed listening to her short speeches and later at the Democratic convention where Governor Stevenson was nominated, thought her introduction of him very moving. She was the first President's wife to reach out constantly to the public with appeals to help the poor and needy.

I felt in that special seventh heaven of the fourth estate when sent to report on an idol, Frank Sinatra, in his first appearance at the Paramount Theater. As he strode on the stage an ovation like that accorded Babe Ruth hitting a homer greeted him. The spotlight shone on his thin body, lean face, high cheekbones. He sang "Night and Day" with poignant intensity, love wrapped in the lyrics. As he reached the words, "You are the one . . ." a boisterous masculine voice from the audience boomed, "Says you!" Hecklers as well as admirers had paid admission.

Sinatra stopped singing. His wide mouth broke into a shy, one-sided grin. He shrugged his shoulders, said, "The customer is always right."

"Attaboy, Frankie!" A scream from the audience,

ninety percent teenage girls. I thought, Sinatra's humor is part of his charm.

I interviewed him in his dressing room as the chant, "We want Frankie!" floated up from the street. He tried to put his success into words: "I see things the way the kids do. They feel that any one of their crowd could do exactly what I've done. I could be from their neighborhood."

That night in my small apartment, a cheerful room filled with the books I liked at that time—*The Great Gatsby, What Makes Sammy Run, The Grapes of Wrath*—I thought of Frank just starting his career. He spoke of, sang with and exuded love. The love of adolescence, I was to learn from John, not the lasting, in-depth love of mature souls who understood both their own weaknesses and capabilities.

After my story appeared, Sinatra sent a courteous note: "Thanks for the fine interview. Good luck." I gave it to my sister Sue, an even more ardent fan than I was.

I also interviewed celebrities of a different caliber, such as the Duchess of Windsor when she and the Duke made their first trip to America following a visit to the Bahamas. Four years before, he abdicated his role as King Edward VIII to marry the former Wallis Simpson, the twice-divorced woman from Baltimore.

I was assigned to follow the Duchess to Inwood House, where unmarried mothers and their babies received shelter, food and treatment. She told reporters who clustered around her, "I am far more interested in social problems than clothes, of which I have been accused of favoring."

But, as I reported, the problem of her wardrobe pursued her, "eclipsing even conversation about birth control in the Bahamas." She answered all questions about the two existing clinics in the Bahamas, similar to

Inwood House. She said they were less adequately equipped, provided only daily visits by mothers and children, not living quarters. One reporter interrupted to ask about her plans to shop in New York.

She said, in sharper tone, "I must have something to put on. I bought a few cotton dresses in Miami but I need several new ones for street wear here."

She was then questioned by a male reporter about the number of pieces of baggage that accompanied her on the trip. She retorted, "I read about one hundred and six but I've never counted them. If you wish to," her eyes flashing slight anger, "I'm sure we could arrange it."

She looked like a fashion plate in a black jersey dress of simple lines, with a draped satin apron front. A tiny veiled black hat fit snugly on her head. A butterfly-shaped pin nestled in the front of the crown of the hat, matching her earrings. She also wore a sable scarf, black suede shoes and white gloves she did not remove.

She seemed warm, intelligent, willing to spend as much time as needed to learn more about taking care of unwed mothers and their babies. I thought she handled questions with ease and honesty. That night I was assigned to cover the royal couple when they went to the Waldorf for a late supper and I enjoyed the pleasure of a smile from the Duke before reporters were barred from the dining room. I was delighted to go home for a deserved night's sleep after calling the city room and delivering the one sentence, "They arrived and are eating."

My finest reportorial hour took place on Tuesday, April 7, 1946. Mr. Joseph assigned me to cover my most overt passion—a baseball game. Not just a baseball game but the opening of the season for the National League at the Polo Grounds. My beloved New York

Giants, whom I had championed since the age of ten, were playing the Philadelphia Phillies.

And not just an opening-day game but a day differing from all other openers. In special boxes sat an unusual group of spectators—the world's political leaders playing hookey from the United Nations, just springing into being at Hunter College's branch in the Bronx, separate from the main site in Manhattan.

A *Times* photographer assigned to the occasion, also a Giants fan, drove me to the stadium. I exclaimed in exultation, "Now I'll see Mel Ott. His picture hung on my wall as I grew up. He was my idol."

At least I thought I would see my hero. But first and foremost my task was to report how the United Nations delegates reacted to a baseball game in America. Trygve Lie, Secretary General of the United Nation's Security Council, confessed to me, "This is my first ball game."

Suddenly, in the first inning, as I questioned the honored guests about their initial reactions, I heard a player's bat crash against the ball. A great roar went up from the crowd.

I asked the reporter from *The Herald Tribune*, "What happened?"

"Ott hit a homer!" he said excitedly.

I wailed, "I waited nineteen years to see that." Then grudgingly, "At least I heard it."

I did not see much of the game, watched Secretary Lie devour two hot dogs and Lieutenant Colonel W. R. Hodgson, Australian delegate, shell peanuts. Conspicuous by his absence was Andrei A. Gromyko, the Russian delegate, who evidently did not care about baseball.

The story brought me a by-line on the front page. The headline read:

HOT DOGS, PEANUTS DISPLACE PROTOCOL AS U.N. DELEGATES SEE GIANTS WIN

My first paragraph: "Trygve Lie, Secretary General of the United Nations Security Council, devoured two hot dogs, one right after the other. Lieut. Col. W. R. Hodgson, Australian delegate to the Council, shelled peanuts, spilling the shells all over his blue suit. Dr. Francisco Castillio Najera ate nothing, kept his hands tight in his pockets. Dr. Eelco van Kleffens munched a chocolate bar."

The second paragraph: "Forsaking for the moment the clash of ideologies for the crack of bat against baseball, delegates of the United Nations turned from Iran to home runs yesterday. They were spectators at a drama provided by men versed not in the art of diplomacy but in the art of the double play."

The next day I received a note from Mr. Sulzberger: "Fine reporting. You are doing well. Keep it up."

I desperately desired to help the war effort, at one point asked to be sent overseas as foreign correspondent. Mr. Joseph uttered a firm "no." Added, "Not for ladies."

But I was selected as the *Times* representative for a group called the Working Press Reporters. I traveled to Washington for six weeks to write publicity for the United States Treasury Third War Loan. Our headquarters was the Treasury building, around the corner from the White House and across the Potomac from Uncle Ed, now serving his country as a general, as in the previous world war he had served as a colonel.

After two weeks I wrote Uncle Ed's sister—my Aunt Grace, with whom I shared many a golf game as I grew up—a letter she saved:

Working in Washington has given me a sense of war as nothing else has. Between visiting the Pentagon and Walter Reed Hospital, I have become war conscious to the extent I feel ashamed to return to New York to cover luncheons and conventions. Corridors lined with 4000 soldiers at the hospital, arms and legs torn off, bodies paralyzed, nerves shot. The suicide ward is always full.

As you're talking to one lad, getting his story of how a shell blew off his arm in Sicily, the boy next to him writhes in pain on his bed. I walked into a room where fifty soldiers sat on the beds, talking casually, playing cards or listening to the radio. Each had either one or both legs missing. The horror of war, all its brutality, that will live for years, not dying when peace comes, is in that hospital. And the toll has only begun.

Then in the Pentagon Uncle Ed and I went through the files of some dead heroes, boys whose parents were given their medals for bravery in action. A Colonel walked into the room bearing a communiqué which reported the Nazis claimed our 45th and 37th infantry divisions in Italy. Uncle Ed and the Colonel went to a huge wall map, spotted the place where the infantry was smashed up. For a moment Italy was in the room. When I walked out of the Pentagon I felt ashamed to be part of humanity.

The day war ended, Meyer Berger, the *Times'* most noted reporter for complete coverage, eloquence and humor, and I were dispatched the few steps to Times Square to describe the evening's celebration as the city rocked wildly to the news of peace. I was in awe of Mike, who sat directly in front of me in the city room. I learned much about writing from him. He believed reporters should reach for the vivid word that gave the story color and action, yet also know what to leave out.

Then without warning I was suddenly attacked by severe sinusitis. I could hardly breathe as I sat at my desk laboriously typing out daily stories that up to then had been simple to write. I consulted several rhinologists, specialists in nasal disorders, who examined my nose, said they could find nothing physically wrong. They suggested I leave New York, head to Arizona or New Mexico where the climate was more conducive to clogged nasal passages. Give up my treasured job? Never. First I would die at my desk from ghostly obstructions in the nose.

As a last resort I sought a rhinologist at St. Luke's Hospital, recommended by a reporter to whom I will always be grateful. He suffered similar pain this rhinologist had relieved. I called the doctor, made an appointment.

After carefully examining my aching nostrils he walked to the window, looked out as though searching for an answer. Then he turned, said, "I really can't find anything organically wrong with your nose."

"What'll I do?" I wailed.

He repeated what the other rhinologists had said. "Move to a hot climate where the nasal condition has a good chance of clearing up. Or—" he hesitated, then went on, "you might try psychoanalysis. Your problem may be emotional."

"Emotional?" I stared at him as if he had suddenly lost his mind. As far as I knew, I did not suffer any emotional problems.

He explained, "Doctors are finding a relationship between blowups of the respiratory system and emotional distress."

I had read Freud at Bennington College. One of the

leading psychoanalysts in the country was Dr. Lawrence Kubie, my father's first cousin. But psychoanalysis was costly and on my forty-dollars-a-week salary I wondered if I could afford it.

I decided I could not *not* afford it. I did not wish to live in the mountains of New Mexico, beautiful though they might be. I would perish without the excitement of New York. I made an appointment to see Dr. Kubie. In his office I asked for the name of a psychoanalyst—I could not afford his high prices, he treated celebrities like Tennessee Williams. I started couch life when Dr. Thurrott agreed to see me.

I died the coward's thousand deaths that beautiful April day in 1946 as I stood outside Dr. Thurrott's ground-floor apartment in the brownstone on East Seventieth Street just off Madison. My nose was too stuffed to take in the soft spring breeze touching trees to green awakening. I rang the doorbell, waited out the terror. Denied the desire to turn and race down the steps into the street.

The door suddenly opened. I saw a slim, rather short man with graying hair and a face somewhat like Fred Astaire's.

"Please come in," he invited.

Sheep to slaughter, I thought, followed him down a dark hall. Turned left into a living room luxurious with flowering plants on tables and windowsills. Reproductions of two Tahitian scenes by Gauguin splashed color on the wall behind a brown couch obviously for the terrified patient.

He motioned me to a large green chair, sat opposite in a brown leather one, lit a cigarette. This gave me sanction to take out one of my cigarettes. He courteously leaned over, lit it for me.

I exhaled the first puff, then confessed in my usual low voice (it had always been difficult for me to speak up, one reason I wrote), "I'm here because I have severe sinusitis, which one doctor said might be psychosomatic. He suggested I try psychoanalysis."

"How did you happen to call me?" Sparkling blue eyes looked into my blue ones, we were a symphony in blue, I thought, he has eyes the color of my mother's and father's.

"Dr. Lawrence Kubie, my father's first cousin, suggested you." Added, "I'm here in despair. All else having failed."

"That's why most people come," he said.

"I don't want to leave *The New York Times*," I went on. "It means the world to me. But it's difficult to cover assignments crippled by these sinus headaches."

He asked a few questions about my family, I told him I was the oldest of four, a younger brother, then two sisters. I also informed him they were all married and I felt like the feminine version of the village idiot.

"Not that I haven't had proposals." Defiantly. "Two in high school, three at Bennington College and seven or eight since then."

"Didn't you want to marry?"

"I did and I didn't. I was never sure. So I didn't."

For the first four sessions I sat rigid on the chair, smoking, shoulders as erect as a soldier facing a firing squad. The fifth session I dragged myself to his apartment at the regular hour of 11 A.M. Luckily he had free time for a morning appointment, it did not interfere with my 1 P.M. to 9 P.M. or later, schedule.

The sinus had launched an all-out attack. If the analysis did not work I would be compelled to forsake Manhattan, whose every block I cherished. Move to some dry, sunny-all-year desert, like the wastelands of Arizona.

I sat on the couch minus cigarette, my stomach queasy from nasal mucous that dripped its way downward from nose to throat to digestive tract. I had whimpered a weak hello, too depressed to toss even one question at him about *his* life, wishing to keep the probing psychic spotlight off mine.

The couch suddenly seemed luxurious, its pillow inviting. I asked, "May I lie down on your couch?"

"Certainly," he said.

I stood up, walked over to the couch, slowly sank into its softness. All at once it became a haven, not a horror.

There was silence. Then he asked in his low but audible voice, "What are you thinking?"

I was worrying lest my black high-heeled patent leather pumps dirty his brown couch. It did not seem good manners to rest your feet on furniture even if this were accepted as high style for psychoanalysis.

"Nothing," I muttered.

"Nothing?" The gentle voice.

"Well . . ." I stopped. Then, defensively, "It doesn't seem right to talk about myself. We reporters look with scorn on the writer who puts everything in the first person. 'What *I* saw.' Or 'How *I* felt.'"

"Perhaps the 'I' doesn't belong in reporting but it belongs here," he said.

"It seems egotistical." Almost a whisper.

"Everyone should be interested in himself, first. Those who refuse to think about themselves realistically never understand themselves or anyone else."

He added reflectively, "Perhaps you were never allowed to talk about yourself and now you feel nobody cares what you say."

Nobody cares. How often I felt no one cared, everybody but me seemed to have someone who cared.

"Maybe you don't care about yourself," he was saying. "If you do not like yourself, you cannot like anyone else."

The first tears in years filled my eyes. I dabbed them away quickly with my left hand, farthest from his sight, hoping he would not notice.

Then I heard my half-choked voice say wistfully, "How could I like myself? I'm full of snails and puppy dog tails."

"That's what little boys are made of," he said. "You were a little girl."

"Yes, I'm a girl." Wondered why I thought of that old nursery rhyme.

"Maybe you don't know what you are supposed to be."

I felt like snapping, A girl, of course, what are you trying to do, make me think I'm crazy?

He spoke on, "Perhaps, as the rhyme you remember suggested, you want to be something else in the unconscious part of your mind."

Hoisted by my own psychic petard. It had exploded, that secret and sinister word, *unconscious.* It stood for the shame and agony and sorrow in men's minds, I wanted no part of it. I knew it lay deep and dank somewhere within but let it lie, trouble enough dealing with the world outside.

He talked on. "The mind may be compared to an ocean in which at times waves bring to the top matter that has been buried. At other times things on the surface sink to the depths and remain hidden. In analysis you bring to the surface buried thoughts and wishes that cause emotional storms."

"But it's my nose that hurts." A complaint.

"A physical pain may be related to experiences of childhood."

"And if I can't remember them?" Almost a cry.

"The feelings still emerge. As you speak of them they lead to earlier memories, though often in an oblique way."

"My childhood was very happy," I assured him. "I never went hungry or worried about money. I always got the highest marks in class. I played baseball with the boys in grammar school and high school. Danced with them, had all the dates a girl could want."

I remembered more. "For the first six years of my life my parents lived in a large apartment on East Ninety-sixth Street just off Central Park. Then they bought a home twenty miles north in Larchmont, named in honor of the larch trees that flourish along its wide streets."

The house was newly built, three stories high. From the attic windows you could see blue patches of Long Island Sound. My father kept adding trees, transplanted a huge magnolia, several tall maples and small spruces. Transformed our front lawn into a suburban jungle. Mother took charge of the flowers, directed the gardener where to place the pansy beds and a forsythia bush she loved. It always flowered first, signaling spring.

Suddenly a scene flashed into memory, forgotten over the hectic years, not of spring but deadly winter. Tears came to my eyes for no reason at all.

"What are you thinking?" The low voice.

"Of the day I stood alone in the street outside the private school I attended in second grade. The snow was piled high around me and the icy wind of January snapped at my face." The school lay in Larchmont Manor, the exclusive part of town, about a mile from where we lived.

I went on, wanting to please him with my recollections. "I waited for my mother to pick me up as she faithfully did every school day to drive me home for lunch. I waited and waited but no mother. My face turned blood-red from the cold. Long after the lunch hour a teacher walked by. She asked why I stood alone in the street."

Silence, then, "Teeth chattering, I said, 'My mother's forgotten me.'"

Remembering more, "The teacher led me indoors, learned my mother had telephoned the school earlier. She asked I be given lunch because she was unable to call for me. The switchboard lady forgot to relay the message. As apology the school fed me a mammoth meal including double dessert. I think it was apple pie."

I sighed. "But the food couldn't remove the hurt in my heart. I was convinced my mother had abandoned me. She liked my brother and sister much better. She never would have left either of *them* freezing to death in the lonely street."

Why is it always me? I wondered, then and now.

A strange thing happened. I started to sob and could not stop. I cried as though making up for all the tears I could not shed that day and over the years of feeling forsaken.

I reached for the box of tissues on the table next to the couch, dabbed away the tears. Then uttered the words agonizedly, "Why did she hate me so? What did I do to her that she should hate me?"

"She didn't hate you." Reassuringly.

"Yes, she did!" I insisted. "My mother hated me." Then heard myself say, "And I hated her!"

I stopped, stunned. What was I saying? What right had he to pull out feelings better left unrevealed? No nice girl should hate her mother or feel her mother hates her, nice girls are brought up to love their mother and father. I hated no one, tried to love everyone, please everybody. Even when I sat typing at my desk in the city room trying to meet a deadline, if a reporter strolled over for aimless chatter I stopped work. Not daring to oppose his wish to speak. Some small fury within wanted to protest the invasion but I bottled it up, smiled with what I trust emanated as pleasure.

Hate inside me? Never. Yet how could I, who demanded explanation for everything, explain why, in one unguarded moment, I had exposed a dart of hatred that had remained quivering inside for years?

I apologized, "Sorry. I didn't mean to cry." I scorned tears, they were for sissies.

"Maybe it's time you cried," he said. "Maybe you have wanted to cry all these years and couldn't."

His words seemed strange, no one had ever encouraged me to shed tears. My father made fun of me if tears came to my eyes, said accusingly, "Don't be such a sissy."

I sat up on the couch, looked at my watch, the fifty minutes had passed. Heaven forbid I should take advantage of him and stay one second over my time.

Suddenly I became aware of feeling strangely lightheaded. My hands flew to my nose. I exclaimed, "I can breathe! My sinus condition has vanished."

Then sharply, missing the peculiar pain of it, "Where *is* my sinus infection?"

"Perhaps it cleared up as your tears flowed," John said.

"I can't believe it," I marveled. "Look!" I breathed deeply through nostrils that had been clogged for a year. I felt as if a thick gag had been torn from my mouth, heavy chains lifted from ankles.

"You probably have wanted to cry for a long time but repressed the wish," he explained. "The tear ducts in some way became dammed up and, in turn, affected your nasal passages."

"That's the relationship between the physical and the emotional, isn't it?" I suddenly understood the feel of the word *psychosomatic*.

"There usually is that relationship," John said.

I asked, "My wish to cry is the cause of my sinusitis?"

"The cause of one thing is many things." He often repeated this when I requested a simple explanation. "Simple" is "foolish," I came to know. We are all very complex, nurture many fears, desires, fantasies.

I had always demanded *the* answer, and quickly. I was to learn there was no one answer, perhaps I would have to wait a long time before I could find more of the answers.

A disturbing thought occurred as I left his office, walked toward Times Square and the city room. I had visualized my childhood as blissful, yet I knew my adult life held conflicts. With the first dim awareness, to which the tears had led, that my childhood was not paradisiac, I had felt better physically and emotionally.

I had to ask, Could I have been deluded about my earlier life all these years? And was I paying a fairly high price for the delusion?

The sinusitis vanished completely, never to return. Its sudden disappearance was the most dramatic moment of the analysis. All else happened so slowly I was tempted time after time to give up in despair. I felt I was searching for a nugget of gold but first must move mountains.

"What am I here for?" I demanded of John. "What must I *do?*"

"Face yourself." Quietly but firmly. "Stop running away from yourself."

"What do you mean—face myself?" I bristled.

"See yourself as you really are. 'The truth shall make you free.' "

I know what I am really like, I thought. Is that what I'm here for? Seems a waste of time and money.

"What do *you* think I'm like?" Defiantly.

"It doesn't matter what I think. You must know."

"Can't you help out?" A plea.

"For one thing, you hide a lot of anger you've never expressed or probably even been aware of."

At this I felt a small rage spurt to the surface of my mind. I squirmed on the couch, protested, "I am *not* an angry person. What makes you think I am?"

I was the good girl of our house, model for the younger children. My father warned me early that I, the eldest, as he had been in his family, would be held responsible and punished when any of the younger ones misbehaved.

John answered my question. "By the way you act here."

"I think I act very properly here." Why was he picking on me?

"You whisper, for one thing. As though you were afraid to reveal your rage."

"I don't whisper," I shouted hoarsely. "I have a naturally soft voice." I would not admit it but people would often ask me to repeat what I said, this increased my fury so I could hardly get words out.

"You sound as though you were scared to death most of the time. I'm not going to punish you or kill you." John's even voice.

I admitted, "I know I whisper. I'm sorry I denied it."

"That's all right." Reassuringly, "You will often reverse yourself here if it's the truth you're after." Added, "Perhaps you whisper when you are frightened."

Slowly I learned to feel comfortable with him. He never judged me or became angry at me, he encouraged me to show anger at him without reproach or reprimand. A strange new acceptance.

He asked one morning, "Why do you think you

never married? You are the eldest of your siblings and they are all married."

I said sharply, "I guess because I'm still waiting for the elusive Mr. Right."

"It's a matter both of seeking and being sought."

"I have my career." Defiantly.

"Why does a woman choose a career?"

"Maybe because unconsciously she doesn't like the woman's role as wife and mother."

I had used the word *unconscious* for the first time in a personal way. I asked hesitantly, "The unconscious—it's a very important part of us isn't it?"

"It's far more important than most people are willing to admit. We think we control our behavior but the unconscious often controls us. We are, in a sense, slaves to our unconscious a large part of the time."

"But we know what we should do—what is right." I felt puzzled.

"Knowing isn't enough. A murderer knows he is wrong when he kills but he is driven to kill by feelings and wishes of which he is not aware."

This took time for me to understand but John allowed me to set my own pace. The "truth" he kept urging me to face could simmer out only as trust in him mounted. Because he relieved pain, I began to trust him. As an animal, whose wounds have been cleansed, licks the hand of the healer.

One day I told him, "If I said everything that came to mind I'd feel like a damn fool."

"Then you'd better get out what comes to mind because that's the only way you'll get over feeling like a damn fool."

Something inside kept whispering, Don't let him talk you into revealing yourself. Control! Control! You have already told him too much. I felt afraid to let my thoughts fly free for fear of what they might reveal

Everything had to make sense, sound logical. Perhaps, I thought, because underneath nothing seemed to make sense.

I was starting to realize I had designed my life to ask, not answer questions. Most of the time I resorted, when pushed to talk, to haul out my prime defense, the question. One day when I asked a question about John's life, he said, "You are not paying me to talk about myself but about your life."

"It's not worth it." A mutter.

"You are no better or worse than anyone else."

I felt victorious the few times I persuaded him to speak of his life. He told me he had been a major in the army, worked with John Huston, the director, on the film *Let There Be Light*, about psychologically damaged combat veterans. It was completed in 1946, rated one of the finest films about the war but not released, suppressed thirty-five years as too "antiwar." Its first public showing in 1981 won the critics' approval.

He also told me he was born in Nova Scotia and his mother wanted him to be a minister. Instead he studied medicine and psychoanalysis. He had been on the faculty of the New York School of Social Work.

I often suffered a sore throat, which protected me against speaking up. I felt I was a "bad girl" when I talked too much, held center stage. Voices of the past rang clear, ordering me to keep quiet. I would discover later on the couch there were powerful reasons I felt constrained to hold my tongue. But I knew with John I had to keep talking if I wanted to understand my childhood and how it was affecting my current life.

He did not mention the psychoanalytic phrase *free association*, speaking your thoughts as they reeled from your mind without censoring one. He rarely used jargon, never referred to "id," "ego" and "superego," those hallowed tripartite divisions of the mind. Eventually I came to know my thoughts would steer, true as an arrow, to the torments of my life. Not the first or third but sometimes the sixth or seventh thought led to the undercover defense, revealing long-buried fears and wishes. What analysts call "the constellation of fantasies," not just one fantasy but the cluster of many, was the cause of my misery.

I told John the one person throughout childhood and adolescence who I felt accepted me almost completely was my maternal great-aunt, who served as grandmother, since my mother's mother died when my mother was two. Granny, as she asked us to call her. Her name was Theresa Prince.

She was a strong-willed, stately woman with a queenly face and body. Some members of the family thought her matriarch and tyrant. She held the purse strings over the small fortune my great-uncle acquired on Wall Street. He was a founder of the firm of Asiel & Company. I never knew him well because he never spoke much. When we visited him his face was usually buried in *The Wall Street Journal.* We children affectionately called him Grumpy.

To me, Granny was a fairy godmother. She bought me glamorous silver lace dresses, paid for my debut at seventeen with an elaborate dance at the Savoy-Plaza. She always insisted I spend part of the Christmas holidays in her elegant Park Avenue apartment, where original Corots mixed with antique Chinese vases she collected on trips around the world.

"I want Lucy with me." Her announcement to my parents just before Christmas.

"Do you want to go?" my mother would ask.

"Of course." I would be crazy not to want to visit an elegant Manhattan dwelling where I would be treated like a royal princess instead of ugly duckling.

Granny and Grumpy also owned a summer estate,

Neldisset Farm, that spread over one hundred acres twenty miles north of New York. It stood high on a hill bordering Scarsdale in the town of Mamaroneck. The latter was once an old Indian village where George Washington slept in a building now called Fenimore Tavern on the Boston Post Road. In honor of James Fenimore Cooper, who wrote a Leather-Stocking tale or two during the first half of the 1800s.

Neldisset Farm boasted four Gothic pillars and twenty-five rooms, "The Big House," as we children called it. It was surrounded by tennis court, rose garden, fish pond, acres of vegetables in the summer, a three-hole golf course and apple orchard, all created by Granny and Grumpy. There was also a farmhouse in which a caretaker lived with his family, encircled by chickens, cows and horses. And two bungalows, built especially for mother and her younger sister, Leonore, who in summers moved their families north to escape the city's heat.

Over the years Granny and I held long philosophical conversations. She advised gently, when I said I wanted to become a writer, "You will never create anything original for there isn't anything new under the sun but you can try to do it in a different way." She never raised her voice with me though I heard it roar at others, particularly bridge partners when they played the wrong card.

It was a special treat to see her sit down at the piano and play "The Moonlight Sonata" with just the right combination of soul and technique. Before marriage she was a successful concert pianist. She appeared with the New York Symphony Orchestra at Carnegie Hall. As a child I met the famous pianist Joseph Hoffman at her home.

When I was ten she sent an expensive piano by truck to our house, ordered mother to find a teacher for me at once. She wanted me to follow in her musical footsteps. I went through the motions of Grieg's *Anitra's Dance* and Chopin preludes but my heart belonged to jazz. I played Sally's daily request for "Glowworm." I preferred my father remain the chief musician in the family. He played a soulful violin. His favorite songs were one that started out, "Daisy, Daisy, give me your answer true" and Irving Berlin's, "Oh How I Hate to Get up in the Morning."

Granny reluctantly over the years gave in to the fact I would never be a classical pianist but newspaper reporter. She died before any of my books were published but she would have approved of my career. Taking her advice I found a different way to interpret psychoanalysis. I was the first to write a successful popular book describing how a patient felt on the couch.

Occasionally I would say vehemently to John, "I want to be a lady."

"What does 'lady' mean to you?" he would ask.

"I don't know." Really not knowing.

One morning, thinking of Granny, I said proudly, *"She* was a lady. She loved me, wanted me to be a lady, too." Wistfully, "She wanted so much for me, her first grandchild."

When I graduated from Bennington she insisted on attending the ceremonies in Vermont, though crippled severely in one leg as a result of an automobile accident. Her chauffeur had not been able to avoid the car swerving toward them in the wrong lane. The day of graduation she handed me a diamond wristwatch, a wedding gift from Grumpy. I was stunned at this glamorous present, protested, "I can't take it."

"I want you to have it." That ended the matter.

Granny died four years later. I could not cry at her funeral. I did not understand why I was unable to shed tears for the one who asked less and gave more in emotional support and gifts than anyone I knew. Even my father, whom I had never seen shed a tear, sniffled. I stared up at stiff, silent trees in Mount Hope Cemetery, Ardsley. My only sensation a shiver as the cold February wind blasted my face.

"Why couldn't I cry?" I asked John.

"Perhaps you were afraid to cry. Afraid you would feel ashamed of your deeper feelings."

I thought I had lost my best friend, someone who cared about me as a person. I felt deserted, drifting somewhat into the darkness of death myself.

But now in John's sympathetic presence I released tears I could not shed at the burial site. To protect myself from breaking down in front of strangers who did not know how much Granny meant to me, I felt icy, like the winter weather, so deep my devastation.

Forgive me, Granny, I thought, for not crying at your funeral, I missed you too much.

"She was the only one who wanted me to enjoy life," I told John, once more drying tears with his Kleenex.

"You seem to feel someone wanted to murder you," he said.

I could not escape the occasional feeling, sometimes bursting forth in dreams, that violence lurked just around the corner. The thought of blood-shed even pervaded John's office, the place I thought fairly safe.

One morning I crawled there, bent over double with the acute cramps that accompanied my menstrual period since ten, even at that age in a hurry to grow up.

I moaned to John, "I'm here though I'm dying of the curse."

He did not even offer aspirin. I thought sadly of the days Mother would wrap me in a blanket, put a hot-water bottle at my frozen feet, a cup of tea on the table beside me and the latest movie magazine in my lap so I could feel miserable in comfort. Illness brought constant attention and love from my mother, she gave physical care graciously. But she was like a stone wall when it came to understanding my feelings and emotional needs. I vowed never, *never* to be like my mother in this respect.

John was saying, "You referred to menstruation as 'the curse.' Women who call it that seem to have the most pain."

"Just a coincidence," I groaned. What an unfeeling creature, he could at least try to comfort me.

I added angrily, "Most girls in college called it the curse. That's where I learned the word."

"I'm sure some girls didn't."

"All my friends did." A retort.

"Your friends were probably the ones who had difficulty accepting menstruation as part of their lives."

I felt too sick to debate, it was not proper to discuss the topic anyhow. He was a man and women did not talk about "those things" with men. I never would have mentioned it except I felt deathly ill. I had bravely staggered to his office instead of phoning to say I was sick. But rather than admiration for courage I received criticism for pain.

"I feel I'm dying," I assured him.

"You know you're not." Reassuringly.

"Well, I *feel* like I'm dying." A mutter.

"If there was an earthquake you'd be on your feet pretty quick."

Was there a difference between actually dying and feeling as though you were dying? Were words that important? Had I blithely adopted the expression "the curse," believing it an accurate description when it conveyed only my fantasy? Did I call the period "the curse" because I felt it *was* a bloody curse? Because I envied boys, wished I were born a boy?

"Physical discomfort is not death," John was saying. "And pain is not death even though to you they may stand for death."

My preoccupation with dying at times seemed strong, judged by the words I used, the dreams I spun. The night before I dreamed I plunged into Long Island Sound from our boat, *The Eddie Boy*, named after my brother. When I surfaced, my back was bloody and clawed as though someone or something underseas had attacked me.

"Two of the cuts were enormous," I said to John. The image of the gaping wounds flashed to mind. "Like a fishhook! That's what I was. A fish, hooked!"

I went on, "On weekends my father insisted on fishing. I suppose it relaxed him after writing legal briefs or arguing in court all week. He insisted I also fish but agreed to unhook any fish I caught. I wanted no part of death. For a fish or me. I thought my father was cruel, killing those poor helpless creatures of the sea. It puzzled me he could enjoy such a sadistic sport."

Silence from the chair behind, I went on sadly, "Often I felt like the poor fish I watched flopping around the floor of the boat. Bloody and helpless."

"And you feel bloody and helpless and in acute pain during menstruation," John pointed out. "A poor fish of a woman instead of a noble specimen of a man."

I remembered further pain. "One summer when I was eleven, I went swimming at the Beach Point Club on Orienta Point. My father helped found this club because Jews in Westchester were not allowed to join the Christian beach clubs. I was climbing from deep water onto the float when suddenly my foot struck barnacles clamped to a rusty chain that fastened the float to the bottom. The lifeguard sitting nearby in a rowboat noticed blood pouring out of my cut foot. He rowed me quickly to shore, poured iodine on the cut, bandaged it and ordered, 'Go to a doctor at once. You need several stitches and the cut ought to be more thoroughly cleaned out. Those barnacles are wicked.' "

I clenched my teeth, said, "Thanks for your help." Thinking, No doctor, he will only make it hurt more.

In the bathhouse I flung off the bathing suit, dressed swiftly. Blood started to seep through the white bandage. I carried one shoe, limped to the phone, called a taxi, as I often did when I wanted to leave. Only our cook, Mae, was home. She was an outspoken young Irish woman I adored, as did my brother and sisters. She designed rich desserts and was our friend.

As I limped into the kitchen Mae was rolling crust for chocolate pie. She looked up, saw the pain on my face. "What's the matter, child?" She put down the rolling pin.

"I cut my foot at the club," I whispered. "I won't go to a doctor. I don't want to be sewn up."

"Go into the living room, sit down and let me look at it." An order.

I walked slowly through the pantry, the hall, sat down on the plush mulberry couch in our parlor. Stared at the bookcases with their sets of Washington Irving and Charles Dickens, which I had read several times. Mae followed with a basin of hot water, iodine, bandages.

I turned my head the other way as she removed the lifeguard's dressing, gently placed the bruised foot in warm water. I felt relieved, the pain eased.

I love her, was my drowsy thought, she will not let me die.

She studied the wound, parting broken skin with soft hands. "Whew, what a cut!" she exclaimed. "You should go to a doctor. It slices across almost half the bottom of your foot."

"It feels much better now." Lamely. Then defiantly, "I'll lie here and die first before seeing a doctor."

She sighed. "Well, I'll do the best I can." She swabbed the cut with iodine. I can bear this pain, I thought, she will take care of me without more hurt.

"You'll have to give up baseball and tennis and hold this foot high on a chair for several days," she ordered.

"Of course." Anything she asked.

I marveled my parents did not haul me to a doctor (they did for everything else wrong) when they came home and saw the bandaged foot. I did not inform them how dangerous the cut, swore Mae to secrecy. But they might have guessed because when I was not asleep at night I remained within the house with my foot propped high on a chair for four days, until Mae dismissed me as a patient. For me to stay quiet in the house for more than half a day meant something was drastically wrong.

I said to John vehemently, "Mae saved my life. I might have died if rust from the chain infected the cut. She wanted me to live. Not like the others, who didn't care whether I lived or died."

"What others?" he asked.

A whisper, "My mother and father."

"They're the only ones that count in a child's life."

"Why did I feel they didn't care?" A stricken voice.

"Because you felt at times they hated you. Hate implies the death wish. They are tied together."

"I sometimes felt their hate. But that they wanted to kill me?" I was stunned.

"Not actually kill you. But they made you feel at moments that their complicated lives would be far easier if you were out of the way and they could live in peace. To a child, this wish by a parent implies death. Abandonment and annihilation."

I thought of my mother storming at times, "You

make me wish I hadn't been born." Or saying angrily, "I wish I were dead!" as she flung me a look of hatred. Meaning, "I wish *you* hadn't been born. I wish *you* were dead."

I remembered with sudden fear "looks that kill," shot out by both my mother and father. I also remember my father shouting, "Don't be crazy!" when I wanted to do something of which he disapproved.

I told this to John, then asked, "Did they really want me dead?"

"They never tried to kill you," he said. "But in your unhappiness it seemed at times as though they wanted you to disappear. In your inner, unrealistic world you believed they wished you dead."

I was silent, this was difficult to accept though I knew I had felt their wish.

"When a parent rages, a child interprets it as the intent to murder. It is hard for a child to distinguish between a real threat of death by a parent and a momentary, unconscious threat, of which the parent is unaware." He added, "Some parents do kill children."

"See your daily paper," I retorted.

"Parents who would never kill a child may possess the wish that the child were out of the way at times but not as intensely as parents who murder a child," John explained.

Words spoken in hate often shield the wish to murder, of which the parent is unaware, but which to the child becomes a murder threat, I thought grimly.

"Children are the barometer of the feelings of parents," John went on. "If a child is happy you know his parents possessed little need to feed on him emotionally."

"You mean cannibalism can be emotional as well as actual?" My voice held surprise.

"You can devour a child, emotionally speaking," he said. Then went on, "No parent wants to hate a child. A parent may become consumed by his unconscious hatred of himself and his parents. Parents often unfairly blame a child for much that goes wrong in their lives. They use the child as a whipping post."

Over the next few months with John's help I also faced the fact that one reason I felt wicked and deserving of death was because I dared possess sexual desires. I felt I must apologize to the world for the strange body hunger that stirred at times.

At first it was painful even to utter the word *sex* in front of him. I would bring up the topic, drop it quickly, like something dangerous. But one morning I dared say defiantly, "I suppose I've got to talk about sex sometime. I've heard that in analysis you're supposed to examine your sexual feelings."

"Please forget what you've always heard," he suggested. "Use your own good mind."

"Let's skip sex," I muttered. "I don't have much to say about it anyhow."

"It's the things you don't say that are important," he reminded me.

"I'm not particularly afraid of sex." I tried to sound casual. "I just don't see any reason to discuss it at length."

"I'd expect you to have some fears about your sexual feelings." Reassuringly.

I finally admitted, "I hate dirty jokes with a vengeance. They're usually sexual. My father used to tell them at times and I felt so ashamed of him. Don't you think it's disgusting for people to sink to the level of filthy jokes?"

"Why do you think it's disgusting?"

"It puts sex on such a nasty level." Indignantly.

"Maybe you believe sex *is* on a low level." His voice was not reproachful, he discussed sex in the same tone of thoughtfulness he spoke of all else.

"Doesn't sex disturb *you?*" I was upset by his composure in face of such a tumultuous topic.

"Why should it? It's a natural function millions of people enjoy daily all over the world. It is neither noble nor disgusting. It just is. Like the digestive system."

"You mean sex is permissible?" A jest that held not humor but fear.

"When kept in its appropriate place. As part of life, not the whole of it. Which it often becomes for those who are afraid of it."

Could it be because I was afraid of sex it held importance out of all proportion to reality—the fascination of forbidden fruit?

I admitted, "Sex to me has always been a secret thing."

"You feel it belongs in the bathroom. You don't see it as a natural feeling in every room of the house."

It is difficult to accept as natural that which I had never been permitted to accept as natural, I thought.

"I'm mixed up about sex and love," I confessed. "To me they are two different things. Love is romance, white chiffon, stardust, soft spring breezes. Sex is sordid, torn black blouses, heat of July."

"Sex is part of love," John said. "The concept that love and sex are split makes for much unhappiness. Some people can't conceive of sex as tender but think of it as dirty and violent."

My mother and father never mentioned sex as I grew up, ignored it as though it did not exist. My father warned, when I was in third year high school, not to give myself sexually to a man before marriage because this led to "sleeping around."

I never dared go beyond the kiss, as endurance with

the lips became compensation for the lack of completion of the sexual act. We went driving in couples, the boys took turns at the wheel so no one would feel cheated out of the backseat. I recall one kiss lasting from Harrison to Larchmont, a distance of four miles. If the driver had not stopped the car, protesting, "It's our turn!" my embraceable partner might have held the kiss as far as New Rochelle, next town down the line. To me a kiss became more than a kiss, it symbolized sex—thrilling, wondrous, forbidden.

Gradually, with John's help, I started to understand that sexual feelings were a part of living. My parents expected me to refrain from any sexual contact until I married. Then, suddenly, in response to the wedding march, sexuality would be permitted to change in an instant from "bad" to "good."

I became willing to learn more and more about my fears and fantasies as I felt John's support of my quest. Perhaps this is part of the analyst's spirit of "hope" for change in the patient, which Dr. Karl Menninger says every successful analyst must feel.

Once I asked John, "Do you think my father really loved me?"

"What do you think?" His oft-repeated answer to a question.

"I think he did. He made me feel important in his life."

"Was it a consistent love?"

"Not always." I fell silent.

"What are you thinking?"

"I remember one evening when I returned from my first four months at Bennington, known for the liberal political attitudes of some professors. I knew my father was an ardent Democrat. Knew I should not say anything to antagonize him. He was famous for the quick temper that accompanied his red-blond hair." Usually calm, he might suddenly erupt in a violent tempest of words, immediately followed by a sunny smile, cajoling manner.

"For some reason," I went on, "this night I expounded at the dinner table on the philosophy of my new professor in political science. He had praised the efficiency of the Communist form of government in raising the standards of the poor. I quoted him as saying in some respects Russia was more of a democracy than the United States.

"Suddenly my father, who sat to my right at the head of the table, turned and cracked me across the face." It had felt like a sharp knife twisting away in my stomach with bottomless hurt. As far as I could remember he had never before raised his hand against me, though he used words to hurt.

I continued, "I looked up and saw my brother, who sat to the left of me, stare at his plate, embarrassed for me. My youngest sister, Sally, across the table, flashed a glance of approval. She stormed at my mother with comparative ease, their fights were legion. I looked at my mother at the other end of the table, opposite my father. Her eyes were blank, a curtain drawn over her usual expressive face. I thought, Mother, you aren't going to come to my rescue, are you? You never protect me against my father's anger."

I took a deep breath, said, "I stood up, dashed from the dining room and raced upstairs in tears, feeling humiliated beyond words. I slammed the door of my room, threw myself on the bed. My father followed at once, opened the closed door. He smiled, said, 'Come back downstairs.'

"I muttered, 'I'll be down in a minute,' started to wipe away the tears. I felt stunned. He had hit me not because of a sexual affair or something unfair I had done to my brother or sisters or for failing in an exam.

But for quoting a political opinion by a professor at a college my father had selected."

I said sarcastically to John, "I didn't realize what an ardent Democrat he was." Then stormed, "I hated him for humiliating me in front of the family."

"I am glad you can admit the hatred," John said. "You feel anger more easily at your mother but I have not been aware of anger at your godlike father. It's more deeply buried and for that reason more destructive. You haven't understood your worship of him contains its share of rage."

He helped me realize my father and I had been, as he put it, "too close for comfort over the years." He added, "Your father made it difficult for you to make peace with your natural Oedipal desire, which then became intense because he favored you."

You cannot possess your father. Those five words infuriated me more than all others put together. It was as though John attacked the only support I could count on in our house. But I gained a glimmer of understanding that my subservience hid the wish at times to destroy him more often than I was willing to admit.

A year of analysis passed as I felt slightly more aware of hidden feelings of rage and sexual desire. Then came another important sign of inner change. At long last I shed the stigma of being the lone spinster in the family. This occurred partially as the result of a newspaper assignment in Dallas.

Because of occasional out-of-town stories I saw much of America. During the war I visited factories in Seattle and San Francisco to report on the need for women workers in the building of planes. Now I was sent to Dallas to cover the annual meeting of the American Association of University Women. Texas was foreign soil to me but I looked forward to visiting Neiman-Marcus. As a result of the analysis I gained a growing interest in the feminine side of me, now rising from repression to a modicum of awareness.

On the second day of the convention I sent a summary of the speeches via Western Union to the national desk in New York, as distinguished from the city desk for Manhattan news and the foreign desk for news from all over the world. Then I learned from a local reporter that ammunition stored in two ships moored in Texas City twelve miles from the Gulf of Mexico had suddenly exploded, killing not only the men aboard but many people in the town of Texas City.

I immediately called the city desk to ask if I should fly to Texas City, 280 miles away, to cover the catastrophe. Mr. Joseph said two reporters were on their way but I should forget the women's convention and the paper would use Associated Press releases. He suggested, "Fly to Texas City at once and send us feature stories."

I flew aboard a navy plane bearing plasma to the stricken area, then hitched an auto ride into the stunned little town. I talked to men bound in bloody bandages, numbed relatives of the dead and missing, dazed owners of shattered stores. There was no place to send the story, no hotel to stay in, but a reporter from Houston, who had arrived earlier, generously drove me to the nearest Western Union office in Galveston, fourteen miles away, to write my story. Page by page a clerk snatched it out of the typewriter to teletype it to New York for the first edition.

I then collapsed on a soft bed in a Galveston hotel room. At 2 A.M. I suddenly woke, bolted upright. An important fact had registered in my conscious mind. I stumbled out of bed, groped for the carbon copy of the story I had filed. Then moaned, "Oh, no!" I had written:

"Terror-stricken Texas City today turned into a gray ghost town. House after house stood in splintered silence, deserted in destruction. In the shadow of the raging fires, a cow munched away at scrubby grass, no one around to milk him."

The "him" glared out like a bull in a china shop. I had insulted Mother Nature. It was too late to phone a correction. The paper had hit the street hours ago, had "gone to bed," as the printers say.

Dejectedly I crawled back to my bed. I visualized *The New Yorker* quoting the sentence with the comment, "Isn't it about time city reporters learn the facts of life?" One of their small fillers at the bottom of a back page.

Fires had blazed away on the *Grand Camp* April 16 and on the *High Flyer* April 17. Five days later, on April 21, 1947, I covered a mass memorial service on the high school football field at the edge of town for the five hundred men, women and a few children who had died in the blasts. I headed for the field, the first moments of leisure in the five tumultuous days of work, along with the two *Times* reporters who arrived shortly after I did.

April in Texas felt like July in New York. My one suit reflected dirt, gore, coffee stains. I was lucky it was black to begin with. I told myself, You sure don't look like a slick New York reporter. Another part of me replied, You're not a reporter. The first asked, Oh, no? What am I then? The second answered, You are a woman, above all.

On the way to the stadium I walked through a building that four days before served as a commercial garage. Now it held row after row of bodies, the identified and the unidentified. Stretched out in death lay workmen of the piers and others who raced to West Bay to watch the ships burn and were killed in further unexpected explosions. Employees of the nearby chemical plant also had been trapped at work when the munitions first burst into the air.

My story started off: "Facing the setting sun, 1,500 survivors of this city's tragedy stood in the local football field this evening attending a memorial meeting for their dead.

"They bowed their heads beneath a sky dark with the gray smoke which still sweeps steadily past overhead. Two separate fires were blazing in the distance. There were few tears among those in the audience. Eyes which had seen only death, near death and destruction for four grim days looked with wonder at the most spectacular display of flowers they had ever seen."

The wooden stadium flamed with the beauty of thousands of massed blossoms. All the towns and cities of Texas, through the Texas State Florists' Association, sent plants, baskets, wreaths. Almost every flower then in season bloomed in a brilliant banner that reached from goalpost to goalpost. Three large crosses flowered across the stadium, nailed to empty seats.

I prayed for those who died and those left behind, "Please God, help these people who have lost their loved ones and bless those who have died."

I also prayed for myself, "And please don't take life from me until I have shared it with someone I love."

The Lord answered my prayer immediately.

I returned to the city room, sat once more in comparative peace at my desk. I thought of the blunder I had made about the cow. At that moment a young copy editor on the national desk walked over to me. He was tall, dark and handsome as they say, in his mid-thirties. I had vaguely noticed him at night. Copy editors arrived late afternoon to work on the day's stories and the fast-breaking evening news.

He announced in a low, rather husky voice, "I was the editor on your feature stories from Texas City. They were excellent. I thought you might not have seen all editions so I saved them for you." He handed me five days' worth of clippings.

He added, a note of humor in his voice, "I also fixed the sex of the cow. Your story made the front page and I wanted you to be correct."

I felt mixed shame and relief. I looked at him gratefully, said, "Thank you more than I can say." Apologized, "I realized the error at two in the morning and by then it was too late to call in." Added, "You saved me from making a fool of myself."

"My pleasure. I only did my job." He turned, walked back to his copy editor's corner of the room.

Three nights later I played bridge in the office with Frank Adams and two other addicts, waiting for a "good night" from the editor. A lone reporter might be typing out a late story of a court case or a political speech delivered at a dinner as, several desks away, a quiet bridge game progressed. Occasionally not so quiet if two prima donnas collided in erratic bidding.

At one point, as I was dummy, I looked up, saw the copy editor who had saved me from ridicule standing beside me. I asked, "Do you want to take my next hand?"

He laughed. "I don't play but thank you."

Then he leaned over, whispered in my ear, "Would you like to have a drink when I get through work in about an hour?"

"I'd love to," I whispered back conspiratorially.

I had never been asked out by a copy editor, only other reporters. I looked up to the copy editor who caught mistakes, supposedly knew the English language better than reporters, though some of the veterans objected to corrections on their copy and quietly or not so quietly cursed the editor who changed one word of the story. I thought most copy editors were calm and courteous, helped us write more precisely. As my new friend on the national desk had done with me.

The game continued for an hour and by then the copy editors had finished work, all stories checked and headlined, the first edition almost on the street. The tall, dark and handsome editor walked over to my desk, said, "I forgot to introduce myself. My name is Paul Freeman," not his real first name.

We walked to Sardi's, around the corner. I learned he was not only a scholar but a soldier, had fought in Germany. Also that he wore glasses only when he read copy. He was a bachelor and his mother, an actress, was appearing in a Broadway play, not as the star but in a supporting role.

Several weeks and several dates later he asked me to marry him. I felt like the belle of the fourth estate. This was the first time I dared dream marriage might become a reality. I had never taken a proposal seriously but no longer was I content to sell my birthright for a mess of masochistic loneliness.

At my next session I told John, whom I had kept abreast of developments in the romance, "Paul proposed last night."

"What did you say?" John asked.

"I want to marry him." I spoke in a strong voice, unusual for me. "We're thinking of getting married in a month."

To my surprise John asked, "Why don't you wait a while?"

"I can't wait." Stubbornly. "I've been an old maid long enough." I relished giving up the role of the family's sorrowing spinster.

I abhorred the idea of waiting, I disliked living alone, as did Paul. We seemed sexually compatible, shared in common the newspaper profession. He was witty, highly intelligent, bursting with energy. Both his mother, an attractive self-possessed woman, and my mother and father appeared delighted with the idea of their lone remaining child finally getting married.

"Are you going to give me up if I marry?" I asked John worriedly. Then I would not know what to do—call off the marriage or end analysis? I heard analysts did not approve of patients taking any serious step, such as marriage or divorce, during analysis.

"No," he replied. "You will still need help."

Mother and I shopped for a gleaming white satin wedding dress, simple flowing lines to the floor. I borrowed a lace headdress, one she had worn at her own wedding, from my beloved Aunt Helen Prince, married to Uncle Ted, Grumpy's brother. Over the years she had vainly tried to be matchmaker, her choices proved neither to my nor the man's liking, but now she felt happy for me.

Mother and I went to the Palm Court of the Plaza Hotel for tea and sandwiches after we found the white satin gown. I felt daring enough in this new intimacy—now I, too, would be a wife—to ask something I had always wanted to know.

"Did you love Laurie when you married him?" I dared.

"Not at first," she said. "But I soon fell in love with him." Added, "I've never stopped loving him."

"Even though you're divorced?" I was astounded.

"You don't stop loving someone because he has stopped loving you," she said.

"I do." Thought of one or two gentlemen who had walked away from me, whereupon I swiftly found a replacement.

"You're younger and more pliant," she said.

Paul and I planned a large wedding. We posted a notice on the bulletin board in the city room inviting the entire staff to ceremonies in the ballroom of the Hotel

Gotham. More formal invitations went to Mr. and Mrs. Arthur Sulzberger, Edwin L. James, the managing editor, and Mr. Markel.

Just before I dashed out of the dressing room Mother pulled from her purse a sprig of orange blossoms, perched it behind my right ear. I had insisted I would not wear one orange blossom, my only break with marital convention, but gave in to her obviously ardent wish. She also poured peppermint medicine down my throat to calm what she thought my nerves, though I believed I was quite composed. It proved so effective I marched like a zombie down the aisle on the arm of my father.

Just before I took my father's arm I glimpsed Warren Moscow, a top political reporter and friend, slip through the door. It was World Series day and the Dodgers were playing the Yankees in a crucial game.

I whispered, as he walked past to take a seat in the ballroom with the many reporters who had accepted our invitation, "Who's ahead?"

"The Dodgers," he whispered back, "and now I can enjoy your wedding."

"So can I," I hissed. I loved Paul but my girlhood dream died hard—to be the bride of Mel Ott, on the Giants but also a National League player. If the Giants could not win, any National League team would do.

My brother was an usher, Sally was matron of honor. She marched down the aisle in front of me, slightly pregnant with her second child, John (now president of Demex, Inc., a large firm in Chicago, married with two young sons).

Rabbi Stephen Wise of Temple Emanu-El in New York City, who knew my father and grandfather, performed the ceremony, approved in advance by Paul, who was also Jewish. I reported to John, "It was a lovely wedding, even if my mother and father did not say one word to each other." By now he had been married to Donna for eight years.

I had asked my half sister Alice, then seven, to be flower girl, had promised if I ever married she could precede me down the aisle scattering rose petals. But when I mentioned this to Mother her eyes filled with tears. I realized I could not hurt her this way, retracted the invitation to Alice. She seemed to understand, assured me she would enjoy the wedding anyhow. She complained later at being restricted to only a few sips of champagne but made up for it by two large portions of wedding cake, chocolate, of course.

Paul allowed me to choose the location of our honeymoon. Without thinking I said, "Let's drive to Williamstown in Massachusetts." When I told John this, I added in alarm, "I think I know why I selected Williamstown."

He waited for my now freer associations.

"It's where my father often took me weekends to play golf," I explained. "He loved that part of the Berkshires, he graduated from Williams College." I grimaced. "I suppose this means unconsciously I wanted to marry my father. Is that it?"

"If that's how you feel, that's it," John said.

Paul and I lived for six months in my apartment on the twenty-fourth floor at Riverside Drive and 103rd Street. Windows framed the slow-moving Hudson and the peaceful Palisades, offered stunning sunsets. Then he decided to buy a small house in Rye, three towns north of Larchmont, set in a wooded area. We furnished it in modern style, streamlined sofa, chairs and lamps. Our joint collection of books filled one room we called his den.

He was outwardly affable but I found him increasingly controlling. I wondered whether he envied me, thought a copy editor was not as important as a reporter. The reporter enjoyed the glamour of covering an exciting story, putting it into dramatic words. A copy editor wrote the headlines and corrected grammatical or other errors such as accuracy of fact or spelling. His name never appeared on the story as the reporter's often did. Perhaps in a subtle way Paul put me in my place when he took over the running of my life and our home. He wanted to be the one to shop for food, cook, select every item we bought for the house. He had to approve everyone who visited, including my mother and father.

One midafternoon when we were both home (our two days off did not coincide except when we made a request for a special occasion) we went shopping at a local grocery store. After the purchases I suggested, "Let's have a chocolate soda. I feel thirsty."

He gave an order. "We're having lobster tonight and you should not spoil your appetite."

I thought of my father, who joyously would have joined me in drinking a chocolate soda any hour of the day or night. I swallowed my resentment, wondered, How long can I stand being told what I may and may not eat and when? Reminder of mother, dictator of earlier days.

For almost another year I tried to deny resentment as Paul continued to give orders, taking over much of my life. The straw, or rather in this case, the plant, that broke the camel's back was added one evening when I returned home on the 9:20 from Grand Central Station as I did five nights a week.

For several months I nourished two ivy plants I had carefully and lovingly hung on the wall of our living room. They thrived mightily, each must have been as thirsty a plant as I was hungry a human. I was proud of my achievement, I had helped something grow, my first horticultural effort.

As I entered the living room I noticed in alarm only a few short ugly snouts now sprouted from the two pots that in the morning were amass with luxuriant leaves to the floor.

"What happened to my plants?" I turned in alarm to Paul, he had had the day off.

"I cut them," he said nonchalantly. "They grew too long. They looked ugly."

He cut them, I thought in despair, he mutilated the plants I nurtured and cherished. If he cared for me, he could not have murdered my ivy. Love me, love my plant. Kill my plant, kill me. I said not a word, turned and went into the bedroom to undress for the night.

The plants never grew, the few sparse leaves turned brown, shriveled. I felt more and more depressed, on days off sat staring out the large picture window into the woods beyond, just as in childhood I sometimes did in Granny's bungalow. I felt I owned things but not myself.

I had married not wisely but driven by compulsive, unconscious needs. If there had been choice, I could have waited as John advised me, come to know Paul's need to control would be unendurable.

Living in such serflike fashion proved so painful I could hardly face Paul when I woke each day, forsaking the fantasies of dreams for unbearable reality. I truly felt like murder in the morning.

Finally I gained the courage to tell Paul I was giving up on the marriage, took full responsibility for my ineptitude in making a go of it. The day I left, after packing a suitcase, I stood on the steps outside the white wooden front door.

I said, "I'll let you know my address when I find a place to live. You can send my clothes and books."

Paul stared at me sadly, asked, "Why are you leaving me, Lucy?"

I was silent, then finally spoke what I felt. "If I stayed, I would either kill you or myself, Paul. I don't know why but that is how I feel. Suffocated to death."

I walked to the waiting taxi, headed for Rye Station and New York. Even though I did not achieve success as a suburban wife at least to try marriage marked new courage, I thought.

Admittedly, not for one second was I willing to relinquish the career to work harder at marriage. At least not unless the husband was less controlling and I was permitted decisions, even though small ones, about matters vital to me.

I told John, "I left because I felt I couldn't even go to the bathroom to pee without Paul telling me how."

"Perhaps his control reminded you too much of your mother as she toilet-trained you," John said.

I sighed. "I didn't mean that literally about Paul. I was exaggerating somewhat."

"Don't denigrate the words you use," he advised. "They tell much about your childhood feelings."

I continued on the couch, I could now give more of myself, felt a wholeness restored. Paul remained in the house he loved, remarried shortly after our divorce, not much more happily. Another divorce later followed. He now joined the business news department, writing his own column, something he had wished to achieve. We saw each other rarely, nodded sadly when we passed in the city room.

One morning I confessed to John, "I feel much freer now that I am on my own once again. Rather than trying to please a man who wants to control me. And I have more time to write."

"Why do you think you wanted to be a writer?" John asked.

"I enjoy writing." Defensively. This was an attack

on the way I earned my living. Attack also on my most cherished way of expressing myself.

"Have you ever thought you might use words as a safety valve?"

"I don't understand!" Belligerently. "I write because I like to write. I get satisfaction using words to convey original ways of describing a scene or expressing a thought."

"Perhaps words help keep you from knowing what you feel," he needled on.

"I *don't* use words to cover up feelings." A retort. "I choose my words carefully. Words are important to me. I live by them."

"Words *are* important," he agreed. "If you use them to know the truth about how you feel. Not to mask feelings."

After three more years of analysis I understood what he meant. The sparkling adjectives I tossed off describing the Easter Parade or what the Empire State Building looked like after an airplane crashed into a top floor did not count because they failed to relate to deeper feelings. The words that mattered were words I dared not use—fear, hate, envy, greed, sexual passion, jealousy—words that ruled my emotional life. Words served as barriers against knowing the hidden self. I threw up a smoke screen of words against the buried pain.

I had taken refuge most of my life in the haven of intellectuality, denying feelings that quivered for release under the surface of words. I argued heatedly about philosophy, politics, psychology, choice of favorite authors in fiction and nonfiction. I used my head for everything but setting myself free of the torment of the past.

I said grimly to John, "My mother and father always had enough words to talk me out of anything they didn't want me to do. Or criticize me to kingdom come."

"They used words that hurt you. It is as though you now say to them, *'Words are important,* even if you, Mother and Father, used them to hurt me. See? They don't hurt when I use them for good, not evil.'"

I discovered words I wrote at twenty-one, from them even a nonanalyst could figure out what marriage meant to me: "Each life is lush with a thousand dreams. And the most delicate disappear when one marries. They do not break—nothing so drastic. They crumble and crackle and corrupt. Slow death to dreams!"

I was obviously describing my mother's failed marriage. After a lifetime of living with people, she was left on her own. Deserted by husband and four children, out on their own. Her home had become two rooms in a New York hotel after selling our Monroe Avenue house with its delicate, graceful willow tree welcoming guests. Now she had nothing to do, no one to care for, she was rootless and abandoned. She sank deeper and deeper into inner despair.

I had picked up some of her moods but at least I had a barbed-wire fence against depression—my work. A certain amount of energy goes into every job but into mine I also poured the passion and devotion most women put into running a home, raising children. Instead, I raced through assignments, took little time to enjoy them, seldom savored the hours.

After fleeing Rye and Paul I lived in a dollhouse-sized apartment on the third floor of a small building on busy Forty-ninth Street between Park and Madison avenues. The four-story building was owned by a shady ex-lawyer turned real estate wheeler and dealer who, for a time, romanced my mother, persuading her to invest money Granny left her in his big deals. She was attracted to him, thought he might marry her. Then he informed her, after losing a large part of her inheritance, he intended to marry a far younger woman. Once again Mother was abandoned, left to fend for herself. It was then Sue invited her to live with her in Hollywood.

And now I lived in misery in Chicago, about to start my second analysis. Perhaps Dr. Emch would help me discover what kept me from being a "proper" wife, understanding what a man needed. I was not quite ready to give up on Tom since he prepared to begin analysis. This meant he, too, was willing to give a final try.

I hoped Dr. Emch would help me understand more of the fantasies John believed kept me from knowing "reality"—whatever that amorphous illusion was. He had introduced me to the idea we lived in two worlds. Of one world we were aware. Of the second world we knew little or nothing but it ruled the world of which we were conscious.

It was this unknown world that caused my misery. I had started to delve into it with John. I hoped to explore it more deeply with this new analyst. Understand why I had made such a disastrous choice of husband, second time around.

5

The Power of
the Unconscious

D r. Emch's home was built of gray stone, a four-story town house on a shaded street bordering Lincoln Park. It overlooked Lake Michigan, now a placid blue before my eyes though it could boil up in a moment with stormy white-capped waves.

On the corner, next to the town house, reposed the Elks Memorial, an impressive white stone edifice flanked by a large lawn browned by winter chill. The bare branches of tall trees hovered over what in summer would be rainbow-shaded flower beds.

I parked the Oldsmobile in front of the town house, walked to the front door, rang the bell. I thought of another doorstep on which I stood trembling seven and a half years before, waiting for the door to open. Then there had been terror of the unknown. Now there was hope at what would become known.

A slim, gray-haired woman, white-aproned, opened the door. "I have an appointment," I said.

"Please come in." A warm smile.

She gestured to a small room on the left. "The doctor will see you in a few minutes."

The room held a green sofa, a wooden-backed chair, a corner table on which rested magazines including, I was happy to note, *The New Yorker*, fan that I was of Audax Minor. I sat down, reached for it, flipped the pages until I found his column, read the most recent thoroughbred news.

The maid reappeared within five minutes, said, "You can go up. The first door to the left."

She led me to stairs carpeted in moss green. The steps spiraled to the left. It seemed strange to walk upstairs to see a psychoanalyst in a house rather than an apartment. Or in an office. Many analysts saw patients away from their homes. I walked up the stairs slowly, wondering what I would find at the top.

Turning left I entered a large room, combination library and study. Rows of books lined one wood-paneled wall from floor to ceiling. In the rear left corner stood a rounded desk, telephone atop it. In the front left corner, facing Lincoln Park, I saw the analyst's chair behind a beige couch. The right side of the room held a large sofa, several light-green satin chairs and an end table bearing a vase of roses.

A slim, blond, very attractive woman stood at the desk as I entered. She walked toward me, held out her hand. Her grasp was firm, reassuring.

She said "Hello," the musical voice I had heard on the telephone. I was so overcome with her graciousness and warmth after Tom's cruelty over the months that I fought to hold back tears.

"Won't you sit down?" she said.

She indicated the beige couch, I sank into it with pleasure, in upright position. She sat in the adjacent brown velveteen chair. I noticed a small clock ticking away the expensive and delicate moments on the table next to her chair.

She was probably in her late forties though she looked younger. The blond hair, slightly curled, framed a sensitive noble face, the features artists often paint. Her eyes were a sparkling brown, her voice vibrant with rich tones, an invitation to the special intimacy only a psychoanalyst can offer. Intimacy without demands, intimacy that offers a trust leading to the acceptance of the hidden self.

"I'm here because I've made an unholy mess of my life," I confessed. "I gave up a successful newspaper career to marry a man I thought I loved. Only to fail at marriage twice. And feel the depths of a humiliation I never dreamed existed."

The tears, near the surface, rushed to my eyes. I drew a handkerchief from my purse, wiped them away, apologized, "I'm sorry."

"Cry all you want," she said. "If you need to cry, you must cry."

She understood my anguish, this gave me the courage to go on. "I could have walked the street, picked the first stranger and it couldn't have been more disastrous a marriage. A crazy thing to do."

Added, "I want to find out why I did it. Maybe we can make a go of the marriage. He is seeing a psychoanalyst, too."

She asked for a higher fee than I paid in New York, luckily I now had money from royalties and advances on new books. She suggested four times a week, one more session than John required.

I asked, "Do you mind if I sit up at the start?"

I was not quite ready to lie on her couch, it seemed threatening to take that supine position once again.

She spoke, a line I shall never forget: "You may

swing from the chandelier if it makes you feel more comfortable."

A bit facetious, this remark, but it brought a laugh I deeply needed. I looked up, a gigantic glittering chandelier hung from the ceiling almost overhead. I was delighted to be psychoanalyzed in a room with a crystal chandelier. It lent an aura of elegance to the hour. It also reminded me of my grandmother's home, as did the Monet on the far wall, a painting of his favorite lily pond.

For fifty minutes I spewed out details of Tom's physical and mental cruelty, my stupidity at failing to heed warning signs. I said bitterly, "I know now what the saying 'Love is blind' means."

As I walked down the spiraling green carpeted stairs and out of the house, for the first time since I originally left New York I had the warm feeling of being comforted.

The next several weeks I did little at the sessions but wail about the unholy state of the marriage. Tom hardly spoke except when we ate, then usually with caustic words. He demanded I tell him every sentence I uttered in analysis, could not understand my refusal as I pointed out this was frowned on by the analyst. My words belonged only in Dr. Emch's room, between her and me.

One morning she asked, "Why do you stay with such a disturbed man?"

"I have to try to make the marriage work," I said grimly. "I took on a commitment when I promised 'for better or worse.' "

"You do not have to keep a bad bargain," she said.

"Maybe I could save the marriage if I understand what he's asking of me."

"Your husband is asking the impossible of you,"

she said. "No woman could give him what he wants."

"Does he think I am asking the impossible of him, too?" This suddenly occurred to me.

"Each may be asking from the other what he cannot give—what nobody could give."

I sighed. "It doesn't make sense. How can you feel one moment the man you love is the most wonderful person in the world and then overnight feel betrayed— by yourself and him?"

Then she said, to me an amazing statement, "You knew unconsciously from the start it couldn't work."

I was confused. "I did? You mean I married him *because* I knew it wouldn't work?"

"Exactly."

"Why did I do such a ridiculous thing?"

"That's one of the reasons you came here. To find out why." Those expressive brown eyes looked straight into my blue ones.

I thought I married because I fell madly in love, could not live without him, wanted to be with him the rest of my life. I had dumped my career down the drain as though it were so much shit. Now I had to unravel the desperate reasons I had raced, without thought, into a pit of fear, terror and hatred.

She asked a question that led toward this deeper understanding. "What was happening in your life at the time you met Tom?"

"You mean that very day?" I wondered what this had to do with the marriage.

"During the weeks or months or even the year before."

Memory reeled backward, stopped one year before I met Tom. I said, "My father died about eleven months before Tom and I were introduced at a party in Chicago after the political conventions."

She waited for me to go on. "That was also the time

my analyst was throwing me out. Said I had enough analysis and should try on my own."

"How did you feel about that?"

"I didn't want him to give up on me. I felt he was getting rid of me." Then triumphantly, "When I met Tom I thought I was getting even with John. Showing him *someone* wanted me."

I was silent, then remembered more. "I saw John for the last time in October. I went to Chicago in November to see whether I loved Tom enough to marry him. A month later we married. I thought I didn't need an analyst any longer."

She said softly, "You fixed the analyst, you thought. But you fixed yourself. Just to get even with him."

I was startled. "I married to get revenge on him? You mean like saying 'You want to dump me but I'll show you what dumping really is'?"

"You may not be aware of it, Mrs. Freeman, but this was probably one of the strong motives that drove you to marry Tom."

"You're saying I acted unconsciously?" Added, "Unconsciously on purpose?"

She laughed. "That's one way to put it."

I thought of another reason I may have fled into the arms of a man without knowing why. "My mother was also forsaking me. She suddenly announced she was moving to Hollywood, Florida, to live with my sister Sue. My father died the previous year and I felt I lost both parents."

"Your mother was moving a thousand miles away, leaving your side, your father had just died and your analyst was going to 'dump' you, to use your word." Sympathy in her voice. "You felt abandoned by the three people to whom you were closest."

"So I did!" In sudden surprise. "I guess I felt I had nobody left in the world."

"Not even your important career could make up for such wholesale abandonment."

"No wonder I fell in love with the first handsome man who looked my way." I felt amazed at this revelation.

"He met your needs at that moment for a mother and father. Only he turned out to be a cruel parent. One who punished you for being a bad girl."

"To think I didn't realize what I was doing to my life." I groaned.

"No one does when they act out," she said.

"Act out? What is that?" Words new to me.

"When you act destructively on the basis of powerful fantasies that keep you from using reason."

I said hopefully, "What happened wasn't all bad. It brought me to you."

She went on, "Perhaps the marriage was also your way of getting further analysis. You told your first analyst you did not feel you were finished. Maybe you had to do something drastic far from home so you wouldn't feel unfaithful to him by going to someone in another city for more analysis."

The nightmare I was living in Chicago seemed founded on many motives, I thought. Caused by sudden traumas in my life I had never dared face.

I realized Tom also acted out as a result of his tormented past. He had told me his mother spent many months in mental hospitals and that his father often deserted the family for long periods. Tom had suffered at the hands of very emotionally disturbed parents.

Slowly, over the next few months, I discovered I had lived in a state of repressed fury at my father for dying and abandoning me to a loveless world. My first reactions had been grief and feelings of deprivation, followed by anger at the loss. But the rage, as always, had been quickly denied, buried in the unconscious.

I was furious too at my mother for leaving New York where I could visit her at a moment's notice, play bridge with her, shop with her, try to find her a second husband. I introduced her to several elderly bachelors and widowers who worked at the *Times*, including my city editor, Mr. Joseph, but nothing romantic ever ensued. And, of course, I now realized I was spinning in a whirling typhoon of anger at John for casting me aside.

I had been so consumed with rage that when the first man came along offering what we both thought love, I flung away career, friends, even in a way, family. I allowed myself to be emotionally raped by an older man, a charmer, who promised paradise. "Let's get married and grow up together," he had urged. That should have warned me we were both children—loveless, angry children, who could not help, only hurt each other.

"I should have had more sense than to marry Tom," I cried out to Dr. Emch.

"Sense has nothing to do with the unconscious," she said. "That is the part of you that deals with nonsense."

She thus coined a phrase I thought apt to describe the world of the unconscious. A world that appeared nightly in my dreams as they whirled with gangsters who attacked me, kidnapped me, robbed me.

She asked after I described one such dream, "Who is the gangster in your life?"

"I don't know any," I said.

"What about your father? Did he know any?"

"He did represent Frank Costello, a leading member of the Mafia, in a legal case," I recalled. "My father was chosen by the firm to help Costello settle a huge income tax problem with the Internal Revenue Service.

My father enjoyed Costello and vice versa. I remember feeling shocked at this. Costello bought Dad a set of magnificent golf clubs, in addition to paying legal costs. And every Christmas he drove up to my father's home in Mamaroneck with gifts of *My Sin* perfume appropriately named I thought, for his new wife."

Dr. Emch said, "Your father is the gangster in your dreams. It was your father who terrified you as an infant and child. Who represented the gangster type."

"Really?" I had never thought of him as a gangster.

"Unreally." She chuckled.

Unreally became a word I adopted to refer to what Freud called "psychic reality." It was my psychic reality we explored session by session as Dr. Emch slowly and skillfully led me to remembrance of terrifying things past.

She thought the non-sense in my life more important than the sense. To her, no thought was random. She wanted me to explore them all, allow words to flow freely no matter where they led. Only as I stopped trying to control my thoughts could I establish real control. I had to become aware of the nature of my unconscious, feel in tune with it rather than fighting it blindly as it won over reason. Which it often did in the everlasting battles among my conflicting emotions.

"Is it difficult to reach the unconscious?" I asked fearfully. The word *unconscious* conjured up maniacal monsters and death-dealing demons.

"Your unconscious lies near the surface, ready to make itself known in many ways," she said.

She held deep respect for the unconscious and, as a result, I absorbed this respect. There was only one sin in her book—to ignore what the unconscious was trying to tell me. She believed the purpose of psychoanalysis was to acquaint me with my unconscious, no matter how terrified of it I felt.

"We are not here to deal with your conscious," she said. "It is what you do not know that harms you."

I had to accept the unconscious as a primitive, greedy, immoral, unlawful part of me, of everyone. But a part from which also springs creativity and imagination.

She never sounded preachy or didactic, never commanded or tried to control, as my parents had. Not once did they apologize for a cruel remark or admit they were wrong. What I would have given for my mother and father to have uttered the words, "I was wrong, forgive me," after an argument or punitive command.

When Dr. Emch once admitted she was wrong, I could hardly believe my ears. After she made a remark I had dared say, "There's sarcasm in your voice. You sound just like my brilliant but often ironic, prone-to-tease father."

"I'm sorry," she apologized. "This is one of the things about myself I do not like and try to avoid. But sometimes it slips out."

The sarcasm seemed inconsistent with her overall warmth and understanding. She seemed almost to place herself in my shoes. The people in my early life appeared as real to her as they were to me. They assumed new dimensions as I looked at them once again, this time with more thoughtful and compassionate eyes.

When I tried to sound moral, saying, "I should have behaved more understandingly," she commented, "You talk like a rabbi." She helped me accept that nothing about myself was "evil" or "nasty." It just *was*, part of being human. John also had this quality of acceptance but hers seemed to strike deeper within. Perhaps I needed such acceptance from a woman, the mother symbol. Unconsciously knew this when I told Mike I wanted a woman analyst.

From Dr. Emch I started to get the feel of my

unconscious as part of me that was unique. That made me different from everyone else, since it contained memories that were mine alone. It held a power beyond belief. It put the conscious to shame when it came to plotting, motivating, deceiving. I felt new self-esteem in becoming aware of the strength of my unconscious, rather than denying I possessed one and living in constant dread of it.

I now became eager to know what stirred in my unconscious. Not to excuse what I did, not to condone, but to understand so my life would be happier. This was inspired by Dr. Emch's ability to float around with me in my unconscious. Lead me to fantasies that had been destructive, as shown in my swift, thoughtless decision to marry Tom.

She also possessed what I thought reverence for the specific. She gave me the sense that every single thing that had ever happened to me, every single person involved in my early life, held importance. I felt she really cared and wanted me to care too about the memories, emotions and fantasies that molded my life, particularly the painful ones that caused fear and distress. She was involved with me and my torments though not involved with me personally.

She never seemed to forget a word I spoke. She remembered something I told her months before, which she then fit into psychic place. She thought of psychoanalysis as a process of development rather than dialogue between two people focusing on the intellectual airing of memories followed by interpretation.

With many a sigh I became aware you cannot hurry a human to grow in an emotional sense, any more than you can hurry a plant. In analysis you learn a new kind of thinking that comes out of just "being." This happens not through words alone, though they are vital. They lead the way to deeper thoughts, once psychically unpalatable, now set free for the understanding of the hidden, dangerous part of the self.

She believed much of what happens in analysis takes place on an unconscious level between the one on the couch and the analyst. This is conveyed not only verbally but through tone of voice, facial expression, lowering or raising of a limb.

I remarked, needing occasionally to show my astuteness, "Analysis really takes place in an eight-way communication, doesn't it? Your conscious speaks to my conscious. Your conscious speaks to my unconscious. Your unconscious speaks to my conscious. And your unconscious speaks to my unconscious."

I went on, "The same is true for me. My conscious speaks to your conscious. My conscious speaks to your unconscious. My unconscious speaks to your conscious. And my unconscious speaks to your unconscious."

She laughed, that soft merry laugh, one of the few times it erupted when I dared an analytic concept. She never quoted theory or threw out professional jargon, nor did she want me to. I felt she had learned all the theory, ignored it when there was a patient in the room. Just related to whoever was stretched out on the couch imploring for help to ease the hurts of a lifetime.

She spoke in terms of my emotions and experiences, using simple words a child could understand. None of the jabberwocky words of her profession. All she wanted to hear from me, in the popular phrase of the day, was "just the facts, ma'am." And the fantasies about those facts. She wished me to spill out both facts and fantasies as though they were nothing to be ashamed of. She wanted only the truth, as far as I knew it.

She seemed more silent than John, who usually tried to fill a void when I felt recalcitrant, as though to reassure me. Perhaps this had been what I needed for a first go-round on the couch, terrified as I was. She wanted me to do most of the speaking, to hear words from my troubled heart. Once when I quoted Freud she said, "If you want a course in the theory of psychoanalysis, why don't you take one at the University of Chicago? It's much cheaper."

Though her voice was gentle, held a shade of humor, I felt rebuked. Instead of praising me for my psychoanalytic perspicacity, she damned me for being intellectual.

She caught my feeling of rejection, said with a sigh, "I wish you'd read Mother Goose instead of Freud."

"I don't get it." I wondered if her mind had snapped under the strain of too many patients like me.

"You will." She settled back into silence.

I thought, It's like what Louis Armstrong said when someone demanded, "Define jazz so I can understand it." The sensitive Satchmo replied, "If you got to have it defined, you ain't never goin' to understand it."

Slightly upset by her attack on one of my most stalwart defenses, I defended myself further in an attempt at irony. "I'm only being considerate of you. Suppose a patient refused to spout theory or give his interpretations, believing this your prerogative and duty. Why, you'd drop dead of the shock!"

"I'd be happy to take the risk." Dryly.

She rarely quoted from any source, psychoanalytic or literary. She used her own sensitive poetic mind. There were exceptions. I have never forgotten her reply when I asked, "Isn't it egotistical for me to be proud of my accomplishments?" after she suggested I take pride in them.

She recited from the Talmud: "If I am not for myself, who will be for me? If I am for myself only, what am I? If not now—when?"

One day on the couch I remarked, telling her details about the Heirens book, "I suppose I have to ask myself, 'What's a nice girl like you doing writing about murder?' "

She said, "You are so angry at your husband you would like to kill him."

"You mean I write about murder instead of committing it?" It had not occurred to me writing was an indirect way of releasing hidden rage at Tom. Perhaps even rage at my mother and father when I was a child.

Sometimes I felt like the officious Red Queen in *Through the Looking Glass*, who explained to Alice, "Now, *here*, you see, it takes all the running *you* can do, to keep in the same place. If you want to get somewhere else, you must run at least twice as fast." Dr. Emch asked that I stop running, slow down, take a deep breath and, in her inimitable words, "Let things percolate."

I had raced from the truth of my life and now wanted to race toward it. Alas, I could not race toward truth, I could only crawl in its direction.

She asked one day, "What made you write your first book, *Fight Against Fears*?"

"It all began in a snowstorm," I said. "I was returning by train from an assignment in Syracuse after covering a meeting of the New York State Probation and Parole Association. It was mid-January and upstate New York was buried in an awesome snowstorm. Our train stopped dead halfway to Albany along the Mohawk River as eastbound trains queued up behind us."

I thought of that moment, an important one in my life, went on, "I had nothing to read, felt I would go crazy. But I had taken a stack of copy paper on which to write my stories before I filed them at Western Union. And three pens. Suddenly I thought, I'll put down what I feel I'm getting out of analysis after being in it five years. I started to write, filled twelve pages by the time we slowly moved toward Albany and ten more by the time we slid into the station."

I smiled, remembering, "I settled down in the private compartment, put my feet up on the bed, wrote away. The words flowed easily. I had enough for an article, I thought. When I got home I typed it, sent the pages to Charles Angoff, editor of *The American Mercury.* I knew he was interested in mental health stories. He bought it."

I told her how shortly after the article appeared I was talking to Daniel Schwartz, then editor of the Sunday *Times* magazine section. I told Dan about the *Mercury* piece, he suggested, "Why don't you get back some of the money you've spent on the couch and write a book about your analysis?" Easygoing, thoughtful, appealing Dan had been responsible for the idea of a book.

Then I thought, Where will I find the time to write it, what with five full days a week occupied with reporting? But I brooded over Dan's idea. I had much I wanted to say about the analysis, maybe I *could* manage a book. It would only be the length of twenty magazine articles strung together. I asked John how he felt about the idea. He had no objections, only asked his name be changed.

Max Wilkinson, just giving up as story editor for Samuel Goldwyn in Hollywood to start his own literary agency, agreed to take me as his first author (he later represented John D. MacDonald and Kurt Vonnegut). Carolyn Blakemore, who became a friend, was a colleague at Littauer and Wilkinson, then senior editor at Doubleday for fifteen years and now is in business for herself as a free-lance and consultation editor for G. P. Putnam's Sons. I remained a permanent client until Max retired in the 1970s to Shelter Island, a far more relaxed life than Manhattan.

Max sent the article to Robert Van Gelder, editor at Crown Publishers, who liked the idea, signed me to a contract with the blessings of the owners, Nat Wartels and Robert Simon. Four months later they had the book, as I took a leave of absence to work full-time on it for six weeks, then slaved nights and days off to finish it.

I told Dr. Emch, "I know now I *had* to write that book. I use words in part to ease the unhappiness in my life. And writing about the analytic sessions with John was one way of reducing the fear of facing myself on the couch. Though I told myself it was the best way to remember all the things he said that helped me."

Added, "And another reason is that I wanted to crusade for psychoanalysis. Many people crusade for economic or political freedom. I crusade for emotional freedom. For men, women and children."

I told her what John thought when I first mentioned my wish to write about analysis. "He smiled, said, 'It's probably your way of dancing.' Meaning I took delight in it. But then he added, as though in warning, 'You couldn't possibly put everything into one book or two or a dozen about an analysis.' And I said, 'But if I tell something about what it has done for me, others may benefit.' He said, 'That's true. And laudable. A gift from the heart, so to speak. No mean gift.'"

When I asked John if he wanted to read the manuscript before I sent it in, he said he would be glad to but would not touch the quotes. He added, "After all, it is your book." He went over it, charged one hundred dollars for his time, which I was glad to pay, changed not a sentence.

His words, "It is your book," meant he trusted me. I never felt my mother or father did. Nor, come to think of it, did I trust them.

Much of what happens in analysis cannot be described. It cannot be put into words even to yourself because the effects are felt in both the conscious and unconscious. As Dr. Emch accepted me—the "good" and the "bad"—I started to accept myself and understand why two marriages failed. They were inevitably doomed from the start, as though two children had tried to make a go of it. Two children consumed with fury.

I now understood something John once said: "When you add or subtract a quantity of fear, many things in a person change." Dr. Emch helped me subtract fear. As I uncovered fantasies that had plagued me over the years, they somehow lost their ability to menace or horrify.

Often the fantasies were tied to time—the unconscious keeps unerring track of traumatic times. This was brought home sharply one morning nine months after I started with Dr. Emch. Until that very day I had continued to sit on the couch facing her. Now after I walked in, without apparent reason I said, "I think I'll try lying down today."

She said, "You have sat up for nine months but suddenly feel confident enough to lie on the couch. Why do you think you chose this day?"

I thought, repeated, "Nine months." Then, "That's the time it takes to have a baby."

Strangely, I felt like crying. I thought, I do not want to be a crybaby. The next thought was, Cry—baby, this has something to do with baby. I told her these associations, then said, "I think I had to find out if you would give birth to a baby and betray me, as I felt my mother did. But you haven't had a baby in the nine months I have been coming here so now I can trust you enough to lie down on the couch."

She agreed with my interpretation. I was proud it was correct. As a child I had felt betrayed each nine months my mother produced a rival. Every child wants to be the only child, cannot understand why he is not. I had to put Dr. Emch through the test.

It was then I could ask, about the handsome man in the United States Navy uniform, whose photograph sat on the table across the room, "Who is he?" It was safe, he had not given her a baby since I arrived.

"That's my husband," she said. "The photograph was taken during the war."

I was as curious about her life as I was about the lives of my parents when I was a child. Polite little girl I was taught to be, I had refrained from asking my mother and father embarrassing questions. But the curiosity later erupted with a vengeance, sparked the asking of endless questions and answers for the whole nation to see in my work as reporter.

One of the most important questions as a little girl of two, then four, then ten, when my mother had produced babies, was, "Why are you doing this to me? Pushing me out of your life and away from your love and care?" I had never dared face my fear of being forsaken by her or the anger that inevitably shadows fear.

Fear is the signal that alerts us to danger, we then use the anger that is part of our aggressive spirit to try to escape the danger. This is healthy when we see a car speeding down on us, out of control, jump away from the menace of death. But unhealthy if we store up anger at unreal menaces. Such anger may warp us, harm us emotionally.

The growing trust in Dr. Emch gave me courage to resolve the most recent conflict swinging back and forth over my terrified head like a perpetual, threatening sword-pendulum. Tom and I lived in silent rage, keeping safe distance from each other for almost a year but now we started to argue.

One evening he snarled, "I don't see any change in you. I don't know why you see that woman pirate. You're only wasting your money." He had quit his own analysis, called his therapist a "fraud."

His words helped me at last to give up the fantasy we would ever understand each other. Perhaps his move to leave analysis was his way of forcing the issue. He now seized another way, a despicable, desperate way.

I had given the twelve thousand dollars I still possessed from book royalties to Tom's stockbroker to invest in an account under my name. This was the first time I dared become a gambler on Wall Street, where the risks were different and many times higher than my bets at the racetrack or living the precarious existence of a free-lance writer.

One morning after Tom left for Boston to survey another hospital I received a phone call from my broker, Homer Hargrave, Jr. He was the son of Colleen Moore, the actress, and Homer Hargrave, Sr., a well-known Chicago broker.

He said in his friendly voice, "I need your consent before I can transfer your money to your husband's account."

I was stunned. "Do you mean my husband, without consulting me, asked you to do this?"

"He called yesterday. Didn't he tell you?"

I said quietly, "No, he didn't." Then, "I can't consent to this. I want to keep my own account."

"I will not transfer it," he promised.

"Thank you for calling, Mr. Hargrave. I appreciate it more than I can say." I felt grateful he had consulted me though this was probably routine in such an instance.

For the first time since I met Tom I trembled not with fear but fury. This was betrayal far greater than a physical blow, the refusal to have sex or the hatred he openly revealed. This was the stealing of money I had earned and needed for my own support and to pay for the analysis.

I could bear the physical and emotional beatings but not open robbery. I had paid from the first day of marriage for all our food, he paid the rent. I contributed the time to shop, to cook and to clean.

Anything a man did was acceptable, I had learned from my mother, who had put up for over a decade with my father loving another woman before Mother asked him to leave the house. But at long last I broke free from following in my mother's path of fear. I now had enough strength to confront a man's duplicity, be it sexual or monetary.

It was then I told Dr. Emch, after describing the call from the broker, "This is the last straw. I am going to find my own apartment and get a divorce."

"Are you sure you don't want to return to New York and your work there?" The melodious voice.

I felt this a shaft in the heart. I did not want to leave her, she was freeing me from much of the pain of the past.

I said stubbornly, "I am not going to give up my analysis with you until it's finished."

"That's your decision," she said.

Leaving Tom was another decision I would never regret. I thought of the words of a friend, Eddie Jaffe, an internationally known expert in public relations. He wrote a moving chapter of his analysis with a well-known New York psychoanalyst in *Celebrities on the Couch.* He tells of his analyst saying to him one day, "You'd better get married or you'll be a lonely old man."

A few months later Eddie followed his suggestion and married. After a number of unhappy experiences with his wife, Eddie remarked to the analyst, "I have to tell you something. I'd rather be a lonely old man."

Perhaps I would wind up a lonely old lady but I preferred that to the devastating existence with Tom. Our relationship could only sink lower, that I now knew.

I was finally able to leave though I could not tell him in advance, fearing his anger, that he would somehow stop me. Through an ad in the Chicago *Tribune* I found a delightful one-bedroom apartment on the second floor of a four-story house on Bellevue Place, one block north of Oak. It was a stone's throw from the Drake, where I had met Tom that fateful evening.

He planned to visit New York for several days to gather more statistics for his hospital survey. The moment he walked out the door I started to pack. I had arranged for a mover to arrive that afternoon and cart to the new home my few possessions, the most important, the typewriter.

The week before I visited fabulous Marshall Field's, a dream of a department store with its wide carpeted corridors and offerings in all departments hard to resist. I picked out a double bed, bureau, sofa, two comfortable living room chairs, four dining room chairs, table and three large bookcases—now I could put the leather-bound Poe and Irving classics out where they belonged. All were delivered to the Bellevue address the day before I moved in. The gracious landlady, who lived on the top floor, offered to show the movers where to place the furniture.

I left Tom a note saying it was obvious we were both acutely unhappy and I was moving out. I gave the address and telephone number. I hoped he would accept the fact no miracle could occur, this was best for both of us. He had to be relieved. Tension would vanish and he would have the apartment all to himself once more.

I felt immediately at home in the new apartment, a haven in the back of the house overlooking a garden. I regained a sense of dignity and self-respect, lost during two years with an angry man. No longer would I have to move carefully and quietly, in constant fear of sudden verbal attack. I savored the purchasing of other items I needed—bedsheets, towels, kitchen utensils, a television set, a rug.

I was through with that time of terror in my life, now willing and able to face some of the earlier terror that had led, straight as an arrow, to the later terror.

After my swift move Dr. Emch said, "You must have been full of piss and vinegar as a little girl."

I felt startled, asked, "Is that an insult?"

"Not at all," she said. "It's a compliment. I mean you are full of energy and imagination. Furnishing that apartment within a week."

When he returned to Chicago Tom called, sounded depressed, said he wished I had not made the move. I wondered why men seem surprised when a woman finally leaves after a stormy relationship, Paul, too, had seemed surprised. As though they had no idea how unhappy the woman had been, no awareness of their behavior as the reason for her leaving.

The next day he called again, this time anger in his voice as he threatened, "You'll be sorry. I don't intend to take your desertion quietly."

I pointed out, "I left you the car even though it is half mine." I now took the bus to Dr. Emch's house.

"You'll have to come up with a lot more than the car," he snarled. "I intend to sue you for every penny you have. You've ruined my life."

"No one can ruin anyone else's life," I said. "You have to take responsibility for your life, I for mine. We cannot make it together, Tom. That's obvious by now."

After similar threats in further conversations over the telephone, he agreed to a divorce. Uncle Ed, guiding me from New York, recommended I settle for eight thousand dollars as the price of peace of mind—Tom demanded twelve thousand but finally agreed to the lower sum. There was also a large fee asked by my Chicago lawyer, a man Uncle Ed suggested, who had represented the firm in cases involving clients from Chicago.

I appeared one day before a judge, explained why I sought the divorce and that ended the matter. I never saw Tom after the decree was granted.

I had been the one to leave, felt slight guilt but proud of my daring to put an end to the two years of horror at 1350 Lake Shore Drive. I was no longer the little girl who remained faithful to Daddy even though he attacked her with verbal assaults and sometimes with his fists.

I was through repeating the script of childhood. Dr. Emch was helping me discover why I married twice disastrously. Helped me accept my responsibility for the domestic debacles. And face other painful facts and fantasies that led to such misery.

6

The Quiet Savage

Slowly I started to realize the depths that remained to be explored if I were to understand the acts that plunged me into grief and despair. Dr. Emch gently led the way, a sympathetic guide. I became even more aware I could in my unconscious possess wishes I thought belonged only in the heart of the devil.

When I first started analysis I would never have dreamed of seeking a woman. How could a woman possibly be as competent as a man? I had fought to be one of the first women reporters on *The New York Times*, believing they were as capable as men in the newspaper field. But when it came to therapy I trusted only a man. Why?

Dr. Emch helped me find the answer. Also helped me understand more of what she called the "unreal" reasons I had hurled myself into a wretched marriage. It was no accident, no whim, no spin of some cockeyed wheel of fate. "Desperation" was the key. Desperate emotions of which I had not been aware sparked the foolhardy act.

I had known Tom five months and then only on the few weekends he flew to New York, except for the two weeks I lived with him. There were clues to which I was blind that showed his incapacity to tolerate a woman. As when I asked where his former wife lived and he said with a bitter laugh, "I murdered her," obviously a wish. Then added, "I mean mentally. At least that's what she told the judge when she sued for divorce. She said I needed a psychiatric aide, not a wife." That he did, I now understood. His demands on me, Dr. Emch assured me, were far from normal.

She helped me know that because all at once I lost the three important persons in my life—father, my mother (off to Florida) and psychoanalyst—I felt lost, without friend or ally. Then, in effect, I abandoned myself. By acting with abandon. Screaming to the world like a helpless savage in the darkest jungle, "I cannot cope with the disasters that have suddenly struck!"

Feeling rejected by those I loved most dearly, I acted out the abandonments by abandoning my newspaper career. As though appealing to everyone, "Can't you see what has befallen me? Please help me."

Consciously I convinced myself I fell passionately in love with Tom. Then unconsciously tried to create with him an earlier, happier time of life when there were only my father and I, or even earlier, Mother and I. In turn Tom acted out his unconscious wishes related to his mother and father as we made fantastic demands on each other. Fantastic, in that they were pure fantasy.

I retreated to that small dark apartment on Lake Shore Drive, shut off completely from a world I thought empty, expecting to find in my husband the loves I had lost. My New York analyst had accused me, even as he ended the analysis, of being incapable of choosing a suitable marriage partner. I set out in revenge to show he was wrong. Only to prove he was right.

I saw Tom through the haze of my unreal demands as the shadow of those I loved and hated in childhood. He was charming, intelligent, articulate, like my father. But also like the underworld part of my father—the bully who thought of women alternately as doll or slave. Tom possessed my father's ability to relate in intense though not loving fashion to a woman. He was also like both my father and mother—rigid, controlling, ready to erupt in fury at anyone who differed in thought, taste, way of life.

We both sought "love" to rescue us from despair. "Save me! Save me!" we silently screamed at each other. He thought because I had written a best-seller about my first analysis, I knew all the answers, believed I could bring him the elusive happiness he sought. I thought he would end my loneliness. We both wanted to take, unable to give. Children looking for the phantom good mother.

Dr. Emch helped me understand that as child and adult I never gave up the hope I could earn my mother's love. I thought if only I could change, be that ephemeral "good girl" she wanted so desperately (and had wanted herself to be in childhood), she would deem me worthy of her love. Should I become somebody special, she would love me.

I had blamed myself for her unhappiness, believed I was at fault. That way I could keep alive the possibility if I became the perfect little girl she would love me. If I could change there was hope, I could not change her. A double bonus awaited if I could also please my father.

But unable to please either, I choked back tears, developed sinusitis, sought the help of an analyst. I thought one analysis would solve all my problems but it had not brought that coveted peace of mind. It did, however, give me courage to seek a second analyst when once again I felt desperate.

Now I was continuing the search for the most important honesty—honesty about the self. I had become aware of the slow progress of analysis. The pace of gaining self-understanding makes the speed of an inchworm seem a meteor, so strong our defenses against psychic pain.

Dr. Emch kept pointing out, as had John, my defense of "supersweetness." My eagerness to agree with everyone, afraid to offend with the slightest word or glance. Not daring to return cruelty with quiet rebuke but offering that other vulnerable cheek.

As child and adolescent I believed life "good," "true" and "beautiful," a fantasy carried to Chicago. The reality of pain, despair, frustration were no part of my world. Frank Adams once stared at me incredulously after I said I thought life was wonderful and exciting, remarked, "Lucy, someday you'll wake up to the harshness of the real world."

It took many years to face that real world, to know what Freud meant when he said, "Mankind is a wretched lot." Meaning men warred on each other, on other nations, killed women, children and other men. Men were selfish, greedy, jealous, murderous, capable of unspeakable savage deeds. And so was I, though the feelings were carefully hidden from my conscious.

Why did I avidly crave murder mysteries? Why had I enjoyed them since the age of twelve? I read them, watched them on television, sought movies featuring murder. I needed the fix of murder performed by others as I needed the fix of chocolate. I even wrote of murder in three fictional mysteries with a psychoanalyst as sleuth—wrote about it instead of committing it.

Dr. Emch helped me know that murder lay in my heart, as it lies in the heart of anyone who feels unloved, hated, abandoned. No one is immune from the feeling of fury that automatically carries with it the message, "Off with his head!"

In the unconscious part of our mind the emotion of hate signals "death to the oppressor." The child who stamps his foot and screams at his mother, "I hate you! I hate you!" tells her he wants her to vanish from his life, stop tormenting him. The parent who flashes a look of hatred at a child gets across the message, "I wish you were dead." Or, "I wish you had never been born," the same thing.

As Auden so tellingly wrote in two lines:

> What murders flash
> Under composed flesh.

Dr. Emch helped me face feelings of hate more deeply than I dared with John. Perhaps because she was a woman and I feared my mother less than my father. Sally's psychoanalyst told her the way she preserved sanity was to openly protest Mother's excessive control. In one way Sally suffered more than the rest of us. At the age of twelve she remained the only one in the house—we all had left—to cope with Mother's sudden bursts of fury.

Her sudden switch from sweetness to almost a savage rage terrorized me. I lived in fear of her anger, like a sudden burst of thunder from a blue summer sky. One day I raced through the upper hall, eager to reach outdoors and play baseball with the boys in the vacant lot behind our house (the Larchmont Public Library today occupies that space). My foot caught the edge of a large sheet on which Mother was stacking the dirty laundry. She hated all household chores but especially collecting and itemizing laundry.

I suddenly tripped, fell across pillowcases, towels

and sheets, upsetting her neat piles. I laughed merrily at the unexpected softness of my landing.

She screamed, "Can't you look where you're going? Damn you. You'll be the death of me."

Murder flashed from the sapphire eyes, I felt her rage as a kind of annihilation. Those full lips sought to devour me, chew me to pieces as she was doing with words. Sticks and stones could only break my bones, which would heal, but her words and looks could kill. The rage she dared not vent at her husband, she unleashed in its fullest fury on the children.

She possessed an arsenal of verbal arrows. There was also, "I'm going to leave this house—you'll never see me again!" (as her mother had left her forever). And, "You make me wish I hadn't been born" (as she must have felt as a child when she faced a wicked, angry stepmother). Her very life seemed to depend on my being a polite little puppet with no emotional needs of my own.

Her only weapon was the scream. She never raised a hand against us, just her voice. I softened my voice to a whisper, as though to shame her. I took the "safe" way, the sweet smile of compliance that hid the sharp teeth of hate.

One day after school I asked if I could visit for an hour my best friend, Virginia Hutchins, who lived two blocks away on Thompson Place. "No, I want you home today," said the commandant of what later appeared in my nightmares as a prisoner's compound guarded by Nazi storm troopers.

I felt a rage so devastating I lost control of the English language, my greatest defense. A flow of gibberish erupted, a mindless foam of impotent fury. I wanted to scream, "You goddamned bitch!" Words I heard my father occasionally use to describe any woman who had in some way offended him. But I could manage only jumbled words of wrath similar to schizophrenic jargon, though perhaps they made sense to my unconscious.

We stood in the hall between the living room, with its blue Persian carpet, and the dining room, its floor covered by a red Persian rug. I could see the Wedgwood plates that graced the high ledge on two walls and the tall mahogany chairs with their red plush cushions.

On the wall of the hall hung a photograph of my father at the age of seven, the colors painted in by some turn-of-the-century aspiring artist. Red-gold curls framed my father's aesthetic, winsome face, streamed over his shoulders onto a black velvet Little Lord Fauntleroy suit. As though defying the world, he stood on a white fur rug, pale blue drape as background. I looked at the tinted photograph, thought, trying to stem my wrath, How could my beloved father have married this witch?

I turned, ran from the sight and sound of her, down three steps to the vestibule. I opened the back door, raced out, slammed it as hard as I could. I expected her to give immediate chase but there was not even the echo of a following scream. When I returned, promptly in an hour, she said not a word.

Sometimes she would impatiently kick a chair that stood in her way. Or curse a sweater that fell to the floor. Or shout at a leather-bound book I left on a table, failed to return to the proper shelf of the living room wall. I would wince as though the leg of the chair, the sweater, the book were parts of me.

But she had a certain way to shred my self-esteem the most deeply. One day I asked, "Mother, may I stay out tonight until ten?"

"I want you in at nine as usual, Lucy." Steel in her voice.

"But the basketball game doesn't end until ten and

then we all go for hamburgers and Cokes." Pleadingly.

"The subject is closed. Nine o'clock."

"But Mother, how—"

She began to hum the popular tune, "My Blue Heaven," hurling melody into my clenched teeth. Other times she would whistle. Her refusal to hear me out drove me into a near-zombie state, I turned mute as a dead clam. I felt wiped off the face of the earth.

I could not fight her. She was like a jellyfish, no spine to strike. Our fiercest arguments were over the matter of time—no accident I became a reporter, whose greatest crime, one that may cost a career, is to miss the deadline. I now used the way she trained me to my own advantage, made a livelihood from it.

In a sense I unconsciously caricatured her by singing in my own style with saccharine words when angry. I still felt the return of fury repressed when someone sang or whistled on the street or bus.

Not able to show anger, it was no accident I took to writing as outlet (any important emotional outlet possesses several roots in childhood). At the age of nine I kept a diary, though I wrote chiefly of love: my first dates and how I adored my brother even though he occasionally slapped his three sisters.

Writing became sweet revenge. Not as rewarding as the revenge that comes from living well, yet a revenge that helps you feel you are at least free enough to create words as catharsis for hidden hate (and occasionally, hidden love).

I told Dr. Emch, "You are helping me know that underneath my sweetness surges a quiet savagery. It has led to rebellion, not wise choice."

She said, "Rebellion holds anger. It is an impulsive act and guilt follows. Choice means you have the freedom to weigh many factors so you can make a thoughtful decision."

I also told her of my mother's panic after she lost my father to Donna. A panic that traveled from my mother's heart to the hearts of her four children as she tried to pull us even closer. She made us feel we were all she had in life, that if she lost us, the ones for whom she had "sacrificed" so much, as she often reminded us, she would die. Unfortunately she depended on us too greatly when Laurie left, unable to go it alone.

She had always been afraid we would disappear. "Be back before dark," she would order. Darkness held some unspeakable evil, perhaps she feared some stranger would kidnap me. "Don't cross the Boston Post Road, there's too much traffic and you might get hit by a car and killed" went another warning. The old Post Road, two blocks from our house, in Colonial days the main highway between New York and Boston, was now the scene of a stream of trucks, buses and cars emitting a constant roar.

Psychically beaten into me as a child was the feeling something dangerous would happen once I left Mother's side. My fear of flying remained until, during analysis, I realized that behind the fear lay the belief that to separate from the safety of my mother brought death.

She often spoke of her mother's death, in anger would sometimes scream, "I never *had* a mother, you children are lucky!" At times I doubted we were, wondered if we did not suffer unduly because our mother did not have a mother for long.

After graduating from Bennington I worked for a year on *The Daily Times* in Mamaroneck, where an astute, genial editor, Richard Campbell, formerly of the *World-Telegram*, taught me the essentials of reporting. I lived with Mother in adjacent Larchmont in a now silent house. My brother had married, was attending the University of Virginia in Charlottesville. Sue was in her first year at Randolph-Macon Woman's College in Lynchburg, Virginia, Sally at a private school in Albany, the only one of us to attend such a hallowed high school. Mother begged me to move in, to her an empty house meant death.

She also created in me a fear of death in another way. I told Dr. Emch, "I have mourned the fact I am the only one of the four children who never had a child. I have been deathly afraid of giving birth."

She waited for me to speak on. "I think one reason is Mother's telling me at times over the years that I almost killed her before I was born. Also that I might have died when she was carrying me."

I recalled, "When she was six months pregnant, she started to suffer intense abdominal pain. The doctors ordered her to the hospital for an exploratory operation. They said they might have to sacrifice the unborn baby to save her life. She told me how she begged them to save the baby. As though she alone was responsible for my being alive. So this would make me love her more. Forgive her for the times she hurt me."

I fell silent a moment, then went on, "I always felt that I, *in utero*, threatened her life. As though she accused me of murderous wishes before I could even think." Added, "The doctors found nothing wrong, sewed her up, and she had a fairly easy birth, she said."

And then, "I wonder if I unconsciously fear any fetus of mine might kill me. That my guilt over hurting Mother even before I was born was so great I dared not risk bearing a child."

I took the chance of dying in another way as I underwent an abortion at a time it was not legal, when infection and death of expectant mothers were not rare. I unconsciously copied my mother—risked the same threat of death (from a fetus) my mother risked with me. I discovered I was pregnant by a reporter on the *Times* about to enroll in the Navy and head for the South Pacific. He proposed marriage eagerly, said he wanted a child more than anything else but I refused. I sought an undercover doctor to perform a criminal abortion in his office on upper Park Avenue.

I was terrified when I first learned I was pregnant, feared I might die from the abortion. I told Dr. Emch, "I walked into the abortionist's office as though to the guillotine, handed the nurse the requested five hundred dollars. I paid, not the father. I refused to accept a cent from him, I felt to blame. She led me down the hall to a small room, ordered me to take off all my clothes from the waist down. Then she placed me on an examining table, where I lay feeling humiliated by an obscene position—as though my legs were raised inside stirrups and I was mounting a horse upside down. I felt disgust at what I was doing and fear at the danger to which I exposed myself."

I feared dying, though more afraid of giving birth to an illegitimate baby. In those days it meant disgrace—certainly in the minds of family, relatives, friends and coworkers at the hallowed *New York Times.*

The doctor, a tall, stocky, dark-haired man in his forties, who spoke with a slight German accent, placed a towel over my eyes. At the touch of his hand entering my body to pluck out the fetus, I felt a shame beyond any I believed possible. Then searing pain, as though a fiery knife plunged into my stomach.

I thought I would faint, then heard him say, "It's over." He removed the towel from my eyes. Remembering how my mother shrieked when I cut a shin as I fell off my bicycle into a heap of ashes, I wondered what sound she would have uttered had she watched the doctor insert the curette into my uterus.

The nurse helped me rise from the table, I felt like a delicate glass vase shattered into sharp bits. The doctor suggested I rest half an hour on a couch in the outer room. I lay numb until the nurse helped me walk painfully out of the office. I caught a taxi to my apartment in Tudor City, threw myself dazed on the bed. The man involved had sent two dozen roses—the color of blood. I hurled them into the garbage, as the abortionist had discarded the bloody fetus.

He assured me I could return to work the next day but that night pain clamped down on my abdomen so I could hardly move a muscle. My feet and fingers tingled as though shot with a thousand needles, I felt poisoned. Blood gushed out in an underground river as if the "curse" had returned with vengeance. I prayed to God, Please save me even though I do not deserve to live, I promise I will never again destroy another baby even if it kills me to bear it.

By morning the pain eased, the river of blood now a rivulet. I dragged myself out of bed, made a cup of tea. Breaking the precedent of never giving in to illness, I called the city editor to say I was staying home two days, sick from food poisoning. Thought, Man poisoning is more like it.

Late the next afternoon I felt well enough to go to the beauty parlor to have my hair, stringy from hours of perspiration, washed and set. I felt like a murderer reprieved. I knew I might have died from the hemorrhage in the abortionist's office or in my apartment. Part of me felt I deserved to die for killing the baby.

Who more appropriate to confess my crime to than that killer-diller, my mustached Lothario of a father, object of my unrequited love and unexpressed hate. The following week I met him for lunch at the National Democratic Club, where he often invited me if he had no important legal tasks and I could take time off from assignments.

After we ordered steak, rare, I said abruptly, "I

just had an abortion." I had been unable to go to him for help or to tell him beforehand, I felt too ashamed. But now I was safe something within wished him to know what I had suffered.

He stared at me in horror, his blue eyes dulled with pain. Then asked, "Who performed it?"

"A doctor. Illegally. I got his name from a friend."

I told him the doctor's name. Whereupon my father said, amazed, "This same man is blackmailing the daughter of a client of mine, one of our country's ambassadors. The doctor performed an abortion on her and now wants more money not to reveal her crime to the gossip columnists."

"What a coincidence!" Even in abortion my father and I were linked.

I told Dr. Emch, "My father asked me sadly, 'Why didn't you come to me for help?' I said I was too ashamed but now that it was over I had to let him know. He said, 'You're my daughter, I would do anything to help you. I could have arranged for you to be in a hospital where you would have been safe from infection.' "

Added, "I told him I was fine. I didn't want to mention the hemorrhage or the pain. I always kept the stiff upper lip around my father."

Had I really heard him say he would do anything for me? I thought, Thank you for the offer of help, Daddy dear, but you killed something in me a long time ago when I could not fight back. Now I can take care of myself, I don't need you. I am no longer that helpless child who did not understand what I was supposed to do or *be* to make you love me.

I was thinking of the time I was two years old, I did not remember it but several times he described it to me as though he were proud of himself. He had warned me the night before that if I wet my bed, in the morning he would have to punish me. When he entered my room at eight o'clock he found the sheet wet, turned me over and struck my rear end hard. I never wet the bed again, he boasted.

I told Dr. Emch of this, then said, "That morning and the time he struck me for talking about Communism were the only times he hit me."

"Why didn't you slap him back when he slapped you at the dinner table?" she asked.

"What?" I gasped.

I pictured myself slugging my father. He could have maimed or killed me with that strong swing he used on a golf ball he sent sailing 250 yards or more. Besides, you do not strike out at your main ally, vicious though he may suddenly become. My father often treated me as though he loved me. He knew I liked to write poetry and short stories, when I was thirteen bought me a typewriter, a gift I adored. It started me on a lifetime of writing, gave me an outlet for my unconscious rage at him and Mother.

At the luncheon where I told him about the abortion, unable to hold back his curiosity, he asked, "Who is the man? Do I know him?" He had introduced me to two young lawyers in his office he thought eligible sons-in-law. I was determined not to marry a lawyer but a reporter, the latter seemed intellectual in my kind of way.

"It doesn't matter." I shrugged my shoulders.

He had met the man one weekend when we drove to Mamaroneck in my Oldsmobile for dinner at my father's home. It really did not matter who the father was, I was ashamed of him, ashamed of myself. Grieving for my unborn baby even though I would have had it no other way. I lacked the emotional strength to tackle both bringing up a child and career.

My father then asked, "Did you want to marry him?"

"No." Quietly, firmly.

"Are you all right?" Worriedly.

"I'm fine. Just glad it's over," I reassured him again.

"Does your mother know?"

"No and I don't want her to." She was too vulnerable, I wished to protect her from pain that would revive her own. I was always trying to rescue Mother, roles reversed.

I told Dr. Emch, "Perhaps I confessed only to my father because of my wish for revenge on his desertion of the family. I knew he would feel upset not only by my act but by my unspoken accusation: If you had stayed at home to protect me, I never would have risked my life in this sordid way. If you had loved me as a father should love a child, I would have been spared this horror."

I felt like a murderer, I do not understand how any woman who undergoes an abortion, legal or illegal, can feel anything but that she killed her baby. Perhaps she spares herself much misery in one way, if she cannot marry the man and give the baby a name but she will have to face sooner or later her rock-bottom feeling— that she has destroyed what could have become a living soul. My guilt ran deep, I had to face and accept it slowly over the years to come.

And yet I also enjoyed feeling I was capable of producing a baby, I was not sterile. This was heart-warming, it did not assuage the guilt but lessened it somewhat.

After hearing of the abortion, Dr. Emch said, "You have to stop playing the victim." Added, "Financially and otherwise." She referred to my paying for the abortion and paying Tom to get free of the marriage. This in addition to paying emotionally for living out fantasies that in both instances were destructive.

Tom had demanded money to "allow" me, as he put it, to get a divorce that would "ruin" his good name. Dr. Emch remarked, "He needed to control you to the last second. He cannot stand an independent woman or a dependent one. Women are dangerous. He feels like destroying them because they cannot be the good mother."

Tom inflicted on me the hatred he felt for his unhappy, disturbed mother. When he screamed "Change! Change!" he was screaming at his emotionally ill mother to change, become normal, so she would not have to be taken to a mental hospital again.

Dr. Emch also said, "He cannot stand the feminine in himself and women remind him of this."

I admitted, "I wondered if he was homosexual. Though just before he met me he lived with a woman five years, he said."

Then I asked, "In extenuation, underneath his bullying and terrorizing, there's a scared little boy, isn't there?"

"Yes," she said. "A frightened little boy who is probably unconsciously copying his threatening father. But you could not possibly satisfy or cope with that hate-filled little boy. You cannot ask yourself to put up with such psychotic behavior."

She was suggesting I no longer allow any man to use me as an emotional boxing partner. Tom and I both placed impossible burdens on each other, trapped by fantasies into the misery of a marriage fated to fail. Knowing from the start we could not make a go of it, though desperately wishing to. Otherwise we could have waited, learned more about each other before reaching a decision.

I sighed, asked, "One dies of violence or of boredom, is there nothing in between?"

Her soft voice. "There does not have to be either

violence or boredom." Then, "What man do you mean who is either violent or a bore?" She always searched for the specific that lay hidden by my generality.

"I feel men fall into two categories. The ones who bore and the ones who resort to violence."

"What men?"

I sighed, gave up. "I guess I'm thinking of my father. He was both. Sometimes he would bore me with endless recital of his law cases. I wouldn't understand a word he said but smiled as though I did. Other times he would erupt in violent temper tantrums."

"And that's the kind of man you pick. One who seems charming at first and then acts out his hostility, as your father did. A hostility you never dared express. Though you enjoyed his display of it as though it were your own."

I was horrified. "You mean I vicariously enjoy a man's expression of hatred?"

"You both enjoy it and need it to maintain your fantasy the man is like your father. Then you can wear a perpetual mask of denial as far as your anger goes. You can continue to play the innocent little girl."

"Sometimes I am like my father," I mused. "When I'm the one to walk out on a man. As I did with Paul." That was unconscious imitation of my father.

And yet, from whom else would I learn if not my father and mother, my only models in infancy and childhood. I acted out parts of my father, parts of my mother, added something of my own in piteous plea for identity. This is characteristic of the child part that remains entrenched so firmly within.

I became fond of Dr. Emch, loved her sympathetic manner, her wisdom, her humor. John helped me face enough of my conflicts about being feminine so I could seek a woman analyst, wishing to identify more with a woman. I could now accept a woman as equal to a man rather than hold contempt for her (for myself, really and unreally) as an inferior creature who deserved little trust or respect.

I was also starting to understand that as a little girl I was at first not aware the bodies of both sexes were different. All children want everything the other child possesses. According to Freud, the little girl believes she was born with a penis and her mother took it from her somehow to punish her when she was "bad," since at that time of life the penis was her most coveted wish. The emotionally stable little girl slowly gives up the wish.

I told Dr. Emch one day, "I think there are many reasons I came to you, a woman, for help. For one, I sought a replacement for my mother, who left to live in a far-off state with my sister. I also felt the men in my life had deserted me. My father by dying, my analyst by forcing me to leave him and Tom by his cruelty."

I then confessed, "I think another reason I wanted a woman was because I could talk more freely about my sexual problems. I always felt a little embarrassed with John."

Just as he did, she encouraged me to feel angry, to speak of the anger. I kept insisting, "But I'm *not* angry." I found it impossible to become enraged at anyone unless, like Tom, he hurt me physically or tried to steal my money. But one day my anger got the better of my denial.

Sometimes she ran behind in appointments, occasionally as long as fifteen or twenty minutes. A patient arrived tardily or she started the day late and gave the first patient full time. This meant everyone who followed had to wait. One morning I sat waiting, waiting in the downstairs room, trying to ward off mounting anger by nervously reading the latest *New Yorker*. Learned the winner of the previous week's big race, then looked at cartoons, the book, movie and theater reviews.

Twenty minutes passed, still no sign of Hilda to summon me, or the patient who was occupying part of my hour stumbling downstairs. I had long finished with the magazine, hurled it to the table. I lit my fourth cigarette, took a few puffs, crushed it angrily against the ashtray. I wondered whether *she* had started the day late or some idiot patient arrived late. Perhaps she had forgotten me entirely, would let me sit there until I petrified with rage.

I stood up, looked out the windows at the clumps of trees in Lincoln Park, trees always pacified me. But today they failed, I thought of leaving at once so I would not be tempted to set fire to the town house. Instead, I catapulted myself back onto the green sofa, demanded loudly of the empty room, "What in *hell* is that bitch doing?"

Then, overcome with guilt, thought, How can I possibly call that brilliant, wonderful, sweet, beautiful woman a bitch? I lit another cigarette, told myself, Calm down, this is no emergency, Dr. Emch probably overslept, though she never has before.

Two minutes later the patient who preceded me stalked out the door, then Hilda entered to summon me to her late majesty above. I walked upstairs to the room with the view of the chandelier from the couch, smiled at *her* with the falsest of cheer, wishing to throttle her on the spot.

"I'm sorry I was so late today." The gentle voice.

"That's perfectly all right." Just as sweetly, as though I had sat through the abominable delay with the aplomb of a well-analyzed patient. "It gave me a chance to catch up with the last *New Yorker.*" Then sarcastically, "Among other things." I thought of adding I also read all seven volumes of *Remembrance of Things Past* but felt that a bit snide.

"You have a right to feel angry," she said.

"I'm *not* angry," I insisted, turning purple with rage. "You must have good reason for being late." Added, "It's really none of my business why you were so late."

I felt it very much my business—the twenty-five minutes had been reserved for me. But I would rather die under flaming torture (waiting was torture of a different kind) than admit anger.

"If you are angry, please say so." Her voice earnest.

I was promptly struck dumb with wonder. Imagine someone encouraging me to feel angry at them, display even a smidgeon of that savage self. John had asked me to show anger but I did not take his request seriously, no one wanted an angry person in the same room. All my life I had been punished when I dared reveal the slightest tinge of rage. Anger was a flash of feeling that had to be swiftly vanquished, signaled danger to my very soul.

She rarely attacked a defense, believed it would fall, no longer needed, as I unraveled fantasies it served to protect. I once said to John when he pointed out my need to be sweet was a defense against rage, "I only become sweeter when you accuse me of it being a defense. The defense will fall when I uncover memories and feelings that lie at the root of it." He had laughed, said, "Touché."

I asked Dr. Emch, "Does my supersweetness and compliance bother you?"

She was silent, as though thinking, then said, "It's a defense difficult to fight because it is so nebulous. It antagonizes people more than anger in which, at least, you feel some direct emotional contact."

She added gently, "Forgive me for pointing this out. But you *can't* be that sweet. You have to be covering feelings of anger."

I sighed. "I think I've spent so much energy over so many years trying to control my anger that I can't change. I associate my mother and father's anger with cruelty and craziness. I always thought as they screamed at me, They are mad!"

Added wistfully, "You'd hate me if I showed anger at you and I don't want you to hate me."

"Why would I hate you for a natural feeling? Today I kept you waiting twenty-five minutes for your appointment. You have every right in the world to feel furious."

The thought that anger was a natural reaction to being kept waiting, a feeling everyone experienced, was welcome at all cost in my world of compliance. We all want to be reassured we are like everyone else, not a freak, at the same time wishing to be treated as unique.

"It's not polite to be angry at one's analyst," I muttered.

"Psychoanalysis is not a tea party," she said. Also words I never forgot.

"But it has been in a sense a tea party to me," I mused. "The tea party of tea parties, a la Alice in Wonderland. I am the dozing Dormouse in danger of having his head stuffed into the teapot by both the March Hare and the Mad Hatter." I knew I referred to my mother and father.

She chuckled, "I will not stuff your head into any teapot. I just want to help you unstuff it of fantasies that torment and hurt you."

Then she asked, "Did your mother ever strike you as your father twice did?"

"I don't think she ever hit me," I said. "Her blows were all verbal." Added, "They hurt too but even so I always felt, as the Bible says, 'honor thy father and thy mother.'"

"But parents have to deserve honor." Quietly. "Sometimes they deserve anger."

Perhaps they occasionally do, I dared think. Perhaps I did not always have to choke back wrath, could allow myself to feel angry at those unfair to me.

I laughed, suddenly aware of how I got even with my father for spanking me when I wet the bed at two, as though he never wanted me to "spill" anything again from my body unless in an appropriate place.

I told her, "I 'wet' things in other ways over the years to protest his cruel act. I spilled milk, coffee, wine, water, accidentally on purpose. Once I knocked an open bottle of ink over the sheets of a hotel bedroom in Saint Petersburg as I wrote my mother a letter. My father shouted, 'You slob! Can't you watch what you're doing?' I secretly laughed, knew he had a fetish about cleanliness and reveled in his rage."

I told Dr. Emch, "He was fastidious in his dress, immaculate in appearance." Added with a smile, "Except when covered with oil and grime while tinkering with the irresponsive engine of his boat. Or perspiring and shirtless in his basement tool shop, fixing some malfunctioning gadget. He could not tolerate anyone who dressed sloppily. I supposed lawyers always had to look elegant in case they were called to court to argue cases, as he often was."

I had wondered why my father asked his children to call him "Laurie," not "Daddy" or "Dad," now realized he wanted to remain youthful, never become a "father."

I went on, "He really was a Peter Pan of a father. He possessed a zest for living found in few men and women. Whenever he walked into a room the air was charged with his charm. He had an engaging smile, expressive blue eyes, curly red-blond hair that turned gray in his forties. His chest, shoulders and arms were sturdy from years of raising a golf club and swimming. He waged perpetual battle against rich, sweet foods, especially chocolate. He was a born teacher, taught Eddie and me to golf, pilot a boat, enjoy traveling, work his mathematics slide rule, value knowledge."

Added, "It's no wonder I have a reverence for trees and flowers. In the early summers of my life at Granny's farm he would take me on walks through the dark forests. Point out beautiful trees and wildflowers. He loved nature—mountains, lakes, the ocean, harbors, clouds, sunsets—and early instilled his passion in me."

Tears came to my eyes, remembering. "It seemed he, the one busy earning a living for all of us, had time for me, whereas my mother, with hours on her hands, was constantly occupied with one of her other children." Added, "Now I understand it was all she could do to cope with one child, let alone four."

In many ways my father was also my mother, I told Dr. Emch. "One morning as I was about to race off to sixth grade, he stared at me. Then he said crossly, 'Why doesn't your mother comb your hair before you leave for school?' I answered, 'She never combs it.' I was surprised, didn't he know she never got out of bed until nine? By that time I was seated in my first class."

I laughed, remembering. "He led me to my small bureau, seized the comb, ran it hurriedly through my hair to the accompaniment of many an 'Ouch!' I felt secretly pleased he cared enough about how I looked to take precious time from his daily race downstairs to gulp orange juice and coffee. Then he would dash to his car and off to legal work in a tall office building somewhere along Madison Avenue."

I told her, lost in the world of my father and mother, "When I was about nine I became aware they were furious at each other. I later learned it was because he had become involved with another woman he would not give up. They both stalked around the house casting stony or stormy looks at each other."

There was no swift severing, only a day-by-day cleavage, prolonged until he left the house. They seemed reluctant to relinquish a precarious anchor even as they strained to be free of each other. They had few interests in common. My father loved law, politics, traveling, golf, his boat. Mother rarely left the house for long journeys except summer vacations to places no more than three hours away. She shunned the outdoors except for tennis, was miserable on the water for she could not swim.

But she did love the theater, often drove to New York to see plays. When she took me to a matinee of *Medea*, as I watched Judith Anderson in the lead, I felt thankful my mother had not set fire to her children as revenge on a faithless husband.

My father hated to write personal letters, said he had enough of writing briefs and formal letters to clients in his daily work. But he was considerate enough to write me, one of the few letters I ever received from him, during my lonely first months at college.

He dictated it to his secretary, saying he hoped I was enjoying myself. Then he added a warning, "Please do not figure with me on receiving letter for letter because this will never work." Referring to a telephone call I made, he said, "I was glad to hear your voice and to learn you are really getting a kick out of things up there." He concluded, "If I can get off, I will come up and see you the weekend after next. There is just a chance. Affectionately, Laurie." I was grateful he visited many weekends that first year, accompanied by Donna, who seemed to enjoy trips to Vermont.

Dr. Emch helped me realize it was the inconsistency

of the love and hate in my parents that confused. The kindness alternating with the rejections. This caused me to build up defenses, never knowing whether I would be in a sense kissed or kicked.

The strength of a defense, I learned, was as the strength of Samson before Delilah took to the shears. Dr. Emch did not use verbal shears to cut through a defense but helpful reassurance and interpretation of my thoughts. As I absorbed her quiet but firm manner, I felt it is not only *what* is said but *how* it is said. Words hurled at me in wrath by my mother and father caused me to erect carefully guarded defenses against my wish for revenge. I also concocted fantasies to block my hurt. I believed defenses had saved my life, not knowing they blinded me to the truth.

I asked, "How did I select defenses?"

"As a child you chose whatever defense you felt offered protection against dangerous thoughts and wishes. You also chose defenses you saw in your parents or others near and dear, like your grandmothers."

She added, "There's only one trouble with defenses."

"What's that?" Quick on the question, a defense that served me well as reporter.

"They never work."

"Why not?"

"A defense is erected to hold back dangerous thoughts and feelings. But the defense does not mean the end of such thoughts and feelings. They reappear wearing disguises that confuse. That sometimes make you doubt your senses."

"Aha!" A cry of triumph. "What Freud calls the return of the repressed."

She did not castigate me this time for spouting theory. She said, "As long as you remain unaware of what you repress, you are haunted by it. The unconscious keeps trying to find an outlet for your pain, again and again, your whole life."

I marveled, "It's like being an unwilling puppet on strings pulled by your unknown self."

Then asked, "How do I recognize a defense?"

"It's easy—in someone else. You seldom see your own without the help of an analyst. But just let another person show the same defense and you react in rage. You are afraid of the feelings it hides within you."

This was an important awareness. If someone enraged me, what I did not like about him was apt to be what I did not like in myself but could not admit. I could not bear women who were, as the expression goes, so sweet that butter would not melt in their mouths. I thought them phony, sickening. Yet this was one of the strong defenses Dr. Emch and John accused me of possessing. Part of me hated myself for being so sugary, so submissive.

I had unconsciously latched on to defenses as a child for protection against hurts, fears, dangerous impulses. I continued to clutch at them with the passion of a drowning person at a rotted plank. Why the sweetness? I did not have to explore deeply to understand that defense. My mother much of the time was sweet, as was Donna, always smiling and gracious. I would naturally try to emulate the women my father loved. The only trouble was it came out caricature, salted as the sweetness was with envy.

Much of Dr. Emch's task was to unearth my torments in the most delicate "drop of water wearing away rock" fashion. She would make the same point over and over and somewhere along the couch-way after she said something five or ten times, I would suddenly hear, think and feel, Yes, that *is* true. Wonder why she never mentioned it before? She is usually so perceptive.

Insights and the feelings that followed started to flash through. Insights alone were never enough, they were intellectual. It was the memories they evoked, then the emotions aroused that were the pure gold of the analytic hour.

After a particularly profound session in which I was able somehow to slash my way through a defense, glimpse the fantasies and feelings beneath, I would feel as though beaten. I wanted only to stagger to the apartment at 24 Bellevue Place, hurl myself on the back room bed. It was an exhaustion different from any I had known. Not the exhaustion of eighteen holes of golf with my father on a blistering July day. Nor the exhaustion that followed sleepless nights and verbal battles with Tom. But an exhaustion that, peculiarly enough, held a sense of victory.

One day, walking out of her house and facing a calm Lake Michigan in May, I thought, For the first time in my life I know what it is like to feel civilized. As though in possession of myself. A moment of true self-esteem.

I was grateful for the sudden entrance into my arid life of a fascinating man, Nelson Algren. He was introduced to me by Harriet Pilpel, a famous lawyer, at that time a member of my father's law firm, today with Weil, Gotshal and Manges. Harriet, long a dear friend, represented Nelson on a movie deal for *The Man with the Golden Arm*, whose lead would be played by Frank Sinatra.

Harriet called one afternoon from the Ambassador Hotel to say she was in Chicago to talk to Nelson about the sale of his book and asked me to meet her at 6 P.M. for a drink. The Ambassador was only a few blocks north and when I arrived I saw Harriet standing in the lobby, by her side a tall, blond man. He had a half-cherubic, half-mocking smile on his strong sensitive face. Rather a Viking face, I thought, it reminded me of stalwart sailors on ancient ships.

Harriet introduced us and after a few drinks we enjoyed dinner at the hotel. Harriet asked how I liked Chicago, I told her I was feeling more at home. As we parted, Nelson asked if he could call me. We had discovered mutual interests, including baseball and the racetrack.

Nelson took me to my first Cubs game at Wrigley Field and to the Arlington Park track, as well as my first—and last—prizefight. I could not stomach the shedding of blood and, gallantly, he left early with me. He also gave me a tour of West Chicago saloons where drug addicts and prostitutes watched as we danced to the jukebox. This was part of Nelson's "wild side" of life.

I truly tried to muster love for Chicago as we walked around the city. Nelson walked, I ran, trying to keep up with his long legs. I felt his reverence, his deep affection for the city, not even his birthplace, for he came from Detroit. I feel for New York what Nelson does for Chicago, I thought, but if anyone could imbue me with love of it, it might be he.

There was not a cliché in Nelson. He would have preferred to perish pronto than utter or write a banal phrase. Original, imaginative, he looked at life with a clear eye that saw deeper than most of us into both its beauty and horror.

One time after returning from a short trip to New York I found a note from Nelson:

Dear Lucy-O,
    Tried to buzz you on your auto-matic telephone, and enjoyed its imperious ring, summoning you from work or play, bed or bread, sleep or wine. But you

didn't answer so I began to suspect that, since you had said you were going to New York, perhaps you may well have went.

But you have to return, if only to shut off the phone, which is buzzing yet. If you do, you might try mine, which is also auto-matic, named Humboldt 9-3584. Simply to summon me from Longshot Louie's Sureshot tips.

Evaire, Nelson

I told Dr. Emch, "I consider it a privilege to know this man." I felt she was happy I was enjoying something in Chicago, her city, too. I shall always be grateful to Nelson for his friendship and sense of fun. Herb Lyon, in his Chicago *Tribune* column, published a note one day reporting Nelson and I had been seen at the races, implying this was the latest track twosome. But Nelson and I were never seriously involved, each sensing the other was trying to handle the hurts of a failed marriage, hardly ready or eager to take on another precarious relationship.

Just as I could not understand Nelson's allegiance to Chicago, so he could not understand my allegiance to psychoanalysis. He was convinced that should he undergo analysis, his creativity would disappear. I once said quietly, "Nelson, psychoanalysis does not take away creativity, it makes you feel more comfortable within yourself so you can create more easily and more happily," and let it go at that.

In his last years Nelson left Chicago for Patterson, New Jersey, to study the art of prizefighting with boxers who trained there, intending to write about it. He moved to Sag Harbor, at the eastern end of Long Island, lived there almost a year, dying at seventy-two. Studs Terkel, author of *Talking to Myself: A Memoir of My Times*, and radio talk-show host in Chicago, wrote of

Nelson in the *Sun-Times* that he had won the first National Book Award for fiction with *The Man with the Golden Arm* and, while he lost at the track and at poker, "he had good reason just to shuffle along like a laughing winner."

I started to come to social life again. I took time to walk next door to dinners held by the Midland Authors Association at a house owned by Mrs. Adlai Stevenson, though she did not live there. I met well-known writers, including Meyer Levin. I thought his *Compulsion* of classic stature, one day told him the way he showed how fantasies of childhood could have driven Leopold and Loeb to murder the young boy was masterful. He wrote a note, "Coming from you, such praise is gratifying," and my morale shot up for an hour.

I wandered through the Chicago Art Institute, entranced by Monet's water lilies, Renoir's colorful ocean scenes—I thought he favored only lush ladies. Whistler's muted, ghostlike paintings of river scenes held a sad beauty.

I was lucky to live on the near North Side, called the Gold Coast, where some of the wealthiest families resided. The Gold Coast was Park Avenue, Sutton Place South and Central Park South rolled into one. In the far north the Edgewater Beach Hotel rose against the skyline as Sheridan Road swept up the lakefront leading to Chicago's elegant suburbs.

Sometimes I would saunter into nearby Stop 'n Shop, indulge in an unbelievable food spree of hot fried chicken, German potato salad, exotic vegetable mixtures, Swiss chocolate ice cream or pies and cakes of rare richness. It was a relief not to cook or face a husband never satisfied with what I served.

I found a special friend in Helen Douglas, who lived five houses away. She had just broken up with Mike

Serota and we consoled each other. Helen was brilliant, thoughtful, witty, worked hard as vice-president of a leading advertising and public relations firm. Many a Saturday evening we would stroll down Bellevue to Mister Kelly's and listen to jazz. One night we talked for hours with Mort Sahl, a friend of Helen's, after he was through entertaining. Another night we drove to Ravinia, Chicago's suburban outdoor music park, to hear my idol, Louis Armstrong.

Helen and I found ourselves part of a committee working on the Freud Centennial in 1956. The American Psychoanalytic Association had decided to hold its annual May meeting in Chicago to celebrate the centennial in majestic manner. I served on a committee to publicize the occasion, along with Helen, who once worked on *Time*, and Arthur Snider, science editor of the Chicago *Daily News*, who wrote penetrating news stories about psychoanalysis.

I sat in on the press coverage of the arrival in Chicago of the main speaker, Dr. Ernest Jones, then finishing his vast three-volume biography of Freud. He had gamely traveled from London to address the convention though suffering from cancer. I never forgot his answer to the question by a reporter, "Don't you think psychoanalysis will soon be shortened to only a matter of months, Dr. Jones?"

The small, indomitable Welshman held his head high, then snapped, "The more we learn about the human mind, the longer psychoanalysis will take."

My analysis now became the whole of life except for writing. I asked myself over and over, What happened to all those lovely dreams of marriage and raising children? Slowly I faced how deeply I had dwelt in the sinking sands of fantasy.

The first time Dr. Emch used the word, I asked, "What *is* a fantasy?"

"You'll find out," That melodious voice, the voice that never sat in judgment or held rancor.

Many fantasies might spin around a compulsive act. Such as overeating when lonely. Inherent in this fantasy was the belief, from early infancy, that though I had lost my husband (originally my mother, the first love of my life), I could still possess him by eating. As though to swallow and incorporate him meant I could keep him inside forever to compensate for his physical loss. Eating also fulfilled the cannibalistic fantasy, one of my earliest, that I could destroy my angry, mean husband by chewing him up, swallowing him, making him disappear.

A third fantasy about overeating was that the added weight symbolized my wished-for pregnancy, which gave solace. I had lost a husband but in fantasy gained a baby.

I became aware of the fantasies behind my fear of flying. I flew all over the country as reporter but died the air coward's one thousand deaths each time I walked up the ramp (plank, in my mind).

"I'm afraid I will die," I told Dr. Emch.

"Why?"

"I don't know. I feel I will never leave the plane alive."

"Do you feel you deserve to die?"

"Yes. But I don't know why."

"Perhaps because you want to kill someone."

Suddenly the words burst out of me, "Why don't the dead let the dying alone?" I started to sob.

When I dried my tears I said, "It was my father who came to mind." Added, "I remembered that when he died I felt I had killed him with my first book. I spoke so frankly of my deep attachment to him. I also reproached him for leaving his family to marry another woman."

"Do you believe you have the power to kill with words?" She sounded skeptical.

"It is a bit fanciful," I admitted.

"You may have wished your father dead at times over the years when you felt a moment of hate for him. But to think your book killed him is attributing false power to words."

"So the pen is not mightier than the sword." Trying to be amusing, to escape pain.

One morning I said, "Last night I dreamed of a painting of a young woman resembling a Madonna. That was the whole dream. Just this painting. It seemed to hang in thin air."

"What does it remind you of?"

I thought for a moment, then said in surprise, "Now I remember! There *was* a picture of a young Madonna hanging in our house. My father brought it home one evening. He had bought the painting after he saw it in the window of a small gallery in New York. It pictured the face and body, down to the waist, of a young woman with dark hair. Not blond like Donna. A white shawl was draped around her head and neck, a nunlike shroud. She looked like a sad waiflike Madonna."

I remembered further, "He hung it in his room at home. When he moved out of the house shortly after, he took it with him. He put it on the wall of the sun porch of his new home. There it gazed out on the world in sadness."

Silence.

"My father adored that painting. The waiflike creature in the white shawl."

"Did your father like sad waiflike girls?"

"My mother had a rather sad and waiflike manner. And she had dark hair like the Madonna."

"So that might be one reason you unconsciously adopted the waif attitude. The sad deprived little girl."

"Me? A waif?" This hardly fit into the image of myself as a sophisticated, daring newspaper reporter, a somewhat hardened dame of the fourth estate.

"You often walk into this room looking for all the world like a waif," she said. "As though no one loved you."

I muttered, "So I've been in the grip of a waif fantasy, along with hundreds of other fantasies."

Then I realized with Tom I acted very much the waif who wanted to be taken in out of the cold, to be cared for sexually as well as emotionally. He could not accept such deep dependency nor should he have to. I might appear to others as an outwardly successful career woman but underneath I felt a waif at heart, still in pursuit of Papa.

That the waif could also hold the feelings of the sometimes angry baby, I also understood. There began to emerge a sense of myself as a small child coming into the world to face my mother and father. She, an uncertain, frightened, beautiful young bride of twenty-one. He, a hardworking, charming, sometimes irascible young lawyer of twenty-seven, who rode to work in the summer on his motorcycle all the way from Mamaroneck to his office on Dey Street, in lower Manhattan, twenty-five miles south.

I tried to see my father in his capacity as chairman of the New York State Board of Social Welfare. There was not a small amount of irony to his task in helping improve the mental welfare of the unfortunate (as the five of us in his home suffered from his neglect, in an emotional way).

He would often beg me to accompany him as he drove long distances to inspect the various state mental hospitals over which the Board had control. He would interview the doctor-directors, then preside over a board meeting. While a freshman at Bennington I wrote, set by hand in the college press, a slim volume of poems. One, titled "State Hospital," included the lines:

A city of red brick set in green hills
Its occupants cry for sanity
Not madness, in this palace of the crazed.

My father set off in me the desire to explore the human mind by taking me early in life on those trips to mental hospitals. For that I would be forever grateful. As a result I could now understand more of the savage in myself as I thought of the men and women in those institutions. Not that they committed savage acts but they showed a word-savagery at times that contained the wish to slaughter themselves and those who had hurt them. I had been fortunate my emotional trauma had not been so severe.

With Dr. Emch I was getting inside my early skin, so to speak, seeing myself as a dark-haired, blue-eyed baby, the first grandchild of doting grandparents. Petted, hugged, kissed, idolized.

Then, crash! The queen lost her crown. When I was one year and five months I saw my mother's abdomen grow larger and larger. When I was one year and nine months a tiny stranger cried his way into the world, shoved me out of my paradise of sole ownership. Not only a rival who took my place in my parents' bedroom, where I had slept every night since I was born, but a rival more admired because he was that superb creation, a *boy*.

Then a second rival, who arrived when I was four. A girl who possessed something special, which set her apart. She was born with bright, gleaming red hair. A glorious shield over which everyone exclaimed with delight. My brother's hair—shining, golden blond—and now this radiant redhead. Then a third rival, six years later, also with a halo of red curls and a face of beauty.

At one session I protested once again my mother's naming me after her mother. I demanded of Dr. Emch, "How could she have felt toward me, giving me the name of a mother who abandoned her by dying when she was two?"

"We can't possibly know your mother's fantasies," Dr. Emch said. "We have all we can do to deal with yours."

But I was starting, fantasies or no, to see myself as less fragmented. One time of life flowing into another, one experience flowing into another. I was accepting more of the child within, rage and all. Learning to live with the rage, control it at times, at other times letting it free if I felt justified. As I had done when Dr. Emch kept me waiting twenty-five minutes.

I could no longer deny that ghostlike child-waif and the fantasies that made her so unhappy as an adult. As I could accept the torment within I would gain new strength emotionally.

There was as yet one important area to explore. An area I had carefully guarded against mentioning except in passing: my feelings about sexual desire and how I coped with what was undoubtedly my strongest impulse. Unless you considered the aggressive impulse on a par or stronger. From my reading of analytic papers, analysts did not seem to agree on which prevailed as the giant influence on our lives, usually giving equal credit.

Toss a coin, I thought, it does not matter which is stronger. Both are vital, both rule our lives.

7

The Death of
an Analyst

Gradually I felt enough at ease with Dr. Emch to talk more deeply about sexual wishes and frustrations. I knew how ardently I had sublimated my sex drive into work—ashamed and afraid of sexual need and fulfillment.

I told her, "It's as though I avoid thinking or talking about sex. As if it's a forbidden subject."

"You are entitled to sexual feelings," she assured me. Then quoted Freud, something she rarely did (left that to me). "Love holds both tenderness and sensual feelings.' "

I complained, "I feel very lonely. I'm sick of sleeping by myself night after night. One toothbrush in the bathroom. One coffee cup on the breakfast table." Added, "My first analysis freed me enough so I believed at last it was my right to enjoy sex. Not hide my head in the sand like an ostrich and pretend I have no sexual feelings."

"But you cannot use someone else as escape from loneliness," she said. She was telling me if I had to sleep alone night after night in the midst of a city of millions, not one of whom belonged to me, the greater tragedy was that I did not belong to myself.

"I've spent most of my adult life alone," I complained. "To endure the long nights with no man next to me is torture. There can't be any worse."

"There is one worse torture," she said. "To have somebody next to you whom you hate. You must know and love the person whose body lies beside you at night."

I complained, "Some escape the loneliness of night with anyone who happens to be near." At times I envied such wantonness.

"That is no answer if you want loving intimacy with one person," she said. "It's the way to avoid love."

I sighed. "Agreed. That is why I am here. Alone on a barren couch. Refusing to compromise. Wanting to know why I have failed in love. Giving it and receiving it."

Sex with someone I truly loved would be the greatest pleasure on earth. At times I felt as though living on the edge of orgasm, impaled on deepest yearning. Other times as if wrapped in a curtain of narcissism, insulated against touch or caress.

I asked, slight edge in my tone, "Do you expect me to have no sexual outlet? What am I supposed to do with my deep longing?"

"Why the urgency?"

"I'll die of desire," I moaned.

"If you do, you'll make history." Slight sarcasm in the soft voice, she could not quite rule it out at times.

Then she explained, "Such urgency is due to other things beside your natural need for sex."

"Like what?"

"You'll find out."

"You *never* give me answers." A wail.

"The answers lie in you. In your thoughts and feelings."

I came to a few of my own conclusions. Because I felt sensual did not mean I had to act on it. To be mature, sexuality was accompanied by tenderness, the sense of caring deeply for the man as another human being, not obsessively desiring his penis. I had to admit, now that I was becoming better acquainted with my unconscious desires, in my relationship to a man sexual desire had often been paramount, tenderness only vaguely stirred the air.

I asked her, "After analysis will the quality of my love change?"

She replied thoughtfully, "I don't think the quality changes. Only the urgency disappears."

Time whizzed by, I completed two more books. I could hardly believe I now entered the third year of analysis with her. I discovered my fantasies of love were indeed of fairy-tale vintage. I would remain forever trapped by them unless I could know the feelings of which mature love was formed.

I thought of the proverb, "In love, it is like the signs on the old inns of Spain—one finds here only what one brings." Each brings to love the feelings fashioned from his dreams and desires, fantasies and fears.

"Do psychoanalysts believe in love?" I asked one day. Expecting silence.

"We most certainly do. Or we would not be analysts." Conviction, as always, in her voice.

I was starting to understand—a big psychic step—that love emerged from the whole of my life. Many memories merged to form my vision of love, which had been somewhat askew. I prepared for love and was prepared for it by my parents from the day I was born. Perhaps even the day I was conceived and as a fetus received messages from my mother's body and brain as to how comfortable she felt about my intrusion into her body.

During what analysts call my "psychosexual" growth (the development of both mind—or psyche—and sexual desire) many changes occurred, "like those in the development of the caterpillar into the butterfly," as Freud put it. He warned if for any reason sexual feelings did not develop at a natural pace (not rushed or retarded), the person would suffer in later years. From a failure to express sexual desire freely, to express it too freely, or to express it in childish fashion, which society calls perversion.

One night as I lay in bed, the radio playing the song "Chicago," I thought of the two anguished years I spent with Tom. I recalled how desolate I felt, stranger in an alien city. Devastated beyond any depth I dreamed possible, trying to make a go of it with a man who had hate written on his face most of the time, as well as emanating from his voice. The song "Chicago" spoke of a man who "danced with his wife." But Tom would not dance with me, sometimes refused to speak to me.

With Dr. Emch's help I discovered the reasons he kept hurling at me the words *change* and *grow* in fiery rage. What did these words mean to him in an unconscious sense? Words he used with fanatic intensity.

I was learning to listen to my words, knew they told me of hidden wishes. I had been unable to listen to his words but now, in recollection, I understood what he really—unreally—demanded of me.

When he shouted "Grow, grow!" he did not mean intellectually. Unconsciously he wanted me to grow a penis so I could give reassurance I was not the castrating mother of his childhood. As a boy (and man) he had the fantasy if he dared put his penis inside me I would somehow cut it off. He confessed before marriage, half-jokingly, that if I became his wife, friends would not think him homosexual. He wanted me to save him from homosexual impulses, perhaps ones that threatened at times to break out of control. I had felt, though never admitted, there was a tentative air about his lovemaking.

He wanted me to solve his sexual problems as I wanted him to solve mine. Act as a shield to whatever shames he hid. He had grown up in a house torn by separations and screams. With a mother so emotionally upset she required hospitalization and a violent father he had unconsciously copied as model for manhood. I knew from my reading of psychoanalytic papers that when a boy fears a castrating mother he turns to his father, the less threatening parent, as the object of sexual desire.

When Tom shouted "Change!" he did not mean in my thoughts or manner or dress. He meant change into a man so he would no longer be afraid of the castrating and castrated, in his fantasy, woman. His violent anger arose because I was unable to rescue him from impotence.

He placed an impossible burden on me. And I flung at him the equally impossible burden of making me feel like a woman. I wanted him to always think me sexy, to respond to sex on demand. We could not possibly keep the unspoken promises we made to each other. Promises impossible for mortals to fulfill.

He tried for several months, then gave up in fear and anger, which brought contempt from me when he could no longer perform sexually. I did not understand his fear of women, a fear that kept him from lasting intimacy with any woman. I did not realize his refusal to have sex with me before marriage was not romantic illusion but the fear that if I knew about his sexual difficulties I would not marry him.

John had sensed the violence, warned, "Do you want to get killed?" At times I courted death through Tom's vicious physical attacks. One night he sneered, "Why don't you commit suicide and get us both out of this misery?" He thought of me as dead and gone forever. When I showed up one day at a session with a black eye, Dr. Emch said quietly, "How much violence are you going to put up with?"

I unconsciously sought violence, I wanted to rejoin in death my beloved father. I did not want to live, as my first reaction to his death showed, in the outburst, "Now what do I have to live for? Who will love me?"

I willingly embraced the first passing stranger who claimed he loved me, unconsciously conveyed to him the message, "I want to die, kill me."

I possessed other unconscious reasons for marrying Tom. He was charming on the surface, violent underneath. I had chosen a man with the negative and positive traits of my mother and father. Tom had shown in spades, dramatized, the surface charm of my parents and the screams of my mother. And the two physical attacks by my father.

In my first marriage I played my father's role when I walked out. In the second, feeling more feminine after five more years of analysis with John, I played my mother's role—the woman scorned by the man. The woman who, for years, endured silent cruelty at the price of deep suffering. To hold what I thought Tom's love, I tried to become his slave, as I felt my mother had been my father's. And as earlier in life I fantasied Mother and Laurie wanted me to be a small slavey to them. I tried desperately to understand Tom's needs and fulfill them but nothing would satisfy him, as nothing seemed to satisfy my parents.

We acted out our subtle games as I played to the insatiable infant in him and he did to me. My Prince Charming turned into a sadist who thought my touch a leprous one. But wasn't that how I felt my mother reacted to my attempts at closeness?

Out of panic I had rushed into marriage with Tom, believing it a safe harbor. Only to find it a treacherous high sea. I thought I would live more like a woman but it awakened unconscious wishes to be a man. As he expected me to provide him with a penis, I expected him, out of my girlhood wish to be a boy, to furnish me with one. It became a deadly game of penis, penis, who's got the penis? As a little girl I felt unloved because I could not possibly live up to the fantasies of my mother and father—be a boy! I sensed unconsciously each wished I, the firstborn, had been a boy. And in marriage I felt I could not live up to the impossible demands of my husband—be a man, "grow" a penis.

I could no longer feel responsible for a man's success in sex. I had always thought if he failed, there must be something wrong with me. As though I were the deus ex machina of his manhood. This was a carryover of the omnipotent feeling of childhood we all possess until we accept reality.

Dr. Emch spent summers at her second home in Estes Park, Colorado, midpoint between Chicago and the Pacific Ocean. She welcomed any patient who wished to vacation there and also see her for two sessions a week, in the tradition of Freud and other European analysts.

That summer I decided to take her up on her invitation as part vacation, part analytic work. She gave me the name of a hotel-ranch near her, I called, reserved a room for three weeks.

After arriving in Denver via plane I rented a car, drove the seventy miles northwest to Estes Park. It

proved a picture-book village set against the first senti-
nels of the Rockies, which end the unbroken plateau of
prairie between Denver and Chicago. I looked out on a
colorful world of nature—lush wildflowers, exotic birds
and deep blue lakes set in the middle of mountains.

Seeing Dr. Emch during vacation gave me a sense
of feeling special. I was one of only three patients, as far
as I knew, who made the trip. As I drove up one morning
to her door, which faced mountains to the west, I saw
her husband for the first time. He stood in the garden,
waved a greeting.

I knew no one at the ranch. I ate alone, went to the
movies at night solo, worked on a new book, the history
of Michael Reese Hospital in Chicago. One evening in
the lobby an appealing nine-year-old girl walked over,
introduced herself as Cate Netchvolodoff from St.
Louis. She explained she was on vacation with her parents but would have more fun if she could find someone
to go horseback riding with her.

"Would you go with me?" she begged.

I felt on the spot. I admitted, "Truthfully, Cate,
while I've bet on a horse, I've never sat on top of one."
I did not want to admit to my newfound friend, the sole
friend in this scenically splendid but lonely spot, that I
was an equine coward. I had assiduously avoided riding
a horse all my life in spite of admiring the large graceful
animals grazing on Granny's farm as I grew up. I felt
aesthetic pleasure in the beauty of a horse, wanted to
keep my acquaintance with horse life on that level.

"Nothing to it," she assured me. "I'll take care of
you. And the man in charge says the horses are very
gentle. Anyone can ride them."

I sighed, thought, I might as well try riding a horse
before I perish. If I got killed they could say I died with
my riding boots on. I felt like the man to whom Freud
alluded as he illustrated how his unconscious dictated

the writing of *The Interpretation of Dreams.* He wrote his friend, Dr. Wilhelm Fliess, who had asked how the book was progressing, that he felt like the man who rode horseback only on Sunday. A friend, seeing him astride the horse, asked, "Where are you going, Itzig?"

Itzig replied, "Don't ask me. Ask the horse."

That was the way it would be with me. As I walked with Cate the next morning to where the horses waited, I was probably the most reluctant rider ever to appear in the west. The owner of the ranch assigned what he thought the proper horse to the proper rider. I told him, "I've never been on a horse and I'm scared to death." He assured me, "Don't give it a thought. I'll put you on Cocoa. She's very calm. And she knows her way blind-fold over the trails."

Cocoa was certainly an endearing name to a choco-late-lover. But all endearment ceased with her name. The minute I was hoisted aboard, we were enemies. She knew she was in complete control of her recalcitrant rider.

She would not move. "You got to hit her with your foot when you want her to move," said the owner of the ranch.

"Hit her?" I was horrified. I was afraid if I hit her she would turn around and bite off my leg.

I explained lamely, "It doesn't seem right to hit a horse. Especially a lady horse."

"Just hit her gentle-like," he said. "You don't have to beat her to death."

I saw Cate high on her horse Burt, way up front as we set off one by one. It was my last glimpse of her the entire trip. Cocoa proved so calm she was catatonic. She stopped dead in the middle of every stray stream. The leader had to halt the rest of the horses, dismount, walk back and slap Cocoa's flanks to persuade her to wade out of the stream. It was a hot day and she wanted to remain in the cool water. I was not about to thwart her. I would have far preferred remaining midstream like a statue, let the others gallop up the mountain trail that lay all too near.

But once out of the water and headed upward, Cocoa took on new power, as though to make up for her lack of daring below. As we climbed higher and higher she seemed bent on showing how near she could step to the edge of the narrow trail without pitching both of us into the void of the valleys that lay miles below. I died the coward's thousand deaths step by step as I inwardly moaned, Cate, where are you? You promised to take care of me.

Once back at the ranch I thought I would never live to see, I lurched off Cocoa, vowing never again to mount a horse. I tossed her a look of sheer hatred that, I suspect, she returned. Though pathetic fallacy does not apply to horses, just to the sky and the wind and the sea.

During the start of my fourth year with Dr. Emch I began to work on my fifth book—*So You Want to Be Psychoanalyzed!*—a partially humorous book. I flew to New York occasionally to consult over luncheon with Leonard Wallace Robinson, my editor at Henry Holt. He was sympathetic to books with an analytic theme.

I also enjoyed an occasional meal at Sardi's, received the usual welcome embrace from Jimmy, the maître d' and Vincent, who owned the famous restaurant founded by his father. I thought of it as home away from home, for I had eaten so many meals there as a reporter. I wandered around Times Square, recalled memorable moments—covering raucous New Year's Eve celebrations, VE Day, VJ Day. Sat on a bench in Bryant Park, mesmerized by the special music of New York, listening to taxi horns as though Satchmo himself played them. Reveled in a room at the luxurious Plaza where Granny often took me to tea.

That summer as usual Dr. Emch went to Estes Park, I stayed in Chicago working on the book rather than going west. She suggested I write her, let her know "how things are going." During a visit to New York I sent a postcard of the Statue of Liberty (what she symbolically meant to me), with the remark, "Half of me is enjoying this visit." When I returned to Chicago I found a note from her: "I hope the 'half' that enjoyed itself in New York manages to dominate matters; if not, write me if you like. And anyway how did you decide that it was 'half and half'?"

This was example of the careful attention she gave each word and what it conveyed about how I felt. I was telling her I was torn about Chicago. Stayed only because she worked there, half of me wished to return to the city I considered home.

I felt relieved when summer ended, signaling my first session with her after the long absence. I had missed her presence, welcomed the feel of the familiar beige couch.

From New York I took back two of the latest style dresses from Bergdorf Goodman. I felt I was at last becoming somewhat of a lady, though I did not give up the silver-sequined blouses and dangling fake diamond earrings I wore to an occasional party. When I told Dr. Emch I covered the fashion world half-time, news the other half, my first six months on the *Times*, she remarked, "To caricature fashion the way you do, you have to know fashion well."

"Me? Caricature fashion?" I thought I dressed conservatively.

This brought to mind a comment relayed to me when I worked on the *Times*. I told Dr. Emch, "Mrs. Arthur Hays Sulzberger, whose father founded the *Times*, was quoted as saying the perfect woman reporter would be one who wrote like me but dressed like another woman reporter who wore trim suits and shirt-waist dresses." I added, "I wouldn't be caught dead at the Fulton Fish Market in her outfits."

Meyer Berger would say with a sigh every so often as we passed in the aisle, reporting to the city desk, "Lulubelle, you're dressing like an Eighth Avenue whore again." I would say with a pleased smile, "Thank you, Mike."

I felt flattered when Mr. James, our horse-playing managing editor, muttered, "Sadie Thompson" when-ever I wore a floppy fur-trimmed velvet black hat I bought on Fourteenth Street.

Wanting to know more about Dr. Emch I went to the library at the Chicago Institute for Psychoanalysis to read articles she wrote for psychoanalytic journals. In one, titled "On 'The Need to Know' as Related to Identification and Acting Out," she explained that "act-ing out" (in which I had engaged at times), the uncon-scious repetition of a destructive act, was a way of trying to master an early situation that frightened, an-gered or confused.

She also wrote about creativity, said it was sublima-tion of an intense, too-early-aroused sexual desire. She believed a sense of "exaltation," tied to the sexual drive, existed in the very early life of the creative child, led to the strong wish to create. Some analysts believe if a mother praises a child for quietly accepting weaning and control of bowel and bladder, this also inspires the child to "produce" artistic creations to win further love and approval.

Soon another icy Chicago winter closed in. Out of the January blue she said quietly one morning, "I have to take off the next few weeks to go to the hospital for an examination. I'm in intense pain and the doctor can't diagnose it."

I was stunned, she had never shown one sign of

suffering. I said, "I'm so sorry. I didn't realize you felt ill."

"Sorry" was only part of what I felt. I wanted to weep because she was in pain. She most certainly did not wish to go to a hospital. But I also felt devastated to be deprived of her. To the child within, she symbolized my mother. Her falling ill was terrifying, a danger to my survival.

All I could utter was an inane, "I hope you'll be out of the hospital soon."

She apologized, "You must know how this distresses me."

I knew what she meant, she believed unconscious wishes were closely connected to physical illness. She added, always the caring therapist, "I am sorry for you that it happens at this time."

We had just started to explore my long-forgotten attachment to my real grandmother, my father's mother, the Supreme Court judge's wife. Dr. Emch believed my grandmother Selina had been a strong influence in my early life. She said, "Sometimes you sound as if you were conducting a dialogue. As though you were two people speaking from the couch. Perhaps she is the other one."

"I seem to remember someone who would talk to me tenderly and to whom I loved to talk," I recalled. "I have a feeling she enjoyed reading to me."

Uncle Ed found old letters she wrote him when he went overseas in World War I, sent one to me. She told him of taking me to Central Park and how, when it was time to go home, I pleaded, "Don't leave me! Don't leave me!"

I did not remember what she looked like but a photograph showed her as an attractive, imposing, gracious lady with glasses, smartly dressed. She was a founder of the Henry Street Settlement House in lower Manhattan and enjoyed the classics. Perhaps my love of them came from her early readings to me, I thought.

Before I was born she suffered a tragic accident. One day at Lake Placid she watched my father, Uncle Ed and a friend of theirs, tee off at the golf course. The friend raised his club, hit the ball and it flew to the right, striking my grandmother full in the left eye. Her sons carried her to the house they rented, a doctor flew up from New York, found her eye so badly injured she would never see out of it again. Thereafter she read with only one eye.

"You were very close to your grandmother, weren't you?" Dr. Emch asked.

"I don't remember but I feel I was."

Sometimes on the couch, as I had done in John's office, I raised my left hand to my left eye in a quick anguished movement as if to cut off vision (imitating my grandmother, who had read to me with that eye sightless?).

One day I mentioned this to Dr. Emch, asked, "Could it be that I am copying her blindness?"

"You might well be," she said. "Especially in times you feel anguished and wish for her love."

I felt in my bones I was identifying with my beloved grandmother. Perhaps trying to bring back her image during painful moments, remembering she comforted me when I coped with earlier anguish—the birth of my brother, my first rival when I was two. It all seemed to fit.

The golf ball disaster also injured her emotionally. This strong energetic lady gradually became an invalid. We moved to Larchmont when I was six and there were no more walks with her in Central Park (where my first love was the youth who ran the merry-go-round). Two years later she suffered a stroke in the rented house in Larchmont where she and Grandpa spent the summers.

She took to her bed, never left it, died that summer, not so suddenly.

Thus the hand to the eye was no chance movement on my part, it was not snatched out of the psychic blue. It was sign of a specific tragedy in my life, the loss of my grandmother, and tragedy in her life, the loss of an eye.

I never properly mourned her death, so deep the loss. It had been trauma I put out of mind. It hurt even to look at her photograph. I tried to believe her leaving me would make no difference, denying what she meant both to me and my father. He felt stricken. Perhaps it was more than a coincidence at this time he met Donna. His mother had forbidden him to marry his Christian-born first love and now with his mother no longer a threat, he found someone resembling his original love.

When I left Dr. Emch that sad January day I asked, "May I phone Hilda to find out how you are?"

"Of course," she said.

Hilda and I had become friends. We both rooted for the Milwaukee Braves to win the National League pennant. One afternoon when Dr. Emch was late (I now had a 3 P.M. hour), Hilda invited me to watch the World Series on the television set in her bedroom, just off the kitchen on the ground floor. Dr. Emch would buzz Hilda to ask her to tell the next patient to go upstairs. When the buzz came for me the Braves were just getting the lead over the Yankees in the decisive game. This was the only time I resented an analytic hour.

The next week in January I phoned, Hilda reported, "Dr. Emch has had an operation and is fine. She expects to be back at work in a few weeks."

The first of February arrived, then the fourteenth. I sent her a bouquet of sweetheart roses for Valentine's Day with a note saying I hoped she felt better. This was my second gift, the first Christmas I handed her a plant embedded in a Chinese vase. She did not want to take it, analysts are not supposed to accept presents from patients.

She said, referring to some primitive society in darkest Africa, "The doctor bestows a gift on the patient when he gets well." Added, "Please give the plant to someone else."

"I don't know anyone in this wasteland of Chicago," I said sadly. I had not as yet acquired a friend.

She kept the plant and vase. I felt delighted a Christmas gift was accepted by someone I loved. It made the lonely holiday easier to bear. In addition to telephone calls to Hollywood, Florida, where I spoke to my mother and my two sisters.

At the end of February Hilda reported, "The doctor is getting stronger but she is not well enough to see patients."

"Do you think I might take a few weeks off and go to Florida?" I asked. "I'd like to visit my mother and sisters." I also wanted respite from the bleakness of the Chicago winter wasteland without the comfort of the couch.

"I'm sure that will be all right," Hilda said.

"I'll call from Florida," I promised.

This I did. I was delighted when Dr. Emch answered the telephone. She sounded well, though the melodious voice seemed softer than usual. After the amenities she said, "I may be a few months recovering. If you want to see another analyst in the meantime, please do."

"I'll wait." Emphatically. I wanted no one else.

When I returned to Chicago in March I phoned at once. I was told, now by a trained nurse, "The doctor is feeling better but cannot come to the phone."

It was then I started to worry, wondered from what illness she suffered. I telephoned two of her patients, analysts in training I had met at parties, but they knew as little as I. Then I received a letter from her:

Dear Lucy,

Finally I am getting to the point where both energy and concentration permit a few letters. No telephones yet except to my mother, sisters, and the cousin who had also to undergo surgery the day before I did. This is to explain that my largest "problem" just now is fluctuation of energy and attention span—believe it or not!

It is this that makes it so impossible for me to plan with any degree of certainty on when I can get back to any kind of routine, even a curtailed "schedule." I am so sorry to say this because I realize it puts you (and others) in a spot—but it is all I can do at the moment.

Please don't hesitate to write me. Even if I don't answer too promptly, I will get to it. I'm glad the work in N. Y. [referring to another trip to see my editor] does not leave you with the feeling of just marking time until we can start again. Or is it still so—underneath?

I'll be interested to know if your uncle really can bring himself to speak of his mother in the years that were apparently blotted out for him—as for others [the grandmother that meant so much to me, about whom I was trying to get more information from him]. But, as I'm fond of saying, whatever it is, just let it "percolate," until your own feelings give you the certainty as to what is (or was) what.

With best regards—and do write.
Minna E.

I answered promptly, told her how grateful I was she had written. Assured her I would wait as long as necessary for her return. She wrote again, thanking me for the letter, said she was still "progressing" and hoped she would soon "have a better idea of when I can get back to work."

I then wrote a newsy letter, telling her that for a monthly column I wrote in a hospital newsletter I had traveled to our atom-bomb complex at Oak Ridge to do a story on the special hospital treating victims of radiation. I did not tell her that while racing in high heels (I detested low heels, would not wear them even on assignments that required vast walking) down a highly polished corridor, suddenly my feet slipped on the overwaxed floor. Luckily I landed on my amply cushioned rear.

As I painfully pulled myself up I thought, Why am I punishing myself like this, isn't life tough enough? Then thought, I feel left out in the cold by Dr. Emch, I am angry she is still not back at work, I also feel guilty for possessing such unwarranted rage, she cannot help her absence. My injury was not serious, I had struck that same spot on my spine during high school days when I crashed while ice-skating at Playland in Rye.

Returning to Chicago I found a letter from her which said, "I wish I could write you now with very definite plans for the fall but it does not as yet seem possible to plan on any kind of regular schedule. Will you let me know what your own plans are and do call me if you are in town, so that if I am up to it, we could at least talk on the telephone. Let me know how things are going and how your present work is progressing too."

She signed the letter, "With every good wish, Fondly, Minna." There was a P.S., "Thank you too for the mysteries. I enjoyed them." I had sent three suspense novels. She once told me she enjoyed mystery books. She introduced me to Josephine Tey, whose work fascinated me because of her understanding of the psychological motives behind murder. I was interested to learn Tey never married, spent her whole life taking care of her father. One clue, I thought, why she might write of murder. Any woman unable to break free from a parent suffers buried feelings of intense rage, prevented from living a life of her own with, as analysts say, "an appropriate sex object." A rage Tey portrayed in her brilliant murder mysteries.

I was alarmed by Dr. Emch's words in the letter, "Will you let me know what your own plans are?" As though I were now supposed to take action. Was I being urged to wait no longer?

I phoned her but once again was not permitted to speak to her. I spent the rest of August in New York getting background for a new book on dramatic cases treated psychoanalytically at Hillside Hospital in Queens, a semiprivate institution. When I returned I found a devastating letter from Dr. Emch.

She wrote, "I cannot plan on any schedule of work for the present. I know it has been a long time to wait, wonder if you might wish to make other plans. Please do not hesitate to write me about your reactions and I shall try to answer promptly." She signed this letter, "Sincerely, Minna." Not "Fondly," as before, and I felt crushed.

I was still determined to wait it out. I would *not* make other plans. I answered by return mail, stating I had waited this long and would keep waiting until she recovered. I asked, "Do you have any idea when you might be back at work?"

There was no answer. After several days I phoned, was not allowed to talk to her. Finally, deciding to act, I wrote her on September 23, 1959: "I want to wait for you but tell me, don't you think perhaps it's wise that I do go back to New York if you plan to be out much longer? Please let me know what you think of this."

Magically, I expected an answer that would inform me she felt much better, it would be only a few days before she once again would make the couch available. Hoping against frail hope.

Two days after I mailed this note I sat in my apartment at eleven in the evening putting together notes on the Hillside Hospital book. Suddenly the telephone rang. I seldom received calls this late.

"Lucy?" The voice of a young psychoanalyst, Dr. Ner Littner, a patient of Dr. Emch. I had been an occasional guest for dinner at his home.

"Yes, Ner. How are you?" I thought this might be another such invitation.

"I wanted to see if you were all right."

"Why shouldn't I be?" Puzzled.

"Did you read the paper this morning?"

"No." Sometimes an entire day passed when I did not leave the typewriter to pick up a newspaper on the street. Somehow news of Chicago was not as vital as news of New York.

"I'm sorry to be the one to tell you," he said. "Dr. Emch died yesterday."

"Oh, no!" A cry of agony, if ever I uttered one. Echo of past tragedy, when my father died and I did not know it until Frank Adams informed me two days later as I vacationed at Fire Island.

"She was very sick," Ner said. "You knew that."

"No one told me anything specific. I would call her home but they only kept saying, 'The doctor can't speak to you.' I never dreamed it was that serious. She wrote such optimistic letters the past few months."

I thought in anguish, Oh God, all those months of waiting, hoping, praying.

"Some of us knew, or guessed," he said. "We started going to other analysts."

"What did she die of?" I could hardly get out the word *die*.

"Cancer. When they first operated, they found so much cancerous growth they just sewed her up and sent her home."

"And she told me she had never been sick a day in her life." Wonder in my voice. It seemed unreal, her kind of "unreally," the unreality of a nightmare.

"There's a lot we still don't know about mind and body, isn't there?" he said.

"Thank you for telling me, Ner." I tried to control tears. "Far better than reading it in the paper."

He then asked, "Would you like to go to the funeral parlor tomorrow? I don't think her family would object if we wanted to pay our last respects."

"I'll meet you there." I wanted in some way, in any way, to keep in contact with her.

He told me where and when to meet him, then hung up. In sudden horror I thought, Good Lord, I was at the track yesterday as she lay dying, what sacrilege! Nelson had taken me, dear Nelson, who hates psychoanalysts but loves horses.

Then I could hold back no longer. I cried as I had cried when I learned my father was dead. I thought, I will never again see her lovely face, hear that soft melodious voice ask, "What are you thinking?" as I lay chained by the silence of resistance.

I cried out of my own heartbreak and then I cried for her. It seemed tragic that she, the youngest of three sisters, be the first to die. To die even before her mother, who I knew from Hilda was still alive.

Part of me, the thinking, conscious part, realized Dr. Emch wanted to live as fervently as I did. But the unconscious, little-child part could accept only the bereavement, the despair and the rage at being forsaken.

I had learned from her that the greatest devastation in a child's life is desertion by the mother. I now understood why men and women commit murder when someone to whom they have felt close threatens to leave or leaves. Desertion is felt as annihilation. I had been reluctant to give up the tattered ties to my husband, not wanting him or me to feel deserted.

Suddenly I thought of the last letter to her, telling her I was leaving Chicago. The letter that now would never be answered. I needed to tell someone of my deep loss, it was too crushing to bear alone.

There was only one person with whom I wished to talk, someone I always called in times of agony. The one I telephoned for solace when I learned of my father's death.

I had never dared call my mother this late at night, it was almost midnight and she was usually asleep at that hour. She might be furious if I wakened her. Sleep to Mother was more precious than gold. Since the first moment of my conscious memory she slept until nine or nine-thirty each morning, then two hours after lunch. She often read until midnight, especially in the years following Laurie's move into the guest room.

I later learned from Donna he had told her he was not sleeping with my mother, when suddenly Sally appeared. Donna was so hurt she refused to see him. He then agreed to move to our guest room and sleep alone. As a child I had been mystified by this move, was glad later to have it explained.

I had been scornful of all the hours my mother spent in bed but I now understood she needed sleep to replenish her psychic energy so she could get through the rest of the lonely day and evening. I also thought she might be copying Granny, with whom she lived from her thirteenth year to her twentieth, when she married my father. Granny always slept a few hours following lunch, did not rise in the morning until almost ten.

I decided to risk my mother's wrath should I wake her. I dialed her number in Hollywood, she answered the first ring.

I asked anxiously, "Mother, did I wake you up?"

"No, dear. I was in bed reading." Her voice sounded loving, not wrathful.

Then she asked, sounding concerned, "Why are you calling at this hour? Is something wrong?"

"I just learned my analyst died." Tears in my voice.

Mother knew how desperately I had been waiting for Dr. Emch to return. She said, "I'm so sorry, dear. You must feel very sad."

There was sympathy in her voice, yet also the same calm as when my father died. Mother was used to receiving news of death with aplomb, perhaps even the first time, when told her mother had died. I felt relieved at her lack of emotion, I was anguished enough for the two of us. She comforted me in her way, told me through the tone of her voice, as she always did when I suffered physical or psychological hurt, that it really was not too shattering. I thought, Natch, otherwise how could she have possibly handled a grief dating back to the age of two.

"Maybe you can now return to New York," she said. She knew how much I missed Manhattan.

"I guess so." I had not even thought of the next step, steeped only in sorrow, part of me not ready to give up the ghost, so to speak, of Dr. Emch.

"Let me know if I can help in any way," she offered.

I knew she meant it. "Thank you, Mother. I had to call you. I knew you would understand."

"Take care of yourself, dear. Come down here if you want. We all love you."

On hanging up, I thought, Mother cannot possibly understand my grief, then thought, Mother understands it only too well in her heart but cannot afford emotionally to admit she understands. I felt relieved after speaking to her, shed a few more tears. Then exhausted, undressed and fell into bed. I would decide what to do the next day, after meeting Ner at the funeral parlor.

I felt like a zombie as I walked, beside Ner, into the room that held Dr. Emch's coffin, stared at the wooden box, which, thank heaven, was closed. I had seen a dead body only once, when Granny died and my Aunt Pat, well-meaning but insensitive sister of Granny's, forced me to look at Granny's face and body. I was so horrified by the waxen lifeless image I vowed never again to stare death in the face.

I hated funerals, tried to avoid them. Yet felt a yearning to attend Dr. Emch's, still loath to let her go. I asked Ner, "Are you going to the funeral?"

He said, "According to the paper the services will be held for the immediate family tomorrow morning at this place. But if you want to attend, I'll go with you."

"I'll call Hilda and ask if we are allowed," I offered.

The moment I reached home, I telephoned Hilda. It was the first time I had talked to her in weeks.

"Hilda! Oh, Hilda!" All I could say.

"I know." I sensed she was crying, too.

"Do you think the family would mind if Dr. Littner and I went to the funeral service?"

"Just a moment. I'll ask her husband."

She returned almost at once, said, "You are welcome to come."

"Thank you, Hilda." I added, "Please tell her husband I am very grateful for his permission to be at the funeral."

The next day before the brief service, Arnold Emch

greeted Ner and me warmly. I recognized him from the photograph in the consultation room and as the man who waved at me as he stood in his garden at Estes Park. He introduced us to other members of the family including Ben Hecht and his wife Rosa, Minna's sister. I managed to hold back tears until Mrs. Hecht put her arms around me as we both cried. I knew how close she was to her sister. When she visited from New York I had seen her walk out the front door a few times as I sat in the reception room.

Ben Hecht delivered the eulogy. He said, in part, "For seven months Dr. Minna Emch, marked for death, and knowing she had cancer, lived with lighted eyes and sparkling voice. Through the days and nights of her dying, our Minna remained untouched and undaunted.

"We heard no fearful sighs, no sound of dread or drama in her voice, no complaint in her words. Our Minna, who had always loved life with all her might, continued to love it with all her might—during her dying. In her sick room we heard only her bright mind speaking, and her spirit sounding—undarkened . . . never darkened during any moment we were near.

"Sometimes humans are sustained in their last agonies by a love of God. Our good Minna was sustained by a rarer love—her love of life. She had a sort of reverence for the mind of man. And she turned her own mind as a searchlight on all the evidences of existence. . . . She saw life as a wondrous and engrossing drama performed by a single actor—the mind of man.

"It had been our Minna's work for thirty years to heal people. She continued in her last months as a healer. Dying, she played doctor to all of us. . . .

"Dr. Minna Emch was a brilliant psychoanalyst whose work was touched with genius. Many honors came to her. Her multitude of patients sounded her praises in all parts of the earth. And the leaders of her profession esteemed her one of their keenest and most talented. She was a joyous-hearted girl, humane and fastidious, full of learning and an unending curiosity.

"I, who loved her, shall remember, however, the manner of her dying as one of the finest lessons of my time. . . . Her death is like a poem that stirs exaltation more than tears. We who are here to bury her are braver by her dying. We have a picture in our hearts of a lovely woman who gave death never a moan—and who departed life smiling gratefully at it."

The service ended, she was soon to be ashes at her request. But I still could not let go. I had to have one last look at the house on Lakeview Drive in which I had spent so many rewarding, challenging hours. The house in which hidden fears, fantasies and forbidden wishes had burst forth in all their terrifying splendor.

The next day I again called Hilda, asked if I might visit a few minutes for the last time. Kind, gentle Hilda (like Mae in my childhood, the cook who healed my wounds) said, "Come whenever you want."

"Now?" I had no place else to go.

"That will be fine."

Then Hilda was opening the door as she did so many times in the past, opening it then to my joy, opening it now to my despair, a psychic era ended. We stood looking at each other in sorrow for a moment. Then sat in the reception room where I had so often fumed when "the doctor" was late.

"Did she *know* she was going to die?" Hoping she did not, hoping all those months she clung to the same faith I did, that she would return.

"She never mentioned it," Hilda said.

I asked if I might, for the last time, see the room upstairs in which I spent so many challenging, illuminating hours.

"Of course," she said, understanding.

We walked up the green-carpeted stairs that curved to the left, into the hush of the wood-paneled library. There Hilda left me, knowing I wished to be alone. It was the first time I entered the room without Dr. Emch standing in it, waiting for me.

I could not bring myself to walk across the room to the spacious beige couch on which I spilled out my sorrows. I stood in silence, not daring to feel, not wishing to move any closer. I sat stiffly on a chair some distance away.

Then, for the final time, I slowly took in the walls of books, the Chinese figurines and tiny carved animals atop the tables. They seemed poised as though waiting for her. I wanted to fix forever in mind everything in that room, though its essence would remain indelibly imprinted on my senses without that final gaze.

I stared at the chair behind the couch, the chair in which she sat, listening, always listening, choosing the crucial words on which to concentrate after I spouted them. Draped neatly over the square back of the chair lay the small brown wool blanket she sometimes used to cover her feet during chilly days. Feet always encased in feminine shoes, my favorite, the powder-blue leather wedgies.

Hilda returned, looked at me questionably, as though to ask if I had absorbed enough of the room's nostalgia. I dared make a request, believing Dr. Emch would have approved (she did accept that Christmas gift from me).

"Do you have anything, just a little something of hers that I could take away with me, Hilda?" I asked.

In our family, when someone died we always sought a small memento, as though it would magically tie us to the lost loved one.

"How about a piece of jewelry?" Hilda suggested. Though I would have loved jewelry, a pin, earrings or bracelet—Granny had bestowed jewelry for years, a jade necklace, a diamond wristwatch, a solid-gold bracelet from which dangled miniature musical instruments—I felt I could not accept so expensive a gift from Dr. Emch.

"No jewelry!" To take jewelry would have made me a thief.

"Let's see what else there is," Hilda said.

She led me up another flight to Dr. Emch's bedroom, which I entered for the first time in trepidation. I stared at the bed on which she spent those last dreadful months, thinking I had no right to be in that intimate room. Yet fascinated by the idea of seeing where she slept, dressed, made love.

Stacks of skirts and blouses were piled neatly on the bed. Hilda offered a white lace blouse Dr. Emch sometimes wore with a brown tweed suit. I could not take this either, it seemed like snatching the very clothes off her body.

Then I picked up a small leather purse of foldover style, it was beige, a color she often wore. The color, too, of the couch. Once I said to her, "I cannot bear to wear any shade of brown. Too close to feces, I guess."

She said, "Beige is a very warm color and looks well on brunettes."

One week later I walked in wearing a beige dress, said, "You are right. Beige is a warm color."

I asked Hilda, "May I have this purse?"

"Of course," she said.

I thanked her, said, "Goodbye, Hilda. I will always remember your many kindnesses," and carrying the small purse slowly walked down the green-carpeted stairs, this time, two flights.

Then out of the house of nonmagic forever. The house where I first started to recognize the difference between fantasy and reality.

As I walked away, I heard the echo of Ben Hecht's words: "She had a sort of reverence for the mind of man. . . . She saw life as a wondrous and engrossing drama performed by a single actor—the mind of man." I had been lucky to find Dr. Emch, I blessed Mike Serota for suggesting her.

A letter I will always cherish arrived the next morning from Dr. Karl Menninger:

Dear Lucy:

Ever since I got the word of Dr. Emch's death I have been thinking about you and wondering what I could say that would be most comforting. I want you to know how sorry I am and how worried I am about you. Write me or phone me if I can be of any specific help.

There now seemed only one sensible act. Return after six years to the city to which I belonged. I sublet the apartment on Bellevue, told friends I was leaving, called Neptune movers (Mother still stored furniture from our home in their New Rochelle warehouse—tapestried chairs, Tiffany china, vases and lamps, paintings). Neptune agreed on its next trip to Chicago to pack and transport to New Rochelle all the furniture, clothes, books, paintings, dishes and other items, store them until I was located in Manhattan.

While waiting for Neptune to set the day, I thought of my mixed feelings about Chicago, which, in a way, I would miss because of Dr. Emch. She taught me about this mysterious feeling called "ambivalence." I loved her, at times hated her—loved-hated her, floundering in the turbulent sea of ambivalence, unable to make up my mind between love and hate.

There were moments I wished to kill her with the letter opener she left so temptingly on her desk, the next moment wished to hug her close. She was wiser than Freud, a bigger fool than Falstaff.

At times I was ambivalent about the analysis. Moments I wished to face the truth, moments I denied it. I had to decide, I did not have to decide. I could not accept a certain thought, I had to accept it. It was agonizing to be on the psychic fence if you did not know toward which side to jump.

Before analysis I believed feelings pure, undiluted. I either hated or loved, believed it impossible to feel two or more contrasting emotions at the same time. How wrong could I be? As a child I felt both love and hate as my mother screamed, my father slapped me.

"Hate and love exist side by side in your unconscious in comfort," Dr. Emch said.

I had muttered, "In my conscious, they fight like hell."

I suddenly realized Dr. Emch's early death reawakened the same sense of shock as when I learned my father had died at the early age of sixty-one after two strokes. All his children, his two wives and members of his law firm had been equally shocked that this zestful, always-driving man should unexpectedly be felled by his body. The worst previous illness he suffered was gallstones in his early forties.

His younger brother, my Uncle Ed, lived past eighty. Why had my father died almost twenty years earlier? Now aware, thanks to analysis, of the close relationship between mind and body, I thought of the emotional stress my father must have endured, the conflict and the guilt at the two separate love lives he led with Mother and Donna. Uncle Ed had always been faithful to his wife, spared the guilt.

I wondered whether my father had any awareness of how he shortened his life by the emotional turmoil he inflicted on himself, Mother and on us four children over the years. We pay for our guilt when we hurt those we love. "Be sure your sin will find you out," the Bible warns. I added, "and punish you," even as I still grieved at the very thought of my father's premature death.

My last night in Chicago was as happy as it could be, given the reason I was departing. My friends Madeleine and Arnold Paley held a small farewell party in their apartment at 1350 Lake Shore Drive. I could now enter the building without bitterness, Tom had moved to New York. Madeleine whipped up her heavenly chocolate mousse, we drank, ate and joked until midnight. Then Helen Douglas and George Taylor, an executive in Arthur Meyerhoff's public relations firm, walked me the two blocks to the Ambassador Hotel. My furniture was on its way to New York, I had moved out of the apartment.

On the plane homeward I thought of how Dr. Emch never reproached me for the most sordid of desires. Always gave me the feeling I had worth and dignity. Never censored me for rage or depression. She exuded a quality money could not buy, she conveyed to me that above all she desired to ease my suffering.

From her I learned to endure what often seemed overwhelming loneliness. I could no longer use someone else to try to escape emptiness within. An empty moment, an empty hour, an empty day did not mean emotional starvation and rejection by the world but could be used just to *be*.

She will always be part of my life, I thought, as I walked off the plane at La Guardia. It was late October of 1959. I had spent almost six years in alien territory. My marriage had ended disastrously, my analyst had died in what I considered the middle of analysis.

I felt like the prodigal daughter returning home, though I had no welcomers. My father was dead, my mother and sisters still lived in faraway Florida. I did not know what I wanted to do—whether go back to *The New York Times,* for Mr. Sulzberger said he would always hold the job open, or keep free-lancing in books.

But, most important, I had to find a place to live. And then perhaps in time seek another analyst to assuage my grief, help me understand even more deeply the truths about a past that still terrorized and tormented.

8

The Sutton Place Couch

The city had not changed except rents were higher and more office buildings of sheer glass were rising. I enjoyed the image of clouds floating across glass walls. The sky brought down to earth, so to speak.

Temporarily I stayed at the Barclay Hotel as a real estate broker searched for a new home for me. Shortly she found a two-room apartment on the second floor of a five-story building adjacent to the Plaza, overlooking Central Park. Within a week I was ensconced within, as Neptune delivered my possessions the day after I notified them.

I settled my conflict whether to return to the *Times* by remembering one reason I left—the sameness of the work day after day. With my literary agent Max Wilkinson's blessing, I decided to keep writing books. One year as deadline for a book was far easier than the daily deadline for a total of almost three hundred separate stories.

I felt pure joy at returning to Manhattan. I recalled
the words of Frank Costello as we strolled through Central Park one day. I was hoping to persuade him to give
me an exclusive interview for the *Times*. The only reason he agreed to see me was because my father had
settled his case with the Internal Revenue Service several years before, possibly keeping him from going to
prison.

As we strolled through Central Park I begged,
"Tell me something about your life, Mr. Costello."

He replied with a laugh, "I couldn't tell you the
truth."

He stared at the skyscrapers surrounding the park,
almost a reverent stare.

"You really love New York, don't you?" I asked.

"Every place else is just camping out," he replied.

That was how I felt in Chicago, "just camping out."
Waiting for the day I could return to the comfortable
complexity of my city. I noticed another change quite
different from the architectural beauty of new buildings, however. The typical New York camaraderie had
grown a bit more primitive.

As I crossed Broadway and Fifty-ninth Street a
truck and taxi vied to be first as they roared downtown.
The taxi cut off the truck. The driver leaned out,
screamed in wrath, "Fuck your mother's cunt!" The taxi
driver was white, the truck driver, black.

Before analysis I would have felt shocked, now I
laughed, thought, as the analytic joke went, "Wonder
what he meant by that?" Obviously it was a vicious
verbal attack, related to the Oedipal taboo against a
man having sex with his mother. Like saying "Go to
hell" in my childhood.

Mother sent a generous check for a housewarming
gift and I wrote my thanks (she saved all her children's
letters, eventually returned them).

Dearest Mother,

Thank you for the money, I bought a much-needed set of lovely plates at Bloomingdale's. Sometimes when life gets me down, I feel I must be a good sport about it and this quality I have absorbed from you. All of us children have this spunk and spirit.

This has been the most difficult time of my life. I felt in shock at the death of the analyst. She helped me so very much. Because of her, my feelings for you, the deeper ones, became far clearer. I am able to see how, out of my selfish needs, I always accepted what Laurie said and thought, which was sometimes very distorted. I have had a lot of growing up to do all over again.

I want you to know you come first in my life and always have, even though at times I didn't act that way. It may have seemed to you I sided with Laurie over the years but I really didn't. Underneath, burned a deep resentment at what he did and I hated him for leaving you and us, though I couldn't admit it. I was powerless to do anything about it so I had to bury my feelings.

You must have loved him very much, Mother. I have never really known your feelings, as I have never known much about you because I have been so angry about things I couldn't quite understand. Someday let's have a long talk about this.

Much love,
Lucy

We never did have that long talk but I think Mother appreciated the letter.

Soon I was hard at work on books that took up most of my time. The months passed swiftly as I made a few new friends. I felt a strange reluctance to call old friends at the *Times* since I was not returning.

I became involved for a year with a young psychologist I met at a party, divorced for the second time. Then I realized he was somewhat like Paul in his wish to control the woman. I thought it was high time to resume my interrupted analysis. I had avoided looking for a therapist principally because I lacked funds, but royalties were starting to come in.

I sought advice from an analyst I knew, a member of the New York Psychoanalytic Institute, the first psychoanalytic institute in the nation. He suggested I call a well-known analyst, who graciously offered a consultation. After asking a number of questions in a concerned manner, he told me he did not currently have an hour available but asked if I could wait six months.

I said simply, "I wish I could. But suddenly I feel as if I am hanging from a cliff by one finger. I daren't postpone further analysis."

My analyst friend then recommended a woman I will call Dr. Elizabeth Mack, also a member of the New York Psychoanalytic Institute (she has since died). She lived on Sutton Place South, a fifteen-minute walk from my apartment. I phoned her, she asked me to come for a consultation, set the day and hour.

I entered her office, part of her home on the tenth floor facing the East River, hoped I would not be rejected by her, too. After a patient left, she walked out of the consultation room, shook hands. She was a tall woman, about five feet eleven inches, in her late sixties, I judged, hair gray, falling to the neckline. She had a pleasant, open face, though lacking the classic beauty of Dr. Emch. Clear blue eyes gazed into my hopeful ones.

As she questioned me about my two experiences on the couch, I felt rather like a prisoner before a judge. When I explained I sought her because my analyst in Chicago died unexpectedly, her expression did not show a smidgen of sympathy either for Dr. Emch or me. At the end of the hour instead of accepting or rejecting me she suggested, "Come back next week at the same time on the same day and let us see if we are suited to work together." I wondered why she did not know after fifty minutes. I wished to be accepted on the first visit as with Dr. Emch and John.

Evidently after the second session, in which I talked about my writing and marital mistakes, I convinced her I would be a suitable patient. We arranged four sessions a week at five in the afternoon, her only free hour. She told me her husband, ill for several years, had recently died. I thought, I find death in her office, too.

At the next session, feeling like a veteran, I headed right for the couch. Suddenly I heard the click of needles, turned to look at her. I was shocked to notice she was knitting. She explained as though in apology, "This way you have my full concentration." Implying if she did not keep her hands busy, her mind would be on matters other than my misery. I was puzzled, my former analysts needed no such diversion to enable them to concentrate on my past misery.

One day she criticized the clothes I wore, suggested I shop in Saks, find a competent fashion expert as guide. I would not have allowed Hattie Carnegie to choose my clothes. Just as I would not let my mother after I reached high school. I enjoyed my own peculiar taste for black in dresses, slacks, sweaters, underwear and nightgowns. As well as sequins and boas for parties.

Dr. Mack would occasionally put down the knitting as the maid knocked on the door, then brought in her supper. She explained apologetically, "After your hour I have to change clothes and go to the opera. I eat now to save time."

I felt uncomfortable at both the clicking of needles and her chewing away as I spoke but held back any comment. Who was I to criticize a leading psychoanalyst?

She also explained that the younger man I occasionally saw walk in the front door using his own key as I sat in the waiting room was her escort to theater and the opera. She told me she had met him when she went to Arthur Murray's dancing school and he was assigned as her instructor.

Thus I was early drawn at times into her personal life, unlike my experience with John or Dr. Emch. My reporter's mind relished knowing the "what" and "why" of the life of someone else so I did not have to face the fear and fury in my own. I was fascinated by any small revelation, wanted to know all about Dr. Mack's life, as I had wanted when a child to find out about my parents' lives (especially the sexual aspects). A strange coincidence made this knowledge of Dr. Mack's "away from the couch" life even more possible.

My current book assignment was to write the life story of the mother of Tennessee Williams, Edwina Dakin Williams, for G. P. Putnam's Sons. I flew to St. Louis, where Mrs. Williams, a generous and gracious lady, insisted I stay at her home when I appeared at her door, suitcase in hand. I had expected her to direct me to the nearest hotel.

I interviewed her for several weeks, day and night, discovered she had more energy than I did, would have stayed up past midnight if I had not tired. She was one of the most articulate persons I have ever met, I thoroughly enjoyed her reminiscences. On my return I told Dr. Mack this and she seemed pleased. She permitted me to take time off without charging.

I titled the book *Remember Me to Tom* (his given name was Thomas) because Mrs. Williams told me she saw so little of him after he became famous that she begged anyone who passed her way and mentioned him, "Remember me to Tom when you see him."

As a result of the book I met Andreas Brown, Tennessee's official bibliographer. Andreas had visited the house in St. Louis just before I arrived. He catalogued Tennessee's letters and manuscripts stored by his mother in the basement, then sent them to the University of Texas. Andreas was helpful in setting me straight on dates, also referred me to some of Tennessee's early poems. Andreas is now owner of the famed Gotham Book Mart, bought it from Frances Steloff, who founded it. Each resides on a different floor of the brownstone at 41 West Forty-seventh Street.

I treasure a letter from Tennessee, to whom I mailed the final manuscript for approval. He wrote:

> Dear Miss Freeman:
>
> I am glad that "Mother's Book" fell into your hands. I think you have caught her personality, her style of speech, with stunning accuracy: the book is both sympathetic and extremely humorous.
>
> If there is any way in which I can be of help to you before the book's publication, I would be only too glad. This book means a great deal to Mother. Unfortunately her present life is rather isolated.
>
> Thank you again for dealing so kindly with a lady who needs so much kindness at this point in her four score years, and best of luck to the book for your sake too.
>
> Yours,
> "Tom"

He signed it "Tom" in deference to his mother's wish to remember him by the name she chose. She told me she always called him Tom, saying "I don't know where he got the name Tennessee."

That spring saw a Broadway premiere of Tennessee's *Slapstick Comedies,* consisting of two short plays. I was invited as the guest of his brother Dakin, a lawyer in St. Louis, whom I had met at Edwina's house along with his wife Joyce. Prior to this, Dakin took me to a New Year's Eve party in New York, introduced me to his famous brother. Tennessee thanked me again for writing his mother's story, said, "You've made her last years happier."

Dakin and I arrived early for the premiere, stood waiting in the lobby with other playgoers. Suddenly before my shocked eyes appeared Dr. Mack, accompanied by Tennessee and her young man. She was dressed in high fashion, a blue satin floor-length evening gown with white boa circling her shoulders. Her false eyelashes of sparkling silver looked an inch long.

We all said quick hellos, then Dakin and I headed for our seats. During intermission Dakin and I crossed the street to a bar, discovered Dr. Mack, her friend and Tennessee there. Tennessee said to me in astonishment, "You look lovely. What have you done?" I had lost fifteen pounds and wore a black velvet dress to look slimmer.

"The results of analysis," I said. He had told me at the New Year's Eve party he had started analysis with Dr. Kubie, my father's cousin, who had originally advised me to seek the couch.

"Analysis works, does it?" Tennessee asked worriedly.

"It does." Reassuringly. Added, "I enjoyed your first of the two comedies."

His face took on a look of concern. "The second is meant to be even funnier. But I'm worried about it."

"I'm sure it will be very moving." He understood the basis of Freudian theory, I thought, more than any other playwright. He translated the trauma of his earlier days into drama enjoyed by millions who saw not only his plays but movies made from them.

Dr. Mack and I smiled at each other from across the small room. She sat at the bar between her young man and Tennessee. Dakin and I left the theater as the curtain fell on the second act to the usual enthusiastic applause for a Williams play, though critics claimed it was not up to his usual brilliance.

At my next session I said to Dr. Mack, "I was surprised to see you with Tennessee. I didn't know you knew him."

She said almost apologetically, "The man I was with is a friend of Tennessee's. I don't often go to first nights." Then, "I enjoyed seeing you there." And, "I don't often wear such dramatic eyelashes but I do dress for theater and the opera."

About a year after I started with her, one day as I walked in the door of her apartment I noticed a letter on the table in the waiting room. I was early as usual and curious as always. Feeling somewhat like a thief, I stole a look at the envelope. It was addressed to "Mr. and Mrs." with a last name I did not recognize. I did not dare mention my act of stealth to her but as I left the building I asked the doorman, an affable elderly man, "Did Dr. Mack get married?" He nodded, said, "Yes, to that young man she's been going out with."

The following session I dared say, "I hear you have married again. Congratulations."

"Thank you." She did not ask how I knew.

As though in explanation of the difference in their age she said, "When you grow older, you marry for companionship."

Not sex, but companionship, she was saying, and I did not see anything wrong with that. I started to identify with her, I realized, when I became attracted for the first time to a younger man, twelve years younger. He was divorced and bringing up three children, one seven, one four, the youngest almost two. At times I cooked supper for the children, who eagerly ate anything I prepared, unlike Tom who wanted only his few favorite dishes. I helped put the children to bed, kissed them good night, a new experience for me.

When I told Dr. Mack, she said, high disapproval in her voice, "You should postpone any serious relationship until you understand more about yourself. You've been in enough trouble with the men you chose."

She went on, "You will only confuse the youngest daughter if you remain part of that household as an interloper. She needs a substantial substitute mother."

This made sense, only at that point I could not follow her suggestion. I thought I loved this interesting man, trying to make a go of it both writing fiction and playing the stock market. I enjoyed the children, the next best thing to having my own.

There were also moments of pleasure in summer as we literally sailed out to sea, the Atlantic Ocean, in Richard's boat, complete with cabin and bathroom. He moored it in Flushing Harbor and we often cruised Long Island Sound, once as far as Montauk. Or sailed down the East River. I would wave guiltily at Dr. Mack's apartment as we passed Sutton Place.

When Richard proposed marriage I was tempted but knew I did not have enough energy to take care of three children, shop for food, cook and write books. There were not enough hours in the day for all these tasks. Richard, with my blessing, found a divorced younger woman with two children of her own, married her.

One day, before I decided to leave him, Dr. Mack threatened, "If you continue to see this man, I am not sure we should continue analysis."

I later discovered it was not wise for an analyst to

threaten a patient in this fashion. I retaliated by deciding never to mention Richard, she would think I obeyed
her, that he and I had split. When a patient holds his
tongue, this is *the* sin of couch sins, I knew. But I did
not want to leave either her or Richard at this point.
Fresh from daily rejection by Tom, I was delighted at
my acceptance by this youthful family. I also enjoyed
the emotional and sexual closeness Richard and I
achieved. We understood each other's frailties, enjoyed
each other's strengths.

One of the pleasures of my life is that I helped for
several years to bring up the youngest child, Mollie. She
was the nearest to having a child of my own, because of
her I mourn less the children I never had. I loved her as
if she were my own. I cuddled her, held her in my arms
when she was frightened or upset. I took her shopping,
enjoyed watching her race down the aisles of Wool-
worth's, picking out a comb, a bright ribbon, a doll.

Mollie brought down the boat in laughter one day
when she was four. We were sailing on a rather rough
Atlantic Ocean. Her father, at the wheel, assured her,
as the boat seesawed to the sky and back, "It's really a
very calm day." With the literalness children possess,
Mollie observed, "It may be a calm day but it's sure a
rough ocean." Richard and I burst into laughter. Mollie
started to cry, felt she was the target. I took her in my
arms, reassured her, "We weren't laughing at you but
the funny thing you said. We love you."

I shall always be haunted by the night I returned
for a visit, absent six months. Richard, not yet married,
had called to ask if I wanted to drop in and see the
children. When I rang the doorbell he and his son
greeted me warmly. I asked, "Where's Mollie?" His son
said, "She's in the bedroom crying because she missed
you so much. She can't believe you're back."

I walked to her bedroom, saw tears in her eyes, took

her in my arms. I reassured her I would always love her, invited her to visit me any time she wished. Over the years Mollie and I have remained close friends. She is now a lovely, sensitive, brilliant young woman who wants to be a teacher and counselor.

Though there were moments I wondered about the validity of the analysis with Dr. Mack, it had its merits or I would not have remained five years. I kept writing books, the writing seemed to flow more easily. She provided further insights about the relationship between my mother and me.

One day after I described Tom's brutality during the marriage she asked, "How could you stay two years with a man who so obviously did not want you?"

I said in surprise, "Those are the very words I said to my mother when she asked if she should divorce my father."

"Perhaps you are punishing yourself in your choice of men for what you thought traitorous words to your mother."

"You mean I choose a man who will leave me, or force me to leave him, because I feel guilty about my advice to her?"

"And also guilt at your earlier childhood wish to get rid of her and have your father all to yourself."

Like my beloved father, who had to be impotent where I was concerned, Tom became impotent. And like my father, Tom at times indulged in violence. Richard and his three children also helped replay the Oedipal battle in which I took my rival brother and two sisters (in fantasy, my children by my father) from my mother. The fantasies of childhood became the heartbreaking realities of later life.

At times Dr. Mack's words made me furious though I did not open my sugary mouth. Once she urged, "Use your good mind," when she wanted me to break away from Richard. I thought how horrified Dr. Emch and John would be at this way of helping me give up fantasies by command. Unless I understood why I put myself in a hopeless situation I could not use my "good mind."

Another time she said of a thought I recalled from childhood, "Other little girls would have felt differently." I did not reply, thought, I am not other little girls, I am me, if I could have been like other little girls I would not be on your couch.

Occasionally I kept notes, as I did with each analysis (turning the table on the analyst). Keeping notes had been part of my life since the early days of the diary, and also a large part of my life as reporter. I wrote on October 27, 1964: Dr. Mack said today, "You always make a narcissistic object choice." I wanted to ask, "What the hell is that?" but queried sweetly, "Can you explain what that means?" Not saying, but implying, To poor, little dumb me.

She answered, "You pick a man who mirrors your image of yourself."

"Instead of what?"

"Instead of choosing a man for what *he* is."

"Isn't sexual attraction important?"

"There is something more important than an orgasm, Mrs. Freeman. Self-respect."

I admitted, "I have always felt my sexual feelings were wicked and evil. Each man I imagined as the first. I blocked out all others who preceded him."

"He stood for the first man in your life. Your father. The man of charm. But also a bastard."

I was horrified to hear her call my father a bastard but even more horrified at her next words. "You had to sleep with every man who came down the pike."

I did not know exactly what "pike" meant but thought it might be the British word for "road." I rose to my own defense, blood boiling. "There weren't that many men, Dr. Mack. My first act of sex took place at twenty-two."

She did not apologize. I continued defending myself. "What about my need for occasional sexual expression?"

"Sex in moderation is natural when you can take it or leave it," she said. "That is desire without urgency. But hungry sex, demanding sex, is another thing."

I do not think I ever forgave her for the unfair accusation. She had practically called me a prostitute, whereas I knew I had engaged in far fewer affairs than most of my female friends between the time I was twenty-two and the recent relationship with Richard.

She went on, "Sex should not be so pervasive in your life. You use sex as an addiction. To relax, to go to sleep."

I had never expressed such a thought, I considered I possessed normal sexual desire, nothing particularly "pervasive" about it. I spent three years in Chicago without sexual involvement, then a year in New York. One day she accused me of "sexualizing" everything, saying, "Sex should be part but not all of your life. You do not know what companionship, friendship and tenderness are."

I felt the fury rise but again did not dare defy the haloed analyst. Perhaps the day would come, I thought, when I could express anger, justified or not. I knew you could not live by sex alone. You cannot put all your passion and energy into sex, much goes for work, for friendship, for creativity, for understanding the self and others.

Actually I had somewhat of a thwarted sexual life. As an adolescent I did not dare go beyond passionate kissing and necking in cars. There were a few affairs as reporter. In my marriage to Paul, sex was satisfactory but his need to control overwhelmed any sexual desire

I felt. Then a practically sexless husband in Chicago. And the recent pleasure with a man Dr. Mack asked me to give up.

One session I dared ask, "Is it possible to find a man who is thoughtful and considerate?"

Her reply, "Some women can find pleasure without pain living with a man. But you are masochistic. You always expect pain. You take pleasure in suffering. You gain a sense of relief when you are forgiven and temporarily loved by the one who beats you. That was your life in Chicago. And as a child, at times, with your father. And your mother, who struck you with words."

I then asked, "How would *you* define love?"

She said, "Right to the genitals is not love." Added, "There is sexual excitement in love but without masochism."

Explained further, "You are afraid of your positive feelings. Like someone who trembles when he calls a person he loves 'sweetheart.' You fear if you declare your love you may get slapped in the face. As your father and Tom slapped you."

I could not argue with her. I said, "It sounds as if you feel sorry for me," wanting sympathy.

"I feel sorry for many people but I don't necessarily support them if I feel they are self-destructive as they mistake passion for mature love."

I wondered if anyone on earth as a child ever received what analysts call "mature love" from a parent. No one, as far as I knew, but perhaps I did not know the less tormented. Blood is thicker than love in those I know, I thought. Meaning the boiling of blood when anger erupts.

I asked, "What keeps me from being afraid to engage in a sexual intimacy that is part of love?"

She replied, "Your whole life lies in the answer to that."

At twenty-two it was easy to believe I loved the first man with whom I had sex. I felt stirred by his embrace as he sought me and I sought him, all my senses responded in warmth, joy and sensual desire. But soon the feeling of fire dulled to ashes and even though we went through the same searching-out movements with lips, tongues and genitals, it was now devoid of the warmth, joy and sensual lust, it became mechanical. There was momentary pleasure in orgasm but the aim seemed to be to reach it quickly and get release, rather than knowing the person better. I had wailed, Why? Why? Why does love change to lethargy so swiftly?

I summoned the courage to ask one day, "Why do I feel angry if the man ejaculates and I have not reached a climax? I feel as if he has left me hanging from a guillotine. The nearer I am to the climax, the more devastating the feeling. Many men help the woman in such a situation but some do not offer."

I thought of all the women who complained about what they believed the selfishness of men who left them unfulfilled sexually. I also wondered if the need to always have an orgasm to complete the act of sex was to deny frigidity, such a fear could lie deep in women.

Dr. Mack then provided another insight. "You experience your readiness for passive abandon in sex as servitude."

Passive abandon? I thought I had been willing to play my part in the act of sex. Tom had criticized me for being "too aggressive" at times but then he could neither be in command nor allow me to be.

Dr. Mack never laughed much, unlike Dr. Emch, whose soft merry peal of laughter I occasionally enjoyed. When I thought I made a wisecrack, there was only silence in Dr. Mack's consultation room. But one day she emitted a warm laugh—not loud but sincere.

I said, "I am learning to pull in my horns when I feel annoyed at something a friend says or does."

It was then I heard her laugh. I lamely rationalized, "I mean I feel less like the devil. Not so fiery and angry."

"And also?" Implying, Please go on.

I sighed. "I know. 'Horns' stands for my wish for the penis. The wish of every little girl after she has seen it on a boy or her father."

"Your fantasied penis," she amended.

My phrase had pleased her, she sometimes reminded me of my carefully guarded wish to be a boy. She also laughed the next day when I referred to a "masculine penis" in a dream where my mother held a golf club. I said, "I think of my mother as masculine. Hiding a penis."

Then admitted, "I want to be the perfect patient and I guess that means penis and all."

She said, "There is no perfect patient or perfect analyst."

True, I thought. John Thurrott was not perfect, Minna Emch was not perfect, Elizabeth Mack is not perfect. I wondered if part of Dr. Mack's imperfection was based on her wish to be a man. She seemed at times quite masculine, unlike Dr. Emch.

I had tried hard to be the perfect child. The perfect adolescent. The perfect woman. My father and mother would have disowned me if they had known of later affairs. Mother had sex only with my father and this ceased when at thirty-one she gave birth to Sally and he moved out of the bedroom. I felt sorry for my mother, deprived of sex at such an early age. But at least she flirted with other men, seriously considered marrying the one who cheated her out of much of her inheritance. In a way she was trying to bribe him by loaning him money. (And I bribed Paul, wanting him perhaps still to like me, allowing him to keep the money [one half of the total] I had put up for our house. And bribed Tom by giving him eight thousand dollars to allow me to get the divorce.)

Dr. Mack helped me understand one reason my self-esteem was low had stemmed from the way my father would alternately show deep affection, even adoration at times, then tear me down in front of others. I realized this was not intentional. It came out of his buried childhood conflicts, perhaps jealousy of his two beautiful younger sisters and of his mother, the controlling woman.

I felt the satisfaction of another insight when Dr. Mack pointed out, "You have hidden from yourself your hatred of your father's second wife. Because you wanted desperately for him to love you alone. You sought this woman's love so she would allow you to keep close to your charming father. If she did not like you, you would lose your father."

"I guess that's true," I admitted reluctantly. "But I also love her for herself. We are close friends today. She refers to me as one of her children. We see each other quite often. I am also close to her daughter Nancy and, of course, Alice."

Alice for a while was my baby in fantasy. I early became her protector, snatched her from the cruel arms of a baby-sitter who would slap her for misbehaving. I felt elated as she once slipped me a Mother's Day card. In later life at times I became the good mother when I helped Alice and Sally find an analyst. Sally said he enabled her to make a happy marriage. Alice also praised him for helping to straighten out her life.

When work on books occasionally took me to Los Angeles, I visited Alice in her home in West Lake Village, thirty or so miles to the north. She moved there after becoming a lawyer, the only one of Laurie's children to accomplish this. She heads the legal department of Filmation, a large company that sells children's cartoon films worldwide. One day at her home I found the copy of *Fight Against Fears* I had given my father. I had forgotten I inscribed the words: "To my father, The most important one in my life and the one I love the most." I felt relieved my mother had never seen that inscription.

I told Dr. Mack, "If it hadn't been Donna, my father would have sought another woman. My mother was not enough for him."

"I am glad you are starting to understand your parents," she said.

I was now sympathizing with them, they no longer appeared such ogres. I might wish they had been more understanding of their children. But they too were beset by deep conflicts. This was part of the reality I had to accept. Along with responsibility for my own life.

Something was starting to disturb me about my relationship to Dr. Mack. It seemed too alien from the analytic relationship with John and Dr. Emch.

I did not feel at ease with her. I refrained from revealing thoughts and emotions I would freely have spoken of with Dr. Emch, who accepted me fully. Did not attack me unfairly as I felt Dr. Mack sometimes did.

I was heading into the fifth year with Dr. Mack. I still could not understand why I did not feel free with her, why I kept bottling up resentments. Why I could not be enough at ease to tell her my thoughts—especially about her.

All I knew was that I was unable to speak of my true feelings. I did not know what held me back.

9

The Psychic Stalemate

A s the analysis with Dr. Mack continued, my doubts about our analytic compatibility grew even stronger. But now I held the slowly growing conviction I should leave, seek someone else.

I moved to an entrancing apartment on the eighteenth floor at 120 Central Park South. It offered a spectacular view of the park, boasted a wide terrace on two sides, ample space for broiling steak or hamburger in the summer. Kitchen, bedroom and bathroom were cramped but the large living room with built-in bookcase from floor to ceiling almost the entire length of one wall made up for it. Seldom do you find everything in a Manhattan home.

After Richard and I gave up on the relationship I became more social. I renewed ties to a few of the *New York Times* staff, including my oldest friend, Ruth Adler, and her sister Frances Lewis, married to Robert Lewis, on the staff of the Sunday *Times.* Unfortunately

Frank Adams and Meyer Berger, my close men friends, had died.

Mr. Markel sent me a note, asking, "How is it I never hear from you? I thought I was definitely and for an indefinite period on your couch." He had introduced me to his daughter, Helen, then an editor at *McCall's*, and we occasionally enjoyed a bridge game.

I wrote Clifton Daniel, managing editor of the daily *Times*, whom I had met before I left the paper, asking if his wife, the former Margaret Truman, would consent to an interview for a magazine article. He replied that she was "flattered" but rarely gave interviews and "hopes you will understand her reticence." He added he appreciated my "taking the trouble to identify yourself but it really wasn't necessary. There is no former member of the staff who is better known or more favorably remembered than you are." I felt grateful for this thoughtful comment, never dreamed I was that memorable. My one regret was that I had left too soon, deprived of working under him as managing editor.

I saw Margaret Parton, formerly of *The Herald Tribune*, a close friend of newspaper days. After reporting news from Japan, then India, she now lived with her son Lemuel in her parents' charming cottage of Revolutionary days in Sneden's Landing, just off Route 9W near Nyack. I recalled the day Margaret and I, after covering an exhibition of art by underprivileged children at the Henry Street Settlement House, wandered to a bench in the sun alongside the East River.

Margaret said, "There must be something better than this."

"What do you want to be?" I asked.

"A foreign correspondent," and she shortly became one.

"What do you want to be?" she asked.

"I don't know," I said. "But I'm ready to take to the

hills if I have to cover one more settlement-house story."

Now we met for luncheons at the Overseas Press Club, to which she belonged, talked of old times. One day she telephoned to inform me of the death of Marguerite Higgins. Maggie, as we called her, a slim Marilyn Monroe-type blond, became the glamour girl of the newspaper world during and after the war. When Maggie broke in as reporter for the *Tribune* I helped her on assignments, the veteran by two years. She was eventually assigned to Europe as head of the *Tribune*'s Berlin bureau, on her way to fame and fortune.

She phoned when I lived in Chicago, asked, "Lucy, could you give me the name of your analyst in New York? The man you wrote about in your book?" Added swiftly, "for a friend." I gave her John's name and address, wrote him saying he might hear from her. I do not know if she ever called.

Margaret and I attended memorial services at the Overseas Press Club, toasted Maggie's memory. She died after contracting a mysterious tropical disease in Vietnam, where for a time she covered the war. How ironic, I thought, the Amazonian Maggie, who survived battlefronts and bombings, felled by the malignance of a microscopic germ.

I engaged in a more social life, remet James Farrell, author of *Studs Lonigan* and other powerful books about Chicago street gangs, at a party at the Gotham Book Mart. Farrell asked, "How did your marriage work out?" referring to Tom. We had originally been introduced at a party for his editor and mine, William Targ, when Bill was vice-president of World Publishers. He later went to G. P. Putnam's Sons, there to become editor of Mario Puzo's *The Godfather*.

"It didn't work out," I said grimly.

"When I went into mine I didn't know whether it was a marriage or funeral." Farrell laughed.

I thought of Sally, who, intending to speak of a wedding sometimes called it a "funeral," then said, shrugging her slim shoulders, "Well, the music sounds alike." I did not feel funereal until about six months after each of my marriages.

I gained new friends as Lillian and Gerold Frank invited me to parties at their home, came to parties at mine. Gerold, author of stirring biographies of movie and stage stars and the harrowing *The Boston Strangler*, laughingly told me about a reporter he knew who once covered a Seaman's Union meeting. He heard the leader of the union warn the other members, after I appeared to report the occasion, "Now don't use any dirty language in front of this cunt from *The New York Times*." I recalled all the union members as exceedingly polite.

Frank and Bita Dobo also became friends. Frank published a book I wrote with Ted Atkinson, famous jockey, called *All The Way!* When I asked Ted the secret of how to win at the track he said cogently, "Two words. Don't bet."

The Dobos invited me to their home one night for dinner, Bita is a superb cook. The guest of honor was Patrick Dennis (Tanner was his real last name), author of the best-seller *Auntie Mame*, based on his adventures as a boy with his aunt. She now lived in Greenwich Village, took care of homeless children as she once took care of the boy Patrick in Chicago.

He was a tall thin man, appealing, sophisticated, almost every sentence a witticism. He drank quite freely and during dinner the alcohol unloosed a hatred of his father.

He asked Bita, "You met my father once, didn't you?"

"We had dinner with him," Bita said.

"You mean you could eat?" Sarcastically, implying his father was repulsive.

He again denigrated his father, saying, "He would vote for a chimpanzee if the Republicans put him up." He told me he had consulted a Jungian analyst. I had the feeling Patrick's childhood anguish, revealed so artistically through humor in his writings, stirred close to the surface.

I expanded my friendship with a few psychoanalysts whom, as reporter, I had met, written about and enjoyed. The greatest compliment of my literary life came the night of January 5, 1963, when I attended the annual Twelfth Night Party of the New York Psychoanalytic Institute. It was given by Dr. Samuel Atkin, then president of the Institute, and his wife Edith, a writer and friend from my newspaper days, at their home on Sutton Place South.

Dr. Victor Rosen, the incoming president of the American Psychoanalytic Association, walked over, kissed me on the cheek, said, "I have a great compliment for you. One of our leading psychoanalysts, discussing the program for next year's international meeting in Europe, said someone should present a clinical case the way you wrote *Before I Kill More*."

I thanked him, pleased beyond words, joked, "Well, I finally made it in my own way as an analyst, didn't I?" This was the first time I revealed to myself or anyone else this hidden wish.

When I came across the words of psychoanalyst Dr. David Cares, "Creativity comes from using primitive impulses in an imaginative way," I felt I did not have to apologize for work that obviously stemmed out of angry feelings and wish for revenge. Like murder mysteries or true crime books.

I wrote my mother regularly, in one letter told her analysis was revealing my deep dependency on her as a child: "Until one can admit such an overwhelming dependency, life can be rough. The first love, the first hate, is the mother. I have been trying on the couch to 'work through,' as they say, my unreal feelings for both you and Laurie. It is slow going because as a child I buried the unpleasant ones and I still fight the analyst when she tries to get me to face them.

"I have the feeling that without analysis I would have died of a heart attack years ago the way I was chasing around as reporter. Living a fantastic, exciting life that was fun but killing myself inside. I now have a far less exciting existence but a more thoughtful, peaceful one, and you have made it possible at times by giving me money when I ran short. Besides, of course, giving me life in the first place. The greatest gift of all."

I said to Dr. Mack one day, "I have only one friend, my mother." Then thought, How can this be, my only friend the woman I profess to hate at times. But by now I knew the hate was founded in large part on childhood fantasies. As I could face them I would see her more clearly.

Another time I told Dr. Mack, "Analysis has helped me feel I am coming out of a long but sometimes exciting illness. One that is emotional, not physical."

She disagreed. "No, analysis is more like growing up. You feel less impulsively driven."

That too, I thought, she speaks in terms of developmental growth, I in terms of psychic illness. To be an adult but to remain emotionally a child *is* a degree of what you might call psychic illness.

At least I was feeling more comfortable with my mother. I telephoned her one evening, informed her the editor of a leading magazine had turned down an original decision to publish part of *Remember Me to Tom*, which would have netted twenty-five thousand dollars. I asked, "Do you still love me?"

Mother replied, "Of course, dear. My love for you does not depend on your selling a magazine piece."

The next day I told this to Dr. Mack, added, "I felt my mother really meant what she said. In spite of her need to push me to produce when I was young. She would ask when I won a prize, 'Will you get it next year, too?' I thought, Is it never enough for Mother, is there no end to her need for me to achieve?"

Dr. Mack said, "Now it is only important how *you* feel about achieving."

"I'm not as competitive as I once was." Defensively. "I believe analysis has made that need less compulsive."

Then I speculated, "I wonder how different my life would have been if I had not left *The New York Times.*"

She said something very important to me: "You cannot live by the 'if's.' *If* only I had done that. *If* only I had known."

The "if" did not help one whit to solve my conflicts, it was only hopeless fantasying, she was saying.

She also gave advice I have tried to follow when she said, "Always move to a better apartment or house, not a lesser one." And: "Accept what was and go on from there. Don't use the past to perpetuate your suffering."

Life becomes tolerable, I thought, when you realize how intolerable it has been in some ways but it was not your fault. This is reversal of what you believed as a child—that you were to blame for everything that happened, good and bad.

She also said something neither John nor Dr. Emch ever mentioned: "You cannot settle for a man because you really desire a woman and you cannot settle for a woman because you are too afraid of your lesbian feelings. So you pick weak, effeminate men who are like women."

This was a verbal bombshell. I had many women friends but never felt the slightest sexual desire toward them. I enjoyed talking to them, playing bridge or poker with them in the company of men. But aside from a casual kiss on the cheek when meeting or in farewell, there had been no physical contact or wish for it. True, I had been a tomboy but since the age of twelve was attracted to boys when it came to dating, dancing, necking. As far as I was aware, I had never been aroused sexually by a woman.

One day she suddenly accused me of wanting a man involved with a woman as a bridge to the woman. I spoke up not angrily but in an assured voice, "All the men with one exception were not married or involved in affairs with other women. And of my two husbands, one was single, the other divorced."

She also said one day in an accusative voice, "You set up the marriage with Tom."

"*I* did?" Bewildered.

"By choosing such a man. He left his wife, he would eventually leave you. Or act so brutally you would leave him. You know by now how strong the repetition compulsion is."

The "repetition compulsion" had become my bête noire—the tendency to repeat over and over an act that is destructive, not knowing why you are driven to do so. Overcoming this compulsion is one of the aims of analysis. By unconsciously choosing men who would leave me, or the few I would leave, I ensured myself enough misery to guarantee assuaging my guilt over childhood desires I thought wicked and evil.

She advised, "Know a man before you marry him. Find out what he is like. How he has weathered life. Whether you could be friends, respect each other, feel companionable. Then decide if you want to spend the rest of your life with this man."

I asked bitterly, "Who would get married then?"

She did not respond well to levity. There was no answer.

I reminisced, "I really went blind into my last marriage. Six months after the wedding march, life turned to a dirge. Tom started to attack me."

Then she spoke. "You race through life as if you wanted to get things over with."

I had to agree I rushed into marriage as I rushed through everything, the hurrying was my attempt to escape anger. Slowing up meant angry feelings might explode.

I told her, "I want to slow up but it's difficult."

She returned to the type of men I chose. "You select men who feel insecure about their masculinity. When they find you have no penis, they feel contempt for you. You remind them of their childhood fantasy that because a woman has no penis, she is ready to snatch theirs. And their contempt mirrors your contempt for yourself because you were born a girl."

So again it's penis, who's got the penis, I thought. The penis is power, without the man's penis no woman can bear a baby. I had thought of a man's penis in terms of the pleasure it could give and felt terrified if, in turn, I did not give the man pleasure. I wanted to be as powerful as I thought he was. When Tom was unsuccessful in sex he insisted there was something wrong with me. I did not love him enough, he could not get aroused. It never occurred to me it might be his fault he felt impotent. I blamed myself for lack of enough allure to arouse him. I believed I was the deus ex machina of his manhood—what incredibly narcissistic thinking.

In her way Dr. Mack served as an analytic haven after Dr. Emch's tragic death, she made many sensitive, helpful comments. When I talked of mother bribing her children with money, Dr. Mack said, "Only love buys love." I thought, Bribery brings guilt, keeps the child an infant.

Toward the end of the fifth year I started to become

uncomfortable about my deeply conflicted feelings toward her. I wrote a note to myself: "What the hell kind of analysis is this? She accuses me of using psychoanalytic jargon as defense, then she uses words like *ego alien* and *narcissistic.* Doesn't she know the patient avidly copies the analyst? If she spouts intellectual words that do not move the analysis along, so will I."

For five years I had suffered many sessions, hearing her eat supper as she sat to my right, slightly behind me. Or heard the needles click as she crocheted or knit, or the scratch of the pencil as she scribbled notes, or her voice when she answered the telephone at times. All forbidden by Freud, who believed the analyst should sit quietly listening.

What did such forbidden acts on her part say to me? That often I lost her full attention during the supposedly sacrosanct moments reserved for her concentration on my conflicts. The hour belonged to me, I paid well for it. I felt she was not fair in diluting attention to personal matters.

And the breaking of sacred psychoanalytic rules increased. Twice I arrived to find a stranger usurping my hour. She apologized profusely, said someone had called for an emergency appointment and she "forgot" I was due. How could she forget a routine schedule of five years? What was she telling me? That I was not important enough to remember?

She sometimes hurled a comment or question in sarcastic tone that made Dr. Emch's occasional quip seem like a sweet whisper. Dr. Mack once asked in contempt, "Mrs. Freeman, when are you going to stop kidding yourself and realize how much you wished to be a boy?" This was, of course, one of my most vulnerable psychic areas.

She seemed very different from both John and Dr. Emch, who stressed uncovering the buried reasons for destructive acts so I could understand and cope with heretofore hidden feelings. Dr. Mack emphasized the need to control impulses, accept frustration, in more of a didactic, intellectual way.

I realized what analysts call a "meaningful transference" did not take place. I did not feel the trust in, the love for her that I did for both Dr. Emch and John. I felt no deep attachment that made me wish to do things for her—such as give up the pain of the past. I thought perhaps Dr. Mack did not fully understand the child in herself and thus could not help me reach more of the child in me.

One day after she again called me "masochistic," this time for marrying Tom, I replied in defense, "Does calling me a masochist help me understand why I am one?"

To my surprise and alarm, she said in an angry clipped tone I had never heard her use, "Let's stop talking about this since you are in that kind of a mood."

I felt aghast, in my years with John and Dr. Emch, I had never heard that venomous a voice, nor been rebuked so harshly for anything I said. I sensed she could not tolerate my expressing even the slightest degree of reproach. I knew it was not proper analysis for her to show rage at my words, she should have encouraged me to express anger, which did not come easily to me. Instead, she took my words personally, blocking the understanding of my relationship to parents who acted as she did at times.

Her use of the word *masochist*, a clinical term, was also taboo. If she could use the analytic language to a patient, I could use it to her. It took years to realize that technical terms did not help me be aware of my inner self. It was the simple words, words children understand, that drew out tormenting feelings.

I wished Dr. Mack would not take umbrage at my

defenses but help me reach what lay behind the need to maintain them. Our defenses against knowing the truth stand like the Rock of Gibraltar, that I now knew. Defenses crumble only with what may seem like sledge-hammer blows of insights on the part of the therapist and a lessening of reluctance on the part of the patient, who now painfully accepts the truth.

Analysis is no soul-searing miracle of Lourdes. It is a grim facing of the painful thoughts and wishes you hide from awareness. Not the pain of bloodletting but of being abandoned and annihilated and the fury that follows. The pain of insane jealousy, of yearnings destined never to be fulfilled. I needed Dr. Mack's full support to face what underlay defenses but felt I did not have it.

I still resented her unfair charge of promiscuity, that I would "sleep with any man who came down the pike." I never forgave this false accusation. I now wondered why she had so thoughtlessly uttered the cruel remark. Was it the jealousy of an older woman married to a man who had become hopelessly ill the last years of his life, as she told me? Or perhaps the jealousy of an older woman who then married a man far younger as second husband, mainly, as she said, for "companionship"? Or had she been a virgin for years before she married the first time and envied me my few affairs?

I also felt upset when she called my father a "bastard." Perhaps he was at times but this was only a small part of him. He showed many fine qualities, supported his children in vital ways. He made me feel loved, wanted, most of the time. He spent hours with me as I grew up, taught me to play golf, handle a boat, ice-skate, took me on countless trips both business appointments and vacation. He paid for my education at a very expensive woman's college, one he carefully selected.

When I told her I was aware I wanted my father all to myself as a child, Dr. Mack said in reprimand,

"You're too old to have such a fantasy now." Dr. Emch would have said, "You are never too old for a fantasy, the aim of analysis is to make it conscious. A fantasy remains part of the child within, you cannot repudiate yourself as a child. As an adult you have to accept this is part of you but you can now cope with it since you are aware of it."

Dr. Mack also spoke of a "weak or damaged ego." I wondered what that meant, visualized my ego hacked by a knife wielded by my parents. Perhaps symbolically this happened, I thought.

I had read our "conflicts" existed among the three mental structures Freud named id, ego and superego. The latter two erected defenses against our fantasies, fears and furies. The analyst has to use his knowledge carefully, sensitively, so he does not increase the pain that originally caused defenses.

As Dr. Leo Rangell, well-known psychoanalyst, said, "You don't use dynamite to remove a wart." Meaning interpretations should not be dramatic or traumatic to the patient.

My "ambivalence" toward Dr. Mack was mounting. I particularly resented her taking notes, I never knew whether about my conflicts or those of previous patients or reminder of personal tasks.

One day I dared ask, "Are you taking notes about me?"

Anger in her voice, she replied, "Must you always be the center of my attention?"

I wanted to retort, I have a right to be when I am here, paying for a session, but could only feel deep hurt. She was telling me the time for which I paid was not always used on my behalf. She was also saying I should not be so egocentric. This was the analyst who crocheted or knit during my hour and when I complained, said she could listen more freely if her hands were occupied.

Then an incident occurred that horrified me, made me decide she was more destructive than constructive. It served as Dr. Emch's death had, though in a different way, to end all contact. Perhaps it signified to me the death of any trust I might have placed in Dr. Mack as I felt aghast at the words she spoke.

I recalled my feelings about a second abortion, which took place at Lenox Hill Hospital, a far safer locale than the dingy office of an illegal abortionist.

I said in sadness, "As I regained consciousness after the anesthetic wore off, lying on my bed in a private room, I cried out, tears running down my cheeks, 'I want my baby! Where is my baby?' "

I heard from Dr. Mack the brusque comment, "You didn't say that."

I could not believe my ears. I thought, She is calling me a liar. She was not present, how dare she speak for me?

At long last able to muster enough spunk to defend myself with righteous anger I said quietly, "Those were my very words."

Took a deep breath, went on, "My sister Sally was in the room. I asked her later if I had cried out for the baby. She looked at me sadly and said, 'I heard you and felt so sorry for you. You sounded as if you desperately wanted a child.' "

There was no reply from the woman sitting in the chair knitting away. From that moment on I did not trust her, if I ever had. She obviously did not trust me.

Afterward I wished I had the courage to ask, How could you possibly know whether I said the words? What made you make such a ridiculous statement? I wondered why she was driven to deny my pain and sorrow. Had she perhaps been through a similar crisis but kept all feelings to herself? Or had she never been pregnant, envied me the experience and needed to cut me down? Or did she have the fantasy no woman would mourn aborting a baby?

That night I dreamed I screamed at a woman, "I will never see you again!" When I woke I knew it was time to leave her. My unconscious told of this wish, confirmed my feeling she was the wrong person with whom to continue analysis.

A few weeks later I told her I was low on funds (partially the truth), had to stop analysis until I received an advance on my next book. She accepted this, said she trusted I would shortly return. I lacked the courage to be honest, tell her I felt I had gone as far as I could with her and planned eventually to seek someone else. But I was proud of the new stamina it took to break away, no matter what the excuse.

A few weeks later she wrote she missed me, that she had not realized how much she would. I later learned these sentiments were highly irregular for an analyst. I wondered whether she truly missed me or was revealing a dependence on me out of her own needs, as a mother might feel when a child left home.

I realized with sudden awareness how much she was like my mother in many ways. Dominating, flirtatious with men, as I saw her with Tennessee, and, most important, never granting me the right to differ from her. And, like my mother, still alive in her early seventies. I had felt Dr. Mack would not die as Dr. Emch did, leaving me destitute emotionally. Or, if she did, I would not mourn deeply.

In a note to myself the day I left, I wrote: "I understand why I am not returning to Dr. Mack's couch after five years, four days a week. I learned much from her, including how narcissistic I have been and my inability to relate tenderly and compassionately to a man. Also, that as a girl I wished unconsciously I had been born a boy."

I also wrote: "But I feel I have not 'worked through,' as she says, many deep feelings. She told me I have mourned my father and Dr. Emch long enough but somehow I have been unable to give up the mourning. I still miss them both very deeply. After all these years I haven't really faced the loss, the sorrow and the anger I feel at my father's death. Or the rage buried deep because he has forsaken me. It doesn't seem logical but I now accept my unconscious is often illogical."

Dr. Mack knew theory but I thought she did not truly feel empathy for me. Whereas Dr. Emch seemed to understand not only me but everyone in my early life, Dr. Mack forgot the name of my sister Sally, though I mentioned her almost weekly.

Many sessions did not seem like analysis but a college course. I felt lectured at, as though I should *learn* from her rather than explore emotions and fantasies. She did not seem one whit interested in my dreams, appeared bored when I brought up one. Unlike Dr. Emch and John, who helped me understand the power of a dream to help reach long-forgotten traumatic memories. I wondered how fully Dr. Mack understood the unconscious or whether she merely gave lip service to its existence and functions.

Desperate for help when I sought her, feeling depressed, I had been only too willing to be accepted by anyone available. I could not blame her or anyone else. I should have walked away the first moment I felt something amiss, such as the daily knitting or the eating of dinners. My need for a good mother was so desperate I dared not make the break. Kept hoping I would feel more at ease. A vain hope as the months, the years, passed.

She intensified my feeling I was a "bad" girl for possessing a natural wish of childhood, such as wanting to be "special," the one and only. Or omnipotent, in control of the world. Or feeling jealous of my brother and sisters. She treated me with disbelief and contempt when I said things with which she did not agree.

One day I said of my anger at my mother, "Doesn't everyone have that feeling as a child at one time or another?"

"How does that help you give up the feeling?" In slightly exasperated tone.

It made me feel more human, more like everyone else, I thought, but did not speak. Also thought, One never "gives up" a feeling, one becomes aware of it, feels more at ease with it, understands it, controls it rather than allowing it to control.

But she had been willing to accept me at a time I felt desperate—any psychic port in a devastating emotional storm. For that I was grateful. Also I had somehow learned more about my buried self, I now possessed a new strength. I had made my own decision in halting a relationship I thought inadequate in terms of what I knew of psychoanalysis.

For a "masochist," as she called me, this was a large step toward inner freedom. One I had never dared take.

The decision proved heartening. It added to my self-esteem. It had been *my* choice. Not the decision of the analyst, as with John. Not because of the death of the analyst, as with Dr. Emch. But a choice made because I believed I had traveled as far as I could with Dr. Mack into the misty realm of the unconscious.

I knew I needed further analysis. I could not leave the couch feeling so unhappy with the analyst. But I would decide very carefully whose couch I would next occupy, which analyst I could trust, someone who would not repeat the experience with Dr. Mack.

10

Of Mourning and Melancholia

I knew I could not leave analysis forever as I had left Dr. Mack—perplexed, angry at her, still not understanding enough about myself to feel fairly at peace. But I now wanted time to myself.

Too, I did not have much savings, rent and the general cost of living were rising, royalties took a dip. Part of me also wanted to be on my own. I even felt a bit soured on analysis after the experience with Dr. Mack.

For the first year away from her I felt new freedom not having to report four sessions a week for couch work. I relished the extra hours for writing. I also had some money to spend on clothes, curtailed drastically for five years.

The hours flew by, sometimes eleven and twelve a day as I met a deadline. I never felt bored or angry while typing, I did not undertake a book unless I found it challenging. Sometimes I worked on two books at once, occasionally wrote a magazine article on the side. One was titled "Electra in the Electronic Age," subtitled in unconscious rage, "I Dismember Mama." I never tried to sell it.

I had always read murder mysteries avidly and now joined the Mystery Writers of America, for which I was eligible because of *Before I Kill More*, a true crime story. I had also written *Children Who Kill*, the account of six children, each murdering a mother, father, sibling or stranger. Dr. Wilfred C. Hulse, a psychoanalyst who treated severely disturbed children, was co-author.

I now started on the book I had always wanted to write—a murder mystery. I chose a psychoanalyst as sleuth, called it *The Dream*. It almost became a play on Broadway but unfortunately folded in Philadelphia after critics blasted the out-of-town opening. The plot centered on how, after a patient in analysis was murdered, the analyst tracked down the killer remembering the patient's dream in his last session on the couch. I wrote two more books in which this analyst played sleuth. After all, analysts are similar to detectives as they try to find the killers in psychic life.

I continued to remain out of analysis, as I found life full, both in work and social activities. I thought, with a twinge of guilt, after two and a half analyses I should be able at least to try solving my conflicts alone.

But I knew I needed further help when a long-term affair, which I sensed from the start lacked even the glimmer of success, ended in angry scenes. I also, for the first time in my life, started to drink heavily at night and this told me I felt deeply unhappy.

It was time after my attempt at false freedom from the couch, to seek what I hoped would be my final analyst in the fall of 1976. I consulted a new friend, Dr. Walter Stewart, with whom I co-authored *The Secret of Dreams*. Walter was a member of the faculty of the

New York Psychoanalytic Institute. He taught young analysts in training, noted for his perceptive interpretation of dreams.

He gave me the name of a psychoanalyst I will call Dr. David Aiken. His office was on Central Park West overlooking the park. I phoned, feeling somewhat anxious at seeking a man. But my luck with women analysts did not appear high. One died, the other disappointed.

Dr. Aiken's voice was warm and friendly. He set an hour for the appointment. I embarked on my fourth, and hopefully my final, analysis.

His large apartment on the sixth floor served as both office and home. I arrived early, sat quietly in the waiting room, studied the paintings. I was fascinated by one of a woman that showed half her face as peaceful, the other half, distorted in rage. There were also Japanese landscapes and posters proclaiming exhibitions of Picasso and Degas.

On time to the minute, the door to his office opened as a dark-haired slim woman in her thirties stalked out. She did not glance right or left but headed for the front door. Then out of the office walked a tall, dark-haired, handsome, bearded man a few years younger than I.

My first reaction was immediate attraction, I thought, He looks like the young Freud. The expression in eyes is important to me and his were friendly, welcoming. They reminded me somewhat of my father's twinkling eyes when he felt pleased, though his were blue and Dr. Aiken's, brown.

I stood up, he walked over, held out his hand. Then said with a friendly smile, "We met in Chicago."

I half-smiled, I was not sure where or when. Chicago had become a blur except for the sessions with Dr. Emch. I said, "I think it was the meeting that celebrated Freud's one hundredth birthday."

He led me into a sunlit spacious room with two

book-lined walls, flowering plants, a few large seashells on the ledges of the bookcases. All the windows over-looked the park, now in lush spring greenery.

I felt nervous, par for first session. I hoped he would approve of me, accept me even though I appeared a seemingly endless patient.

I sat uncertainly in the chair he indicated. He took a chair facing me. I started off, "I've been married twice unhappily. The second time I left my job on the *Times* to live in Chicago. This hasty marriage lasted only two years and I went into analysis with Dr. Minna Emch. She suddenly died and I came back to New York. Then I went to Dr. Elizabeth Mack, whom you know, of course." They were both members of the hallowed New York Psychoanalytic Institute. "I learned much from her but I felt something missing between us and left after five years."

I sighed, said, "I thought I could make it on my own. But after trying, I need further analysis." Added, "I knew that when I left Dr. Mack, it felt like unfinished treatment."

He was easy to talk to, those earnest brown eyes took in my every word. I was afraid of him—afraid of all powerful men—but felt this my last chance at happiness or whatever one calls that elusive state of euphoria that seems to escape so many.

I also told him, seeking sympathy, "My mother has become a veritable vegetable. She lives in a nursing home in Daytona Beach, near my sister Sue."

Then confessed, "Before I started to look for another analyst I consulted Dr. Lawrence Kubie, my father's first cousin, who originally recommended I seek help. I asked whether I should go into still another analysis."

I had met Dr. Kubie at the annual American Psychoanalytic Association's December meeting at the Waldorf. He invited me to lunch, where, mustering courage, I asked over a tuna fish sandwich, "Do you think I should try a fourth analysis if I need it?" Added hastily, "The second analyst died in the middle of my analysis so this would really be only the third." He said enthusiastically, "By all means, if you believe you need it."

I told Dr. Aiken, "I can only afford three times a week." I hoped that proved enough.

"I have an eleven o'clock hour open Mondays, Wednesdays and Fridays," he said.

"That will be fine." I smiled inside, I had been accepted without needing to return to see if we were "compatible," could "work together."

Done and done, I thought thankfully, as I walked away from his apartment house. I felt triumphant at taking a difficult step. I also felt a bit traitorous to Dr. Mack, yet knew I was in the right to change analysts. It would have been, to use one of her favorite words, *masochistic* to stay.

Seeking Dr. Aiken proved lucky timing. My mother's doctor had warned us, because of a severe attack of pneumonia, she did not have long to live.

My feelings about her imminent death occupied my first sessions. While I thought her infuriating at times, I benefited most in one way as a child—I had her all to myself for the first year and nine months of my life, a time she may have been happiest. She did not have many responsibilities nor was she depressed at the thought my father had chosen a younger woman to love.

"She was good-natured much of the time," I told Dr. Aiken. "Generous in both attention and money. Always ready for company and a party." Added, "She taught me in an easy, comfortable way to play tennis and bridge. She bought me books galore on rainy days so I would be content to sit quietly in the playroom, not run out in the rain. She hated rain, she thought it brought death. She had seen her cousin and an uncle die of pneumonia after being drenched in the rain."

Two more thoughts. "She encouraged me to spend time in the new public library that rose behind our house. And she welcomed all my friends, as well as those of my brother and sisters, to our home."

I described the day she taught me to respect my religious heritage. After I finished sixth grade at the Chatsworth Avenue School, a few blocks from the Boston Post Road, she and my father wanted to send me to exclusive Rye Country Day School, where my best friend Virginia Hutchins was enrolled. Mother called for an appointment to see the principal and then she and I drove there. She left me in the car, walked inside to confer.

Within fifteen minutes she returned, a strange look on her face, a face that swiftly conveyed her feelings. I asked anxiously, "Did they take me?"

She stepped into the car, turned on the motor. Then she said slowly, "They will accept you if we change your last name."

"I don't understand." I felt puzzled, what was wrong with Greenbaum? It meant "green tree" in German and I loved green trees, thought of Granny's vast forest in which I walked, sometimes ran happily many a summer day of the first six years of my life, with my father and Grumpy as companions.

"They don't accept Jewish students," my mother said. "But because your marks are so high, if we allow you to use a Christian last name, they'll take you."

"Did you tell them you'd change my last name?" I thought, Of course she will agree, she wants me to have the finest of educations.

"I couldn't do that," she said quietly. "I wouldn't want you to go to a school that holds such an attitude."

She said no more but I understood. To assume a

false name, to pretend I was not Jewish, would have demeaned her, the family, me. I never thanked her for this but I believe she knew how I felt because I did not protest.

Mother was in her prime when it came to the rescue of my friends if they faced crises, I told Dr. Aiken. A tall striking-looking athletic girl named Beatrice Rosofsky and I were close all through high school, practically lived at each other's homes. When I entered high school I lost Virginia, three years older, as she commuted to New York for further education. Bea and I played tennis every morning before class, at noon recess after gulping a sandwich and at the end of the school day, relinquishing the court only for snow or a heavy rainstorm. We also took turns at the piano, banging out jazz.

Bea's battles with her mother made Sally's with our mother look like halcyon encounters. The familial fight of our decade occurred a week before graduation when Bea and I were to appear onstage in the dramatic event of our high school years. She was the star of the play and under her urging I was to make my first (and, as it turned out, last) reluctant stage appearance.

The evening of the performance as I dressed at home for the role, no glamorous sequined costume but a plain blue cotton dress worn by a girl my age in contemporary society, I heard the telephone ring. My mother answered, called out, "It's for you, Lucy."

Bea's familiar voice held an unfamiliar pitch, one of sadness. "My mother won't let me wear the dress I want," she said slowly. "She thinks it's too revealing. So I won't be in the play tonight." A small sob.

"You *have* to appear," I insisted. "The show must go on, even if you're dying. Clara Bow wouldn't let a thing like the right dress stop her."

"I'm not Clara Bow," she wailed. "And I will *not* appear in front of an audience in the leading role wearing that old rag my mother picked out. She never wants me to look pretty."

"Let me speak to your mother, Bea," I begged.

There was silence, then the voice of her mother, low, depressed, "Yes, Lucy?"

I pleaded, "*Please* let Bea wear the dress she wants, Mrs. Rosofsky. We can't put on the play without her. And if we don't give it, graduation will be ruined. We've worked very hard at getting it perfect."

"She's a bad girl," her mother said. "She has to obey me."

How often I had been defeated by those very words. Perhaps the dictator in my house could outcommand the dictator in Bea's house. I said sweetly to a second hated tyrant, "My mother wants to talk to you. Just a moment." I ran to my mother, begged, "You've got to help," explained the situation.

Mother took the telephone, tried equally without success to reason with Bea's mother. Mother found her match in what one psychiatrist calls "the stubbornness of the emotionally weak." I heard my mother say, "We'll be right over."

My father, always busy at night with law briefs, had been persuaded by mother, against his better judgment, to attend the evening performance. Mother now asked him to drive his own car and meet us at the school, warning him not to be late. She and I sped off in her car for Bea's house.

"What are you going to say to Bea's mother?" I asked nervously.

"I'll try to reason with her," mother said.

Inside the Rosofsky home we found Bea's mother, still unbending, and Bea in tears and in her underwear, two dresses flung on her bed. One was a drab gray with long sleeves, the other, bright red with short sleeves and a low neckline.

Mother led Bea's mother into the kitchen, saying, "Let's have a cup of coffee." Mother's solution to all conflicts. She gave me a wink, nodded her head in the direction of the front door. I understood her directions, pulled the filmy low-cut red chiffon dress over Bea's head. She grabbed her purse and we both ran out of the house and the three blocks to the school, leaving Mother to make peace with Bea's mother.

Somehow everyone in the play remembered their lines, the curtain fell to loud applause as we bowed, smirking. I ran to find my father and mother, thinking, They must be very proud of my debut in the dramatic world.

I caught a glimpse of my father struggling up the aisle against the parental mob that flocked toward the stage. As I reached his side he said impatiently, "Let's get out of this crowd, it's late."

"How was I?" Expecting him to say, Better than Garbo.

He muttered, "How would I know? Couldn't hear a word you said. Get your mother and let's go home."

"Couldn't hear?" I was stunned. "Were you sitting in the last row?"

"Third row center. It was late when I got here. I couldn't find your mother and they put me up front in the one remaining seat."

Thus ended my dramatic career. When I caught up with my mother she said, "You were fine but I wish your part had been more than a few lines."

"Thanks, Mom." I was grateful for her kindness, though in a way she was complaining, as she always did, that I had not achieved enough. I added, "And thank you for saving the night. Without you, there would have been no performance."

"I was glad to help," she said. "Bea's mother is a

very interesting woman. She's had to struggle very hard to make ends meet."

"Did she come to the play?" I thought of course she would want to see her daughter, the star.

"She refused. She said she was ashamed to see Bea in that obscene dress."

Mother accepted Bea as a fourth daughter after Bea's parents suddenly died of heart attacks within a few weeks of each other while I was at college. They owned a large stationery store on Mamaroneck Avenue, had worked long hours for years. Bea's younger brother Ned, when the house was sold by his older married sister, lived at our home for several months while deciding what to do with his life. This was another sign of Mother's caretaking of children. She had been a waif and she took in waifs.

Nine years later, at the *Times*, my telephone rang suddenly as I wrote the details of an interview with the poet Marianne Moore. As I entered her Greenwich Village apartment earlier in the day she said apologetically, "I had a sleepless night and woke up feeling like a run-over daisy." Apt description of how I felt after too little sleep.

My mother's voice. "It's me, Lucy."

She seldom called the office, respected my work hours. I knew this must be important.

Without preamble she went on, "I thought you should know. Bea was hit by a car this morning and died in a hospital."

"Oh, no!" I felt deep anguish.

It seemed incredible that vivacious, irrepressible Bea could be destroyed. She had married twice, both times unhappily. Following a miscarriage and the decision to leave her second husband, she sought a sanitarium for "a rest."

I asked my mother, "How did it happen?"

"Her sister said Bea was to be sent home tomorrow from the sanitarium. This morning she walked to the nearby town and crossing the state highway saw a car bearing down on her. She dashed in front of it, then changed her mind suddenly and headed back. The confused driver swerved and struck her. Her sister says it wasn't the driver's fault. They didn't even hold him. Bea shouldn't have been crossing that highway."

Two days later (I asked for the day off, something I rarely did) Mother and I drove to a funeral parlor in Yonkers. We arrived in that city early, stopped for coffee at a restaurant. I thought of the way Bea died, a heedless act—did she wish to die? Someone put a nickel in the jukebox, out flowed the melody of Gershwin's "Someone to Watch Over Me," a song Bea often played on her piano with a wistful expression.

The last time I had seen her, in her modest Lynnbrook, Long Island, home, she lay on her bed, a sheet pulled up to her chin, as though she wanted to hide from the world. A stricken look came over her face when I asked how she felt. She did not answer, not daring to put her misery into words. Once outside the room I asked my mother, who had driven with me, "What's wrong with Bea?"

"I think she's upset over losing the baby," Mother said.

I told Dr. Aiken I was grateful to Mother for easing much of my pain as I grew up. I said, "I would feel obliterated though when occasionally she would forget who I was and call me Sally or Sue." As though denying my very existence.

While at moments I felt she hated me, I never stopped seeking her love. The first present I ever gave anyone was a small jeweled box I made for her in nursery school the summer I was five. All my life thereafter

I bought her gleaming gifts—necklaces, pins and more
jewel boxes. I wrote poems to her.

The cruelest thing she ever did, though unaware of
how deeply she wounded my spirit, occurred on
Mother's Day when I was nine. I handed her a poem on
which I spent hours composing loving sentences telling
how much she meant to me. She read it, turned to me,
asked, "Where did you copy it from?" She was calling
me a thief of words, the insult of insults.

"I have never forgiven her," I told Dr. Aiken vehemently.

"She was praising you," he said. "She thought the
poem so mature that a renowned poet must have written
it."

I granted grudgingly, "I never thought of that."
Forgave her somewhat.

I told him, "I was very close to my brother. We
spent much time together in our early years." Eddie
taught me to drive a car when, at thirteen, he received
as gift from Laurie a little Austin to guide around the
gravel roads of Granny's summer home. In turn I
taught him to dance, occasionally helped him with home-
work. Sue and I enjoyed an amiable, warm closeness in
spite of fights about dresses and underwear, as one
"borrowed" or "stole," as the case might be, from the
other at times. I protected Sally, ten years younger,
helped her learn to walk, talk, leave the house to enjoy
flowers and trees along Monroe Avenue as it led to the
waves of Long Island Sound.

In my adolescence Mother and I became almost pals
at times. "She had to find someone with whom to talk of
her pain," I said to Dr. Aiken.

I described an unforgettable September night of
my life. I was seventeen, about to leave for college. I felt
hungry around ten o'clock, crept downstairs to raid the

refrigerator. As I sat at the small wooden table devouring cold string beans Mother walked through the long pantry and into the kitchen. We were both dressed for bed, she in a long white cotton nightgown, me in sheer sky-blue pajamas. She poured herself a glass of milk, sat opposite me.

"Want some beans?" They were her favorite vegetable. On Mae's day off Mother and I sometimes prepared them, my job to snip the ends.

"No, dear." She looked at me sadly. Then asked, "Lucy, what will I do?"

"About what, Mother?" I consumed a few more green beans encased in caked cold butter.

"About your father. I don't think I can stand it much longer."

I had known of course what she meant, there was anguish in her voice. I stood up, walked over to her. I sat on her lap like a child, put my arms around her to comfort her. I said in all earnestness, "Mother, how can you stay with a man who doesn't love you?"

It was straight out of the true-confession magazines I pilfered from her closet. But I honestly thought nothing could be more demeaning than to try to hang on to a faithless man.

She kissed me on the cheek, said, "I think you're right, dear," and for the moment lost her sad expression. I returned to my chair, offered her the last forkful of beans, thinking she might be hungrier now she had settled her burning problem. But she said, "No, dear, you eat them. You love string beans." That was my mother, dominating at times to an infuriating degree but generous to the last bean.

It took her seven months to act. Meanwhile I adjusted to my new temporary home in the Green Mountains and the slow pace of a small but stimulating college where you learned because you were interested in the subject, not because you were forced to study it to get a degree.

No hated math or science for me. Instead, American literature as I read Melville and Faulkner with rapture, learned of the revenge of a man seeking a whale who had devoured his foot, and of rape with an ear of corn. I also studied political science as seen through Charles Beard's pungent philosophy and the psychology course gave me a taste of Freud—foundations of my future thinking.

Bennington has a two-month winter period for students to work on special projects or professions in which they are interested. I chose to write a thesis on *Beard's Economic Interpretation of the Constitution*. As my father did when I was in high school, he asked me to accompany him and Donna on their three-week vacation in Florida. I eagerly accepted, knowing I could write about Beard just as well in Hollywood as the chill of Larchmont.

I told Dr. Aiken about one of the most tragic experiences of my life. The day we were to leave I packed a few summer clothes as I had done previous years. Then I walked down the hall to Laurie's room, watched him finish his packing. Mother joined us, sat in silence for a few minutes.

Then she said quietly, "Laurie, if you take Lucy with you this trip, don't come back."

As if to say, No more self-deception, wise guy, about Lucy the shield. If she goes along, you think I won't believe you have sex with this woman, though I know you do. Lucy is growing too old to be subjected to such deception and sexual stimulation (my innocent mother not knowing the emotional damage first occurred at the age of eleven when I accompanied them on out-of-town trips).

In his casual manner my father appeared not to take her seriously, though I felt deep alarm. As we said goodbye I heard her warn again, "I mean it, Laurie. I won't let you back in the house if you insist on taking Lucy."

I asked him, worried she might carry out the threat, "Shall I stay home?" Even though I enjoyed traveling with my father, I did not mind giving up the trip if it meant outright war—and his banishment from our home. It was one thing for mother to throw my father out because he was in love with another woman, quite another for her to force the issue over me. This guilt I did not need, I was burdened with enough.

"You come with me," my father commanded. Refusing, as always, to be intimidated or *told* to do anything. He spent his boyhood rebelling against a dominating mother, once ran away he revealed, "in protest." When I asked "Protest against what?" he replied with a slight blush, "Soup." "Soup?" I exclaimed in wonder. "I wouldn't drink the soup the maid prepared, I didn't like barley," he explained. "Mother insisted I eat it so I got up and left the house for a night or two. Slept next door in Arthur Sulzberger's guest room."

During our three weeks in Hollywood, a city of spreading palms shading wide streets and mansions, I did not speak of Mother's threat though it haunted me. I worked hard interpreting Beard's economic philosophy, swam intermittently in the Atlantic, walked the beach picking up an occasional seashell. As always when with my father, I felt a mixture of elation (unconsciously taking my father from my mother?) and depression (only to hand him over to another rival?).

We approached home in Larchmont after dropping off Donna at her house, five miles north of where we lived. When we entered our driveway I noticed the long branches of the magnolia tree my father had lugged home as a sapling were iced. Snow banked high on the flower beds lining the front windows.

My father turned off the motor in the backyard and I stepped out of the car into black night, suitcase laden with seashells for my brother and sisters. My father by my side, lugging his heavy suitcase, we walked in the dark. It was nine at night. I thought of my mother's last words, terrified lest she still meant them.

My father unlocked the back door and we entered the vestibule, put down our suitcases. Mother walked toward us. Her face held a look of calm, one of the few times I ever saw her so composed.

She said to my father as though to a burglar, "Please leave the house." Added, "And your keys."

Her voice was low and firm, not loud or angry. In sudden fear I wondered whether she meant me, too. I waited for the ultimatum.

As though sensing my fear, she turned, kissed me on the cheek, said, "I'm glad to see you, dear. We missed you. There are lot of messages on your desk from your friends."

I stole a frantic look at my father. He seemed stunned. He took a set of keys out of his pocket, rolled off two, one for the front door, one for the back, lay them on the telephone table in the vestibule. It was the first and only time I ever saw him not in control of a crisis by temper tantrum or edict. He said not a word, either in plea or argument.

He picked up his suitcase, turned and walked out of the house—forever, as far as my mother was concerned.

For one uncertain moment I wondered if I should leave with him. He looked so vulnerable, so lost. I felt he needed me more than Mother did, she had the three other children. I waited for him to ask me, as I always waited for him to lead the way, but he said nothing.

Mother had finally taken the step that severed her

from the only man she ever loved, a man who thus far caused her ten years of humiliation in the eyes of friends, relatives, her children and herself because he refused to give up "the other woman."

The next day my mother summoned her four children to the living room. She announced, "Your father has left us."

"Will we ever see him again?" Sally asked.

"I'll invite him for supper once a week on Fridays," she announced. "I just don't want him to live here."

Now that Laurie was gone I felt as though I had to summon extra strength to help Mother and the three children. I also felt a sudden strange freedom, even though I adored my father and knew I would miss him desperately. I thought, One tyrant has been deposed and perhaps the other tyrant, liberated from living with a tyrant, may be easier on us.

Just after I returned from college for summer vacation, on a Saturday when all the family except me were out, my father phoned, asked if he could drive over and collect some of his clothes and tools. I let him in the house, eager to see him. He gathered sweaters and jackets from the closet in the guest room, where Mother had left them hanging and tools from his cellar workshop. I felt this another sad day of my life, now there was nothing visible in the house to remind of him.

On the way out he stopped in front of the pallid green and blue landscape of Mount Whiteface that hung in our living room. It originally belonged to his mother and father, one of their wedding presents to Mother and him.

"I'd like that painting," he said wistfully.

I could see Mother throwing a fit when she came home to an empty space above the fireplace. But I knew for him the painting held poignant memories of boyhood summers at Lake Placid.

He hesitated, as though waiting for me to stop him from taking the painting. I said not a word. He lifted it from the wall, carried it reverently to his car as I walked beside him.

"Thanks, sweetheart." He kissed me goodbye.

That evening Mother asked in offhand manner, "By the way, Lucy, do you know anything about the disappearance of the painting over the fireplace?"

I winced. "Laurie took it."

"How did he get in the house?" Her voice sounded not angry but curious.

"I let him in." Then apologetically, "He called and asked if he could pick up his tools and summer clothes. He also wanted the painting because it belonged to his mother and father." A pause, then, "I didn't think you'd mind. Just one painting."

Silence, then, "I'll put the Snake Lady there."

Reproduction of a classic painting, a dark-haired woman with a live snake curled around her neck and bare bosoms, hung on a wall across the room. As a child I often stared at it, wondered why a beautiful half-naked lady would wear a snake around her neck. It took five years of analysis to understand the symbolism of the snake as woman's penis envy displaced upward to the neck.

I was grateful my mother thus dismissed the minor theft. I had expected to be reprimanded for letting Laurie steal the painting. But Mother seemed to accept I would continue to live under my father's spell, would follow him into the flames of hell, if ordered.

I told Dr. Aiken that over the years of analysis I understood my rebel father more, as well as my intense attachment to this seductive, sometimes sadistic man. He was very spoiled as a boy, according to Aunt Grace, and all through his life relatives, friends, colleagues and clients continued to spoil him. He acted much of the time as if life were one big party, except for his law work. As though he would never have to pay the psychic piper.

Mother's sense of failure as a wife and now the increasing sadness within her, made us children feel repentent for past misdeeds. One day I apologized, "I'm sorry for always taking Laurie's side. I shouldn't have gone with him that final trip."

She said thoughtfully, "I understand how he charms you. He could charm his worst enemy."

I early had the fantasy if my mother could not make it in marriage, how in the world dare I try? It took my analysis with John to give me at least slight assurance I might somehow be successful but I failed twice. In a sense I rushed back into the arms of my mother.

My first months in college, finally free of what I considered her daily dictatorship, I could not understand why at times I felt so lonely I often wished for an attack of appendicitis so I could be sent home. I thought of myself as a prisoner, surrounded by hostile strangers in this small women's college cloistered in the Green Mountains. In the distance lay the battlefield where Ethan Allen's courageous Green Mountain Boys routed the British in the Battle of Bennington, as they earlier did at Fort Ticonderoga in New York. I learned much of Revolutionary days working on my senior thesis, an analysis of Vermont's first newspaper. Its publisher, a courageous printer named Anthony Haswell, fought via headlines for freedom from England and the right of Vermont to become the fourteenth state. (And was I so interested in victorious battles that led to freedom from the tyrant mother country because I had been unable to wage successful battles against my own mother-tyrant?)

I visited Mother many a weekend, racing homeward in the green convertible Oldsmobile with top down one hundred and seventy miles south. After I graduated it

was difficult to make the physical break from her, knowing somehow I had to escape what I felt would become
a life of stagnancy by her side. Devastated by the divorce, she obviously did not want me to leave, needed
me to grieve with her, help counteract my father's abandonment. She even offered to give me "the big room"
Sally and her nurse once shared.

Knowing my mother's devastation would be deep if
she were left alone, I moved in for a few months. It did
not matter I had complete freedom four years at college.
She still expected me home early from dates. Refused to
sleep until I appeared to kiss her good night on the
cheek as dismissal—hers as well as mine—for bed. Then
arrived the invitation to join the city room of the *Times*,
after an interview by Bruce Rae, assistant managing
editor.

"I realized it was a matter of salvation that I flee my
well-meaning, very vulnerable mother, even though I
knew this would hurt her at a time she felt deserted,"
I told Dr. Aiken. "I grieved for her but I could no longer
sacrifice myself—whatever that self was—to save her.
Saint Lucy was shedding her halo."

"She certainly knew how to make you feel guilty,"
he said.

With all four of her children Mother was consistent
in one way—encouraging us to be dependent on her.
Possession may be nine-tenths of the law, as Laurie was
fond of quoting, but it is not nine-tenths of love.

From what I learned in analysis, emotional separation from my mother should have started when I was
five or six months and led slowly but surely to a spirit
of independence and sense of self. But Mother overin-
dulged us, bribed us with money and gifts, over-
dominated, overprotected us (unconsciously fearing
[wishing?] something dreadful would happen). She did
not know, because of her emotionally terrifying child-

hood, how to help her children separate emotionally from her. How could she know what separation was? A child cannot separate from a phantom mother.

Panic propelled her to pull us close, a panic that traveled from her heart to ours. She became anxious and angry when, as a child, I made tentative attempts to be on my own, and her anger frightened me into submission. Any rage that rose to my breast had to be denied if I were to live in peace with her. Make sure she would take care of me, not toss me out into the heartless world. Her sudden ability to switch from sweetness to maniacal rage if I dared defy her, paralyzed me, whereas it stimulated Sally to fight back with a courage I did not possess.

It was difficult, even after years of analysis, to view her objectively. So powerful and so complex, as well as so entrenched was she in the emotions and the fantasies of my childhood. With my little-girl eyes I saw her simplistically—good or bad. She either gave pleasure or inflicted pain. I hated her or I loved her. One moment I overidealized her, the next, thought her sinister.

Mother encouraged me unconsciously to fear marriage, one of the toughest tasks most of us face. I was the last of her children to embark on it. She told me just before I married the first time, "You don't *have* to get married," perhaps sensing my high ambivalence.

"But I want to," I protested. "It's lonely living by myself."

I wondered, What the hell is she saying to me? That I should have learned from her experience no man is to be trusted? That now divorced and alone, she wanted me for herself, as I had wanted her all to myself as a baby and child (and even now)? For seven years the career had been enough to fill my life, before analysis with John I thought I did not need a man to share the pleasures and inevitable pain of intimate living.

When I married a second time, Mother lived in Florida with Sue and seemed in a less depressed state than during my first marriage when she lived alone in New York. On one of my visits to Hollywood, when I told her my second marriage was doomed she asked in a soft, appealing voice, "Why don't you move down here and live with me? We'll take a little house."

I told Dr. Aiken, "I couldn't believe my ears! Didn't she know how eager I was to leave her? That I could never return?"

I stood in the bathroom putting on lipstick when she called out this question from the living room. I wondered what to say that would not hurt her. I replied jokingly, "I couldn't, Mother. It would end in matricide." The true feeling oft spoke in jest.

Only silence from the living room. Then she queried in a tone of curiosity, "Tell me, what does matricide mean, Lucy?" From my childhood on she would sometimes ask what unusual words meant, appealing to my supposedly superior intelligence.

I wondered whether I dared tell her, then thought it would be an insult not to answer with honesty. I said, "Murder of a mother by a son or daughter."

"Oh." Her voice seemed calm.

I raced to the living room to see the expression on her face. Would it be shock or would she be stricken at the thought of raising such a thankless child? She smiled as she said, "It was just an idea, dear."

But my one sentence, uttered jocularly, unveiled an underlying fear of my life—I might murder my dominating mother who, I felt, sometimes suffocated me emotionally.

I saved her from what might have been serious injury as I visited her following the divorce. We were alone in the house one morning, Sue and George long gone to the large department store they owned. As I read the local newspaper in the living room suddenly I heard my mother exclaim from the kitchen, "Oh!" A cry of pain.

I rushed in to find broken glass spattering the sink and the palm of her right hand covered with blood. I pulled back with a shudder. I might be an intrepid reporter afraid of nothing while on the job but I was distinctly a coward when it came to looking at any mutilation of the human body—the last profession in the world I could handle would be nurse in a surgical ward.

Mother looked at me ruefully, said, "A glass broke as I washed it. I think I cut myself pretty deeply. Will you take a look at it?" As I had asked her in childhood to look at my wounds.

I had never seen her bleed or appear so helpless. I mustered total courage, stared at the cut. The gash was about two inches long and bright red blood gushed out.

"Wait here." My first command ever to Mother.

I raced to the medicine cabinet, seized cotton, alcohol, gauze and adhesive. I washed the cut with alcohol, the first time I ever performed first aid on her or anyone. I bandaged the wound. But the blood kept seeping through.

Mother went regularly to a doctor who gave her injections for a thyroid condition. She asked, "Do you think we should call Dr. Jones?"

"Do you know his number?"

"You'll have to find it in the telephone book. His first name is Walter." Her face paled, she seemed about to faint.

I found the number, dialed it. I told the nurse this was an emergency, gave mother's name. The doctor came to the phone. I said, "Mother has cut the palm of her right hand on broken glass and it's bleeding badly. Do you have time to look at it?"

"Bring her right over," he said.

I hung up, told Mother, "Come on," seized her good left hand, raced to her Pontiac. When we reached the doctor's office, I helped her out of the car. He took six stitches in her hand.

Back at the house as we sat in the sun surrounded by the red beauty of hibiscus and poinsettia, sipping instant coffee, she said, "Thank you, Lucy dear. I don't know what I would have done without you."

I was happy to hear these words. Glad I helped ease her pain. For the first time in my life I felt I had the power. Up to now she was always the one in power. I had used my power wisely, not as, in fantasy, I feared it might be used to destroy her.

"Mother, it was nothing." I felt embarrassed. "I only drove you to the doctor."

"But if you hadn't been in the house I wouldn't have made it on my own. I couldn't have driven, I was too upset. I might have bled to death."

A sudden feeling of love surged through me. And with it, a sense of vulnerability, not quite daring to trust the love. Knowing I would feel the old anger and rejection as soon as she gave an order I felt unfair, or showed a preference for my brother or sisters.

And yet when I felt terror, I longed for her touch. She had the power to hurt as no one else could but she also had the power to give comfort and reassurance as no one else cared to.

I told Dr. Aiken, "I never dared talk about sex with her. I thought her the prude of prudes in contrast to my sexually acting-out father. To her credit, though, she did tell me in advance about menstruation, in contrast to her silence with Sue and Sally, who had to find out from friends."

Thus at ten, I did not think I was dying when blood gushed out of a place I already believed dirty and evil. The "curse" hit early, perhaps part of my precocious desire to grow up fast and head for a spot in the world where I could breathe more easily.

Though I never dared ask such questions as "Is it harmful to neck?" or "How far can I let a boy go?" she encouraged me to go out with boys as long as I did not allow them to "make advances." Even though she might be in a vile mood she turned seductive in a second if a man appeared on the scene. At the sight of the delivery boy she would become a flirt, whereas a minute before she was shrieking at one of her children.

She thought of love in terms of the romance in magazines, the fantasies of adolescence. One secret I believe she never told anyone except me revealed her attitude toward sex. She and Laurie returned to New York at the end of their honeymoon in Washington, D.C., to learn that her cousin Leonard, Granny's twenty-one-year-old son, who had just graduated from Williams College, had suddenly died of pneumonia. Mother had been close to him during the years she lived with Granny.

Mother said to me, disgust in her voice, "And your father wanted sex the night of the funeral," as though it were inappropriate to perform an act of life in the face of death. As though sex were a gift to bestow on a man when *she* felt it proper, rather than a mutual act of love after two weeks of marriage.

Frightened of her sexual feelings, Mother also must have lived in fear of rape. Otherwise how could one explain her compulsive closing of all the downstairs windows in the house each night, even in the heat of summer, so a Brutal Stranger could not burst in and rape the women?

Dr. Aiken pointed out to me I absorbed psychologically the feelings and attitudes about sex held by Mother. With his help I started to realize Mother was my first sex model as well as sex object. What she thought of herself sexually, how she treated her body and mine, whether roughly or tenderly, how she reacted to men, crucially influenced my sexual feelings, fantasies and acts. She molded my sexual desires from the moment I lay at her breast.

From her I also learned the look and feel of love, as far as she could show it. The degree of tenderness she expressed, profoundly influenced whether I could feel tender toward myself and others.

My belief, based on how I saw her act with Sally, is that when I was tiny she kissed and hugged me but as I became more of a person she seemed afraid of touching or being touched by me. After all, no one touched her in tenderness following the age of two, and perhaps rarely before. She never let me kiss her on the lips, always turned her cheek. Her hugs were perfunctory, not warm embraces like my father's. The touch is important to a child, it makes him feel loved and wanted. Luckily my father's frequent hugs and kisses on the cheek made me feel desired by someone.

There was no doubt Mother used me and the other children as the target of her anger. We provided an outlet for, as well as a defense against any danger she may have felt in expressing sexual feelings. Anger may be used as a defense against sexuality, just as expression of sexual wishes may be used as a defense against violent feelings.

Dr. Emch had pointed out my mother may have been using me to carry out her sexual fantasies as she permitted me to go on weekend trips, as well as vacations with my father. First, alone with him, as though I were taking her place, then later with him and Donna, as though I were my mother's surrogate voyeur.

We four children valiantly tried to make Mother's last years as comfortable as we knew how. She started to lose her memory, suffered several small strokes, finally spoke in streams of gibberish. Once in a while she seemed to know someone she loved was near. She might suddenly say as we left her, "Come again," her first lucid words in hours, or call us by name.

One night the telephone rang as I worked on *Sparks*, a collection of unpublished letters and articles by Dr. Karl Menninger, with additional interviews about his life by me. I thought he might be calling from Topeka as he sometimes did to ask how the book was going. I picked up the receiver, expecting his cheerful, enthusiastic, deep voice, one that always buoyed me up.

But it was a woman's voice, my sister Sue, calling from Daytona Beach. A frightened voice.

She asked, "Can you fly down right away? Mother had a bad stroke today. The doctor doesn't know whether she'll pull through."

"Where is she?" I felt sudden, deep fear.

"At her house. We have a nurse around the clock besides Mother's companion taking care of her."

"I'll be down on the first plane in the morning."

"We'll meet you at the airport."

Mother was living in an attractive small house on Dundee Road that Sue and George bought for her. The companion took care of Mother, cooked nutritious food under the orders of a doctor who checked Mother every so often.

Per Sue's request I caught the early plane to Daytona Beach airport. Before I left I called Dr. Aiken, told him there was an emergency involving my mother and I would be gone for two or three days. Sue and George Junior met the plane, we drove straight to the house on Dundee, not far from the Ponce de León inlet, the historic spot where the first white man stepped on American soil.

I walked into Mother's bedroom. The companion, a trained nurse and George stood by the bed on which Mother lay stretched out like a corpse. Her throat bulged as though a rubber ball were caught in it, her beautiful blue eyes closed against a world she feared. Her breath came in agonized wheezes even as she received air through an oxygen tent.

I burst into tears. George took me in his arms, said understandingly, "Go ahead and cry." He was an unusually sensitive man.

I dried my tears, George gestured toward Mother, "She hasn't eaten in forty-eight hours."

I turned to Sue, suggested, "Don't you think we should call the doctor and ask him to arrange for Mother to be sent to the hospital?"

She looked relieved, said, "That's the reason I wanted you to come down. I didn't want to take full responsibility."

She called the doctor, who at once arranged for a room at Halifax Hospital three miles away. Within twenty minutes an ambulance arrived at the door. I rode in the ambulance with Mother, siren shrieking as we raced over the bridge to the mainland, through the quiet streets of Daytona to the hospital, which lay to the west. Sue and George followed in their car.

After examining Mother the doctor at the hospital told us it was only a matter of hours before she would die, her pneumonia attack so severe. He suggested Sue and I immediately buy a coffin, select one of Mother's dresses to bury her in. We held back the tears, we had work to do, could not afford at that moment to grieve or feel sorry for Mother or ourselves.

We drove to the Haigh-Black Funeral Home, whose owners Sue knew socially, selected a coffin with an inside lid decorated by an eternal flower sewn into the blue satin fabric. Then we drove to Mother's house, looked through the few pathetic dresses in her closet, chose a print with purple background, Mother loved the color purple.

Later that afternoon I stood alone by her bed in the private room, empty for the moment of nurses. Mother's blue eyes were closed as though she lay in her final coma.

I stroked her gray-streaked dark hair, the first time I dared do this, thought of how I always believed my father so affectionate, Mother so cold, the true untouchable.

And I said two things to her.

I said, "Thank you for having me."

Then I said, "I'm sorry I've been such a bitch."

I do not know if she heard me, no one knows whether a stroke takes away complete consciousness. Perhaps somewhere in the crevices of her mind she heard. And forgave. Or perhaps thought there was nothing to forgive.

But because of strong lungs and heart, Mother somehow pulled through, recovered temporarily from her death-battle with pneumonia, the illness she feared most. Sue and George placed her in a nearby nursing home, something they had avoided, but now had no choice because she needed constant medical supervision.

Before I left for home, at sunset time I sat on the terrace of Sue's house overlooking the Halifax River. A scene of quiet except for the whistle of a whippoorwill or the toot of a horn from a yacht cruising the river, part of the Inland Waterway from Miami to Chesapeake Bay. The Halifax flowed up to Sue's front lawn, exotic with hibiscus and bougainvillea. George Junior, seven years old, whom I loved, even as a child he had the mind of an adult, walked out. He sat in harmonious silence, eagerly refilled my glass of wine when it emptied, the perfect host. Sue's elder son, Bobby, who had his own family, also lived in Daytona.

Then it was back to Manhattan and Dr. Aiken's office, where I could shed all the tears I wished, not feel ashamed at showing my grief. Like Dr. Emch, he believed if I cried, I needed to cry, a need in some way connected to my earliest years when I lacked the words to tell of it, as well as grief at a current loss.

Five months later Mother died alone as, in a sense, she had lived alone since the age of two. Her last breaths were taken within the sterile walls of a nursing home she probably never saw. No one at her side to kiss her cheek, hold her hand, stroke her forehead. Not one of her four children, whom she needed so desperately, there to comfort her.

George arranged for her body to be shipped north. She was buried at Mount Hope Cemetery in the Prince plot, a few feet from the huge mausoleum that held Granny and Grumpy. Just down the hill under a tree lay Laurie. In death, as in most of her life, Mother would be separated from my father but, I thought, At least they lie not too far apart in the same cemetery.

"I mourn her death deeply," I told Dr. Aiken. "I am haunted by the sadness of her life. The sorrow in those sapphire eyes." Added, "My writing in a sense is a memorial to her. She first encouraged me to keep a diary."

Writing, as psychoanalysts say, is often an attempt to restore "the lost object," the mother of childhood. My words on the printed page may be an attempt to keep her alive through memories, some conscious, some with unconscious roots. I hated her at times but I loved her far more than I hated her.

Most of all I mourned her inability to convey her feelings. We never really talked about what was most important to each of us. Life was a game, a party, soap opera, roles to be played. Chin up, no tears, march on.

I said sadly, "I never understood her pain, nor she, mine. I had no awareness of her desperate need for love."

I recalled, "One day at her house in Daytona she

and I sat close together on the same outdoor lounge chair. I suddenly felt her stroke my dark hair, heard her say, 'My Lucy!' I thought in bitterness, It's too late, baby, it's too late. The words of the popular song sung by Carole King. I had to feel bitter otherwise I would have cried like the unloved baby I felt myself to be."

I thanked my lucky stars (growing inner strength?) I had returned to the couch and found Dr. Aiken. He helped me mourn my mother's death. I did not feel, as with Dr. Mack, that I was not allowed to mourn the death of someone I loved. Perhaps she sensed how much I loved Dr. Emch and in comparison how ambivalent I felt toward her, she seemed to resent the very mention of Dr. Emch's name.

In a way Mother's death, which I had the chance to mourn slowly in advance, was less of a shock than the death of my father. I wrote of this to my new pen pal, psychoanalyst Dr. Lawrence Friedman, in Brentwood, California. He replied, "You will find the entire process of analysis contains mourning because you have to give up infantile attachments."

I also wrote Larry, author of *Psy'cho-a-nal'y-sis*, "I am finding this analysis far more profound and pleasurable, if I may dare use that word about analysis, than the last couch experience."

Dr. Aiken helped me understand more of the complexity of my relationship with my mother. How unknowingly she contributed to the unhealthy tie between my father and me. She could have forbidden him at the start to take me on trips but either she was afraid of his wrath or believed my presence would somehow lessen her fear he would leave her for the other woman. Mother did not realize my erotic feelings would be aroused as I slept in a room adjoining the one my father occupied with his "friend."

Dr. Aiken possessed the same quality of empathy

as Dr. Emch, not the sometimes punitive feeling that emanated from Dr. Mack. But to have one out of four turn a bit sour is not a bad percentage, I thought.

I faced Dr. Aiken almost a year before I could lie on his couch. He allowed me to sit up until I was ready to turn my back on him, in the analytic sense. Which paradoxically meant that the unconscious part of my mind would open up more readily. With Dr. Emch it had taken nine months, the gestation period.

I said, "Dr. Emch died after I lay on her couch and, come to think of it, the year of sitting up with you may have been my mourning period since I have talked a lot about her death and my mother's."

"It is important to mourn as fully as you can," he said.

I thought, Most people I know have difficulty mourning, they have been taught, as I was as a child, to hide feelings of mourning and loss.

Thus Dr. Aiken led the way to my awareness of the high psychic price I paid for denying feelings of mourning. We explored other essential emotional territory as the months raced by. But the experience of unearthing buried grief at the death of my mother and father, as well as earlier, different kinds of losses, was a completely new one. It proved a vital one in my struggle to understand the pain of the past.

There was one area each analyst had stressed from John on but I had only scratched the surface of its well-concealed depths. My hidden rage. I had protected well against it. Could Dr. Aiken help me finally release my locked-away anger? Rescue me from the heavy burden of concealing it at the expense of self-esteem?

11

The Right
to Feel Rage

I knew intellectually my long-congealed and concealed rage reached back to the years before I could
speak a word. I had been trained early to hold my
tongue and my tears.

Both John and Dr. Emch tried to help me express
even the slightest show of rage. But it was so deeply
embedded, so well-defended against for so many years,
I could not sustain it. The second I felt the touch of
anger I banished it automatically to the unconscious
part of my mind.

I knew I was furious at Dr. Mack much of the time
yet I did not want her to hate me more, to feel further
obliterated, so I carefully guarded against any show of
anger. I walked away from rage and eventually her.

Freud said it was not intellectual awareness of a
fantasy or memory that helped the patient but a "living
through" of the emotions connected to the fantasy or
memory. The horrors I fled, the tears never shed, the

torment never faced, the hate buried deep, the sexual desire denied—all the unspeakables. "Living through" these terrifying, tabooed feelings was the pure gold of psychoanalysis but I seemed destined to settle for tin.

Slowly, almost imperceptibly, however, I moved toward knowing the anger I hid. Dr. Aiken made this possible by just waiting it out.

I enjoyed his sympathetic, sincere and soothing voice. It was a voice I loved to hear though at times he could be silent almost the entire hour. One day he uttered not a word for forty minutes. At first I displayed my usual servile attitude, buried the rage at feeling slighted so long.

Finally I turned my head to the right, where he sat behind me, hurled the insulting query, "Are you dead?"

I thought in further anger, Jesus, can't he give me one word of reassurance or interpretation after listening the whole hour? Am I speaking just patient-bilge, wasting valuable minutes?

He still said nothing, nor did I. It was enough I could dare even a small flare of anger.

Slowly I accepted, as Freud said, that the words the analyst spoke were not the essence of analysis though I treasured them as such. They provided insights which led to further revelations of fantasies and conflicts. But it was primarily the feelings evoked that healed the emotional wounds of the past. Feelings I could now slowly and painfully accept as I could trust the analyst. I felt Dr. Aiken had hope in his heart for me, that I was not "stupid," my father's word for me at times.

Now there rose to the surface thoughts I had denied, emotions that had whirled in my unconscious for years. I wrote Larry, my West Coast psychoanalytic correspondent: "The analysis goes well but at times I reel home from a session in subdued shock. The result,

I guess, of an insight taken to heart. Or awareness of some formerly forbidden feeling or thought."

Larry replied with his definition of what he called "the goal of existence." He wrote: "To find a satisfactory solution for one's life in spite of or within the framework of our limitations and the necessary restrictions."

The "satisfactory solution," I thought, may differ with each of us. It may lie in marriage or out, in the choice of marriage or profession, or both. The better we know the nature of our infantile attachments, the more capable we are of feeling free to decide wisely. We are no longer at the mercy of parents or circumstances. Children are not allowed choices. Adults are.

I recalled how devastated I felt when I first left home for college and suddenly realized I could choose to eat whatever I wished at any hour of the day or night. I no longer lived under my mother's restrictions. Part of me felt aghast, as though she no longer cared. How could she so easily have forsaken me? Then I realized college meant new strength, the choices—wise or unwise—were now up to me. What I ate, what boys I chose to date, how late to stay up, what clothes to buy.

We cannot choose our parents but we may choose our marital partners, friends, employers. Though our choices as children were almost completely influenced by parents, as adults we do not have to repeat the past. We are free to make choices if we understand the feelings and fantasies that have kept us tied to parental voices.

As I spoke up from the couch many new memories slowly edged out into the open. Sometimes they were reawakened as I sat in Dr. Aiken's waiting room by sounds emerging from the home part of his apartment. Once in a while the voice of a child or woman, at rare moments a melody played on a piano.

I envied those near and dear to him, the envy, as I spoke of it on the couch, brought back scenes and fantasies valuable to the understanding of my jealousy of my brother and sisters, especially my brother. When he was born, to make way for the needy newcomer I was deprived of sleeping in the same room as my parents, a monumental insult to the fantasy I was the one and only.

I now became more acutely aware of childhood fantasies that crippled, affected the type of man I chose. I told Dr. Aiken, "I see now the two times I got pregnant I did not select responsible men, knew it and refused to marry them."

Added, "Isn't it ironic the two times I married and tried to have a child I could not conceive?"

"You did not want to be like your mother," he said.

"That's for sure," I agreed. "I made that vow early in life."

I felt too angry at her, headed directly for the career I cherished above all else. No male intruder was going to deprive me of it no matter how intensely the woman trapped inside wanted to bear a child before she left this earth.

I admitted, "Mother did have a large heart and sympathetic understanding at times of need. When I was little and even after I grew up, if something tragic happened, like the death of Granny or a broken love affair, my mother's way of comforting was not to encourage me to express grief but to hand me a piece of her jewelry."

Added grudgingly, "It was comfort of a sort. Better than nothing. Her way of showing solace was through gifts. Not dangerous words or hugs."

Recalled further, "She would sometimes push me away when I tried to hug her. My father was far more affectionate, I never felt I repulsed him." In later life, nothing made me angrier than when I started to hug or kiss a man or woman on the cheek and they withdrew swiftly, a look of reproof or revulsion on their face.

I waited for Dr. Aiken to speak, again there was no sound. I forged ahead, "I suppose because of her painful early life Mother's defenses were like iron. As a child no one was there to reassure her when she felt hurt. Mother never dared mourn and her intense need to do so, especially after the death of her mother, must have been overwhelming."

More silence. I filled it. "The first time I told her I had an abortion, expecting her to show she understood how devastated I felt, she did not say one word. Her expression did not change to sorrow or pity. Instead she headed for her jewelry boxes, picked out an expensive amethyst bracelet, handed it to me to ease the loss of the baby and the pain."

Grimly, "Physical *and* emotional pain. Pain I never knew existed. Try having an abortion without anesthesia. No words, no show of feeling from Mother. Just cold, hard amethyst."

Then grudgingly, "I guess I should be grateful for that. Mother did not dare be aware of her feelings of grief, much less mine. We shared an unspoken compact. Neither would tell of her losses."

He spoke at last. Said simply, "You wear her sadness."

Not that I wore her bracelet, her necklace, her ring—but her sadness. A far more important aspect of life than jewels.

"I never thought of that." Then defensively, "I don't consider myself a sad person. Everyone always remarks how cheerful and optimistic I am. Like my father." I sighed, gave in to the truth. "Maybe I have tried, like my mother did, to hide my sadness from the world."

Silence. I went on, "Maybe the black outfits I eternally wear is to tell of my sadness. My mourning costume for all the lost loves."

"All the lost loves standing for the one lost love of childhood," he said.

He added, "Your black outfits are your uniform. They tell of your mourning."

"I always thought black was sexy." My voice held surprise.

"That, too."

I thought of the word *overdetermined*, which analysts use in their clinical talk. A thought, an act, a wish, a conflict was determined by several fantasies, not merely one.

"My first black dress was a low-cut satin evening gown for the high school junior prom," I recalled. "It had a silver rope of rhinestones as neckline. Donna shopped with me after my father gave her the money. He said in his caustic way, 'Buy something that looks good on her for a change.' Meaning neither my mother nor I had taste. Donna always dressed like a movie star, in lovely silken latest-style outfits."

Mother did not approve of the black dress, I saw revulsion in her large blue eyes. She wanted to keep me unsophisticated, not flaunt the garb of a wicked woman of the world who would compete with her for my father's coveted approval.

I fought my mother all the way in trying to grow up—style and color of dress, lipstick, rouge, bra, high heels, sheer stockings and staying out past nine at night. The black satin dress was my first subtle act of sabotage. Since my father had paid for it she could not complain. She defied him only once, as far as I knew, when she asked him to leave the house.

Black was sexy but paradoxically, as I told Dr. Aiken, black also symbolized sexless to me, and therefore safe as far as my erotic feelings were concerned. The nuns who lived in the convent next door wore long black dresses and were part of my very existence from six years on. Daily I watched their stately walk in pairs around the grounds. Sometimes they said a gentle "good morning" as they neared our low hedge.

Dr. Aiken helped me understand another source of hidden rage. There were times my mother regressed, became like a baby, made demands on me as though I were her mother. I could not bear Mother acting the child. It seemed obscene and I fled the scene.

I thought once again, tears in my eyes, What a lonely death in that nursing home, no one she loved to comfort her in the final hours of what, to her, turned into a pitiless planet. There was cruel symmetry between her early life and departure from life.

Dr. Aiken patiently helped me become aware of the rage I hid from myself and tried to hide from everyone else. My biggest psychic defense, as each analyst informed me, was my inability to know my carefully guarded fury. It bubbled slightly more to awareness with each succeeding analyst but for the most part still cowered in the mind's lowest depths.

My task was somehow to know the murder that flashed in my heart under that "composed flesh" Auden mentioned. To become aware the wish to kill when angry or hurt was part of my survival mechanism. We all need the capacity to feel that instant killer surge in case our life is realistically threatened so we can defend ourselves, stay alive. If we deny this impulse to protect ourselves and the concomitant strong emotions it stirs, anger may control us rather than our controlling it.

Before I could freely feel the hate toward my mother and father in childhood, first I had to become aware of and express anger at the analyst. Know he would not rage back, threaten me with punishment or wish to kill me. This awareness slowly arrived during the years with Dr. Aiken.

He helped me understand more fully the grief and rage I hid when my father died. There was a dual loss at his death. Not only what I felt his abandonment but my mother's strength now slowly became sapped in a deep depression that felt like abandonment of her children. Within me, parts of my parents I had emotionally absorbed seemed to die a little, too.

Dr. Aiken helped me know another aspect of my rage. One night playing bridge I listened to a man issue constant "dos" and "don'ts" to us three other players. "Stop drumming your fingers on the table," to an opponent. "You should have played the Queen, not the King, to inform me you had both," to his partner.

The next morning I described the scene to Dr. Aiken, complained, "He sounded just like my mother. Do this, do that." Then asked, "The dominating, overpowering mother chains the child to her, doesn't she? The child then feels angry and dreams of revenge on this assault to freedom. As I did last night at times with this overbearing man."

In his thoughtful way Dr. Aiken remarked, "The wish for revenge is also a bond. The desire to get even keeps the parent alive in your thoughts." As I could give up this wish I would give up the hurtful attachments to my dominating mother.

I also came to know one of the most dangerous things for an adult is to face how infantile and primitive he feels at times. This means becoming aware of fantasies we believe "unthinkable." Fantasies of greed, the wish to kill those who have hurt us, childlike dependence on our mother, our wishes to be special and omnipotent. How ugly and selfish the unconscious can be, I thought. Yet this is part of being "human." To deny these feelings is to deny a vital part of the self. Some impulses *are* barbaric. We can never do away with the primitive inside us. But we can learn to control our dangerous feelings more wisely by becoming aware of them.

I described a television movie I had seen the night before that inspired a dream. I recalled, "The movie mentioned 'the white city.' This alluded to a city in Central America that sold cocaine to our country. There were scenes of pathetic young women holding their babies as they went to jail for trading cocaine to get money to keep the babies and themselves alive. I thought how tragic it was these mothers had to take part in a criminal act just to live."

Added, "And just before this film I saw part of a documentary on Freud. One scene pictured Freud standing before a painting in Florence of the Madonna holding the baby Jesus. Freud said the child looked as though he 'lusted' after his mother."

Then I described the dream. "A huge crab crawled toward me, menacing me. The crab looked deadly. I was afraid it would devour me."

Dr. Aiken waited for the golden thoughts that would lead to awareness of what the dream was trying to say, only sketched in the surface action.

I went on, "I think of the 'white city' of cocaine and the starving young mothers. Looking at them I thought of a phrase of Freud's mentioned in the documentary. 'Landscape of ghosts.' Ghosts are 'white.' Ghosts are scary. Ghosts can kill, like cocaine."

Added, "Scary like my mother. Ready to kill, like my mother. Who today is just a ghost. Dead and buried."

Dr. Aiken said, "Your mother was the 'devouring crab' of the dream. A crab you feared would eat you up physically and emotionally."

"You mean I thought of my mother as a crab?" I had fantasied her in many ways but never as a crawling, man-and-woman-eating crab.

"You have often talked of her 'suffocating' you, destroying you." Then he said, "You quote Freud saying it is the child who 'lusted' after the mother. What about your wish to devour your mother?"

He was saying that though I might at times fantasy she wanted to devour me, I as a baby also fantasied devouring her. I sighed, said, "I have to stop blaming my parents for my unhappiness."

He was quiet a moment, then, "Blaming them is also a way of keeping the attachment strong."

This was an important new thought. Unless I could give up blaming my mother and father I would remain emotionally tied to them. A cripple of the past instead of a healing, more whole person.

"I blame them and I mourn," I confessed. "I seem to be mourning all the time. For the beautiful babies I see on the street that are not mine. For my dead mother and father. For the exciting days on *The New York Times.* For the men I did not marry and the ones I did, from whom I split." And, though I did not say it, mourning for what I knew would eventually be the end of this analysis. One that brought out all the mournings of my life.

I had been entrapped in the love-hates of childhood, unable to undertake a lasting marriage, no children, no family of my own. Feeling rejected, in turn I rejected.

I wailed, "The bottom line is rejection."

"And the anger that follows, which you have largely repressed."

Then quietly, "You'd be happier if you could stop fighting your mother and accept her as she was."

"The trouble was I couldn't fight her." I sighed once more. "Sally was the only one who could. Sally's analyst told her she survived Mother's emotional outbursts because she screamed back, ran out of the house, did what she wanted. I lacked such courage. That's why I have such a hard time even knowing I am angry. Much less express it." Added grimly, "Here or anywhere else."

I had to face head-on my terror of my mother and father's anger, a terror that haunted my adulthood. I was afraid to speak up, say nay to anyone. It was a mark of analytic success I could finally address an audience, look into that sea of faces wearing the mask of the faces of my mother and father sitting in disapproval, waiting for me to make an error.

My mother's name was Sylvia, Shakespeare asked, "Who is Sylvia? What is she? That all our swains commend her?" As a child I could not fully commend my Sylvia but at last I started to make peace with my feelings about her. A few justified, many mere fantasy.

As I uncovered the deeper feelings of hate and rebellion and the wish for revenge, I also uncovered the deeper feelings of love and yearning. I sensed my strong passions as a child when they came into conflict with hers. I stopped blaming, started to understand.

My mother and my father, though the latter more subtly, were experts at what analysts call "soul murder," the small slicing away at the child's soul that parents may inflict day to day, causing the child's fear, hatred and distrust. It may run from the extremes of incest and violent beatings to verbal assault or neglect.

Little by little, with gentle encouragement, Dr. Aiken helped me feel safe enough to experience and express buried anger. Such anger was similar to the shower in my bathroom that sometimes took five minutes to get warm but then became hot enough to scald me.

One day after he kept me waiting ten minutes, a very unusual occurrence, for he made a point to be on time, I muttered to the air in his waiting room, "You bastard!" Just as I had lost my temper at Dr. Emch for the same crime.

After five minutes on the couch, steeling myself with small talk, I announced, "I thought of you as a bastard for keeping me waiting as I sat outside." I expected him to strike me, as my father once struck me when he thought I defied him in words—he probably would have killed me if I had called him a bastard.

Instead, Dr. Aiken said quietly, "Congratulations."

He knew how difficult it was for me to express the slightest flicker of rage. This was a mental milestone.

I would not have believed the fantasies of murder in my heart. It was no accident I wrote the true life story of the young killer in Chicago, projecting on him my wishes to kill a young woman (my mother, as in her early twenties she gave birth to two other children). I had felt my anger a bomb that would blow me up should I expose the wisp of a signal of its potential power. The thought of possessing buried fury terrified me. Now I knew denial of it caused a lowering of self-esteem and independence. Not to mention that third indicator of integrity—sense of identity.

Dr. Aiken also helped me understand how I used sex partially to express anger. The sexual affair offered one way to release some of the rage as either I or the man eventually broke off the relationship. I could feel anger justifiable and leave him, following what I thought his betrayal, if in some way he did not live up to the image I fantasied. Or, if he abandoned me, I could feel rage at the "bastard." In fantasy he became my father, the "red-headed S.O.B.," as some of his secretarial staff called him at times because of his violent temper when they misplaced documents or were not swift enough in carrying out his commands.

Mother hid many of her violent wishes except when

she screamed or threatened, "You'll be the death of me!" Then added aggrievedly, "You're lucky you had a mother. I lost mine when I was two." And I thought at such times, I wish I had lost you when I was two, signal of my anger.

When she threatened at one point to kill the woman who had "taken Laurie away," I felt she wished to kill me, the little mistress who championed her father over the years. I was terrified of my mother, the would-be murderess. Yet felt deserved to be eliminated because of guilt over childhood wishes to take him away from her.

When she finally ordered him out of the house I thought in a sense she was trying to kill him. He did not want to leave, that I knew. Difficult as it was, he had made his peace for ten years, keeping two women, five miles apart.

I told Dr. Aiken, "After he left I saw him as much as I ever did."

"You remained your father's little mistress in his fantasies and yours," Dr. Aiken said.

A touch of incest in the minds of both, I thought. Said, "I'm finally becoming aware of that."

"He made you a participant in his love life."

"He was cruel at times, wasn't he?" I mused. "One day Dr. Mack called him a bastard. This shocked me because I worshipped him, though I was also very frightened of him."

I wondered whether, as a result of some people referring to my father as a bastard, I rose to his defense, admired the bastardly part of him. Sought other men who sometimes acted as bastards.

I admitted in a low voice, "I'm frightened of you at times." As though calling him a bastard.

"Why are you frightened of me?" The gentle voice.

"Because you are a psychoanalyst."

"No. Because you are still frightened of your father. You felt annihilated when he became angry at you."

"The only time I cried was that day he became so enraged at the dinner table," I admitted. "I never cried when Mother was angry. Only acted more submissive and sweeter."

At long last I started to face that angry, vindictive little girl and her wishes to hurt, destroy. Wishes I had needlessly and with unnecessary guilt punished myself for feeling over the uncertain years. They arose from fantasies of vengeance at both real and imagined hurts inflicted by both my mother and father. I had not understood as a child (how could I?) my role in the ménage à trois among Laurie, Donna and me and prior to that, Laurie, Mother and me.

Mother at least found partial outlet for her anger, sometimes unfairly, at the expense of her children. I fantasied at times her serpentine tongue might suddenly lash in and out in an orgasm of words dripping in venom from an imagined penis. Her anger was masculine, whipping, commanding. Not gently reproachful if we deserved reprimand.

I had not wanted, ever, to show such ugly fury. Then no man would love me, stay with me forever. Over the years I buried anger wishing to be completely different—I am not my mother, I am myself. But I did not reckon with the parts of her I had emotionally absorbed that helped form my character, spurred angry acts at times. I remained furious at those features of her I hated, ones I unconsciously had taken unto myself as defenses, fantasies, wishes.

At sixteen I dreamed of marrying a boy in high school I thought I loved passionately, bearing his children, enjoying a wifely life. Why had I not fulfilled this

THE RIGHT TO FEEL RAGE

daydream? What went wrong? That, too, was what analysis was all about.

The daydream mirrored deeper fantasies about my father. I placed him on a pedestal, denied even a hint of rage, put Mother in the pits. I adored my "resourceful" father, as one lawyer who knew him well described him—a quality essential to a lawyer. Blocked in one argument while waging verbal war during a case, my father would explore another argument and, if need be, a third and fourth, according to Theodore Jaffin, who says my father taught him all he knew about law when he joined the firm as a young man.

While I knew at times I hated my mother yet concomitantly I became her protector. I thought, If I ever forsake her, emotionally speaking, she will die, as her mother died, and it will be my fault and I will die too, her revenge. When her need for me became too voracious after Laurie left, I fled to survive before she swallowed me emotionally. I thought of her at times as a simmering volcano threatening to erupt. Yet I also knew there was another mother, a vulnerable little girl of a mother. It was this pendulum switch of her moods that scared me all my life.

I fled two torturers who occasionally turned their weapons on each other. My father would attack Mother verbally. He once told me nastily, "Don't be like your mother," and at that moment I felt her champion. He had called her the "no woman," pointed out her first response to anyone's suggestion was usually no. Though she could be talked into changing her mind if something pleasurable was involved.

"It is no wonder I ran swiftly to a career," I said to Dr. Aiken. Thought of Freud's words, "In the heat of battle one does not notice one's wounds."

Added, "Only after I have done my work can I enjoy shopping for pretty dresses."

He commented, "When the masculine job is finished then you can take care of the little lady inside."

"That sure shows the split in me." Ruefully. Then bitterly, "Why would I ever want to be like my depressed mother?"

"You no longer have to be," he said. "When you were a child, you had no choice."

During one session I was surprised to hear him remark, "I learn a lot from patients."

No analyst had ever said that to me. I told him, "It's hard for me to believe I could give you insights." The inner waif who sought to be given to.

One day I had the courage to say, "You know, it is not always *what* you say but the *way* you say it. Your tone. Whether the words are spoken with quiet conviction or, once in a while, perhaps a bit cutting." Added hastily, "I know an analyst cannot always be empathic. That's like asking him to be perfect. Which you assure me analysts are not, they are human, too."

"Indeed they are," he said.

As a result of his help I found a new closeness to my brother and sisters. I now saw them as complex human beings who wanted to love and be loved as deeply as I did. Who faced the same conflicts, the same fantasies. They, too, endured suffering, tried to get what pleasure they could out of life. Their childhoods were no more joyous than mine.

As children we were naturally jealous of each other, vying for our parents' love, but we were also strong allies against warring parents. Our two powerful enemies had early split into opposing camps. Each tried to entice us into his special emotional province. We were used by our mother and father in different fashion and, to protect ourselves, joined forces. Over the years we have remained close. Sally and I live in Manhattan, Sue in Las Vegas, Eddie in Clearwater, Florida.

I now became aware my mother was not the same mother to each child. As Sally said to me astutely, "Your mother wasn't my mother."

No mother *is* the same to each child. Every child relates to the mother differently, as does the mother to the child. She may love one more than another because the child looks like her or does not look like her. Or looks like her husband whom she loves. Or she may hate a child who looks like her husband if she no longer loves him.

One child may be born when she wants a baby and she will love that child. Another may be born when she does not want a baby and she will reject this child. Or she may love a child who is powerless as an infant, hate the child when it shows a will of its own or sexual activity. There are many reasons, conscious and unconscious, why a mother may prefer one child to another and this affects how the child feels about her and itself.

I decided to ask Eddie, Sue and Sally how they felt about Mother when they were children, to describe their relationship to her. Here is Eddie's answer.

> My three sisters say I was mother's favorite. The beloved boy. I knew mother loved me. She was always a very good mother to me. I thought she was a good mother to all her children.
>
> I was never afraid of her. Even though she might oppose me at times, I always felt she would give in and I would get what I wanted. To me, she was not a dominating mother but weak in ruling. True, everything was "No!" at first. But then she would allow you to have your way.
>
> Whereas if our father said "No!" this meant "No!" No appeal in his court.
>
> As I grew up, I couldn't see why my father ever married my mother. They were far too differ-

ent to get along. I felt he never really loved her. When I first heard it had been chiefly a marriage of convenience, arranged and supported by their parents, I understood why the marriage had not worked out.

He was a great teaser, had a lot of personality, was very charming and well-liked. He was what in those days they called "a ladies' man." I accepted this characteristic in him, and was not really shaken up when I heard about another woman in the picture.

I felt sorry for mother, of course, because I believed she really loved and cared for him and I sensed this love was not returned. I thought mother a good person, a kind person but, as I said, rather weak, in that people could walk all over her.

As to Laurie's qualities as a father, I felt he set high standards for me but that whatever I accomplished, whether it met his high standards or not, he accepted and loved me because I was his only son. I also thought I let him down at times because I did not meet the high scholastic standards he set. Nor did I become the lawyer he wanted me to be. I was a fair golfer, which pleased him. I enjoyed being with him on the golf course or his boat. I have owned a boat much of my life. He instilled in me a love for the sea.

I loved him, liked to talk to him, enjoyed his keen sense of humor. And yet, with dad, I also always felt a certain amount of fear. I thought of him as a powerful person—chairman of boards, a prestigious lawyer, initiator of new ideas, a fierce Democrat, always for the common man.

Whereas with mother, I felt no fear. Nor did Sally, who, when mother ordered her to put on her rubbers if a drop of rain fell from the heavens, would sullenly pull them on, walk out of the house, then when she reached the high hedge that bordered the front lawn, hurl the rubbers back over it. Sue and Lucy were too frightened of mother to defy her, though Lucy told me that when she was a reporter on *The New York Times*, she would cover assignments when it rained, deliberately minus umbrella or hat, exulting in the feel of the rain on her face and body as she felt free of mother's domination.

I have been married three times, have seven children by my first two wives, both of whom have died since our divorces. I have found real happiness with my third wife, Dorothy. We live in Clearwater, Florida, where I have my own business. I am also a licensed real estate broker.

I feel I have led three lives. My first marriage, an elopement, took place when I was seventeen, while I was attending the University of Virginia in Charlottesville. My first wife, Lorraine, was fifteen. We met in high school, fell deeply in adolescent love. We had four children before we divorced after five years. The second marriage, to Madeleine, also from Larchmont, lasted twenty years and we had three children. I have been married to Dorothy ten years.

One of my most poignant memories of mother is visiting her in her New York apartment the day after my father died. I said to her, "I'll pick you up tomorrow and we'll drive to Westchester for the funeral."

She said calmly, "I'm not going."

"Not going?" I was shocked.

"No," she said. Then she added quietly, "I'm glad your father is dead."

I felt even more shocked and protested, "How can you say such a terrible thing, Mother?"

"You don't understand," she explained. "I mean that now that he's gone, nobody else can have him."

Then I understood how she felt. She had been the woman scorned. She was showing us all the abandoned wife's primitive need for revenge on both her ex-husband and his second wife. Many former wives may deny this but it is natural for the woman scorned to feel this way. Some have even acted on it. They kill the husband who wants to leave them, or murder their feminine rival. I have noticed many stories in the newspapers about men killing women with whom they have had an affair when the woman threatens to leave them or go out with another man.

I leaned over, kissed mother on the cheek. I don't think any of us children ever kissed our parents on the lips. I said, "I understand how you feel, Mother. I also understand how much you loved him and that's all that matters."

When she died, I thought of the lonely life she led after his death. But perhaps it was no lonelier than her life before. Perhaps she started to be lonely when Laurie left our house in Larchmont for good, or when Laurie left their bedroom. We older children were in our teens, Sally was eight, and we all tried to give her as much support as we could. For a few years she tried to live alone in Larchmont, then New York City but only felt more and more depressed. Sue then practically ordered mother to join her in Florida and mother from then on felt more alive.

I know she enjoyed many moments of happiness with her grandchildren, especially with my oldest son Danny and his younger brother Bruce. And, I hope, when her four children were growing up, we helped add to her enjoyment of life. She certainly looked happy as we danced in the living room to Benny Goodman records or played tennis with her on the Beach Point Club courts. Her later years were often sad, though to the last, she was there for us if we needed her. As we were, for her.

Sue then spoke of her feelings about mother. Sue is now a licensed real estate saleswoman, selling condominiums in Las Vegas. Her husband, George Polera, owns a booming Vegas business, the Ready-Mix Concrete Company. George Junior has his vitamin mail-order company.

I remember when were were children all of us had to go into mother's room every morning before school to kiss her goodbye on the cheek. She kept her eyes closed, gave no sign of being awake. But if we forgot to kiss her, we heard about it when we returned from school. She liked to sleep a lot. She got out of bed about nine in the morning. She'd sleep for two hours after lunch every day. If we were all going out at night, like to the Beach Point Club to see the firecrackers on the Fourth of July, we'd have to rest in the afternoon along with her.

Sometimes mother would scream when she got angry but I didn't mind. I never hated her. Not for anything. She never infuriated me to the point of rage as she did with Sally. I guess I'm not the same temperament as Sally. She would talk back, sometimes even curse mother, say, "God damn you!" which mother might have said to her first. Sally would scream in a voice you could hear down Monroe Avenue, loud enough to wake the sleeping nuns.

I thought Sally sometimes treated mother like shit. I thought of Sally as "the brat." To me, mother was never a tyrant even though Sally and Lucy say she was. I got along the best with her, maybe because I didn't go against her wishes. She never got angry at me, probably because I never talked back. I don't remember one fight with her though Sally says she remembers me throwing a clock at mother. If I did, it was only that once when I lost my temper, whereas Sally broke mother's heart by openly defying her all the time. They say tempers go with redheads but I didn't get angry.

Mother was what some might call overprotective and dominating but I didn't mind. To me, that's a good parent, to worry about your child. A good mother is protective of her child. My feeling is that the way things were with Laurie, mother put all her love on us kids. I never resented the attention she gave us. She was always there when we needed her. Always very concerned about us—where we were, when we would be home, what we did.

Mother was generous to a fault with her children and grandchildren. We never needed for anything, she never begrudged giving us money when we ran short. Not when we were little or when we grew up. I felt she loved all of us and when she punished us it was for our own good. We were just children, we couldn't expect to get our way.

I envied Eddie being a boy and allowed to do things girls were forbidden like staying up late, carousing with his friends, owning a motorcycle. I loved Eddie dearly. When he married it broke my heart. I was so jealous of Lorraine I could have killed her. Lucy told me she felt the same jealousy and so did Sally. Eddie might have been mean at times or hit us occasionally when he felt angry but we passionately loved him. He was our little Prince Charming, charismatic to the core.

Our dining room was always fun at night as we talked about what we had done during the day. Mother would summon the maid by pressing the buzzer under her foot and in would come meat, potatoes, vegetables and eventually a fancy dessert, usually chocolate, which we all loved. It was a pretty room with white curtains. The windows looked out on the trees of our front lawn, including a magnolia Laurie had planted, as he did the willow under which Virginia and Lucy acted out plays they thought up. After Laurie left us I missed his presence at dinner, as I am sure the rest of the family did too.

Our house was a veritable zoo. We also had a parrot perched in a cage in the downstairs porch, which held our player piano, wicker chairs, flowering plants and red tile floor on which we danced. The parrot would call out "Mama! Mama!" imitating our voices. Mother never knew whether it was one of her children or the parrot calling her.

I guess we girls were spoiled, brought up in a home where there was always a cook, maid, a chauffeur at times and, when Sally was born, a nurse for two years. Lucy says she dreads going into a kitchen because everything in it is waiting to attack her and usually does. She took her first apartment one summer when she worked at the Mamaroneck *Daily Times*. Mother closed the house to vacation with Sally and me at Virginia Beach so there was no place for Lucy to live— mother refused to let her stay in nearby Mamaroneck with Laurie and his new wife.

Lucy's apartment, all of one room, was a quarter of a mile down the Boston Post Road from our house. Mother got a phone call one night just after we returned home, Lucy's voice asked, "How do you light a gas stove?" Mother said, bewildered, "What have you done all summer?" Lucy said, "Ate out. You know I hate to cook." Another night she called to ask, "How do you know when water is boiling?"

Mother begged, "Come over for dinner, forget about the stove." Lucy soon took an apartment in New York, a trolley ride across town to the *Times* and boasted to me she ate every meal out, including breakfast. I envied that.

Mother was not above having a drink or two of rye, her preferred taste, though I never saw her take more than two drinks an evening and rarely during the day. Lucy says mother would bring a small flask with her when they went to the Belmont Racetrack, which they did a few times a year. Lucy tells of the day they drove to the track on the spur of the moment, lost the first six races. As they studied the card for the seventh, mother said, "There are two long shots at ninety-nine to one. I'll split a two-dollar bet with you on the one named Prince George." Mother bet any horse with Prince in its name since her mother's maiden name was Prince.

Lucy placed the bet, heard Bryan Field, to whom she often had waved across the city room before he left the sports department to become track announcer, call, "And they're off!" Prince George ambled in dead last. The other ninety-nine-to-one shot won. Lucy and mother looked at each other, burst into laughter and mother hauled out the little silver flask she carried for just such emotional emergencies. She offered it to Lucy, "Have a drink, dear." When I heard what had happened I said, "You should have bet on both long shots," and they agreed. I am the practical one of the family.

Mother was a social drinker, never an alcoholic, though she drank more after Laurie left, especially when there was company. I remember a Wall Street broker over six feet, named Sidney, who spoke with a thick German accent. He met mother on Granny's tennis court and proposed to her. But she laughed gently. He didn't have Laurie's charm.

When Laurie married again, I lived for a while with mother. At night I would hear her sobbing, sometimes even throwing up her supper. I felt betrayed. I thought Laurie had betrayed the whole family by what he did.

After seven years of caring for mother in my homes in Florida, I called Lucy one day and pleaded, "Please do me a favor. Just take mother for a little while. I'm worried about her, I think she's had a few small strokes and should see a good doctor in New York."

"You've done more than your share," Lucy said. She flew down at once, took mother back to New York by train, found her an apartment at the Chatham Hotel and a live-in companion. Lucy also tried to get her to go to a psychiatrist who specialized in treating the elderly depressed with psychotherapy but mother refused to go after two sessions, insisting there was nothing wrong with her.

When mother became even more depressed in New York George and I bought a small house in Daytona Beach in mother's name and hired a companion to care for her. The companion and I flew to New York to bring her back to Daytona. Slowly she started to lose her memory, had several more small strokes, spoke in unconnected words. About a year later on June 17, 1972, she died in the nursing home.

But she is with me daily in spirit as well as memory. In our Vegas home her picture hangs on one wall of my living room. It is a reproduction of a photograph, enlarged, two feet by three feet, with the authentic colors painted on. Her purple dress, her favorite gold chain with the cameo around her neck, her blue eyes, her hair that even at seventy-seven retained much of its brown, peppered with gray. Not a wrinkle on her face. She is smiling, always very much the lady, as she sits regally in the tapestried chair, a wedding gift, now part of my living room.

I miss her more than I can say. The years do not dim the mourning. I feel anguished that she had to suffer so during her life. But she also knew happiness and I think some of it came from bringing up four children with all the care she could muster. A care she had never known as a child.

I believe I have led a run-of-the-mill life, but what's wrong with that? It's all I ever wanted. I didn't seek great wealth but just enough money to live comfortably and do what I wanted. Mother gave me far more than she received from her mother or those who took care of her after her mother died. And I consider what she gave me the greatest of gifts. First life, and then how to live it.

Finally I asked Sally to tell me her feelings about Mother as she grew up.

Mother was both my mother and father since my father had, in large part, abdicated when I was born, given his involvement with another woman.

Later in therapy I realized any good qualities I might have had were a result of mother's caring. My father gave me his willingness to fight for my rights, his seemingly endless energy, his interest in other people and his coloring of red hair. I was the only one of the children to have brown eyes, the rest all had the blue eyes of our parents, which led to the family joke that mother had been involved with the delivery man, who had sparkling brown eyes.

Though mother was physically there for me, she was emotionally inaccessible most of the time. When someone says "mother" my picture is of a woman lying on a bed in a darkened room. I feel that mother slept most of my early life away.

I was the fourth and final child, born when mother was thirty-one and aware my father had fallen in love with a younger woman, whom he eventually married. I felt mother did not want me, that I was an awful drag on her. That she couldn't cope with herself, much less me.

At times I even hated her. I felt suffocated by her. It took years before I could wear a turtle neck sweater or a scarf. Smother love, Philip Wylie called it in his book about mothers, *Generation of Vipers.*

My two older sisters remember chiefly the good about mother but I remember chiefly the depressed woman. They knew her in her happier days. I felt little rapport with her. I rarely talked *to* her or she to me. I never knew, with both her and my father, whether I was going to get hugged or kissed or screamed at. Mother never hit us but threatened us. She was not physically violent, just verbally abusive.

"God damn it!" she would scream in a voice of fury, which to a child means "I hate you!" When she touched me, I would cringe. Sometimes I felt she was a crazy lady. I also thought of her as frumpy, dowdy, unattractive. I understood how my father could have wanted a more beautiful, less depressed woman.

When mother was angry she looked ugly to me, though she had an attractive face when it was not distorted in fury—as it would be if any of us got in her way as she counted the laundry in the upstairs hall of our house.

Mother constantly threatened, "If you won't do this for me, I won't do that for you." It was the barter system. But she rarely carried out her threats. I don't remember being deprived of many pleasures. But often she frustrated me more than I could stand. She could be utterly unreasonable. It was always "No!" Negative. That was her attitude toward life. My father was outwardly the merry optimist, mother was the sad pessimist.

There were times I felt she did not have an ounce of rationality in her. She couldn't listen. She would hum or whistle when I tried to talk to her. Her life was ruled by the clock and if I wanted to go to bed five minutes later than she commanded, she turned on me with the shout or the scream as I felt she wiped me out completely.

I lived in the terror something was going to destroy me. Today, many years later, after therapy, I know I displaced my fear of mother on the rats that lived in the large attic above us. I had the fantasy they were running through the walls and might attack me, bite me and kill me. This was also, in fantasy, what I wanted to do to mother because of my fear and anger.

I knew I had been conceived merely to hold the marriage together. She did not say that to me but she told the other children who repeated it to me, and unconsciously, of course I knew it, *especially* because she did not put it into words. How could I help but know? The message got across in many subtle ways as I grew up. Each parent made me into the messenger to the other as they lived apart and did not speak. It was always bad news I was asked to transmit. Usually mother asked for money or Laurie made a demand for a divorce which at times she fought.

As an adult I wanted to change, I knew there was a better way to feel and to live. When my first marriage broke up I went to a psychoanalyst in Hollywood, Florida, then to another in New York when I moved there. The latter helped me look at my mother and father as objectively as I could. He freed me considerably from both as I slowly realized we four children had all felt miserable because our parents were so unhappy, especially mother. I am grateful that I believed there was a better way to live because I don't think too many people ever become aware of this.

One day in analysis I was crying because I thought I had treated mother abominably, cursing back at her when she screamed curses at me. My analyst reassured me the only way I could have survived her emotional illness was to fight back. Eddie was goodhumored about mother's anger, as though he didn't take her seriously but that's how he felt about life, his father's way much of the time.

Eddie was the first to escape mother, marrying when he went to college. I was envious, he was free of mother. Sue stayed by mother's side much of her life. She was able to tolerate mother more than the rest of us could. I was a dreadful daughter. I felt I didn't give mother anything.

Mother grew up blind to her childhood depression and her children and existed trying to survive her depression. I probably suffered the most—even before I was born mother knew she had lost her husband. I was her last hope, so to speak, and I failed to bring him back. I thought she hated me because of this failure. What with her earlier devastating loss of her mother, the loss of my father proved overwhelming and that was why she retreated to sleep much of the time, I thought.

Sue and I never got along well as children, I felt she hated me. Lucy was my good mother. She tried to rescue me from our mother's superpossessive touch. I remember Lucy taking my hand and leading me out of the house and down the street on my first walk away from mother. I adored Eddie as we all did.

During analysis I realized there *were* times I enjoyed mother. She had her merry moments. She was a very generous woman. She always welcomed my friends to the house. They have memories of mother smiling, dishing out mounds of chocolate cake, cookies and glasses of milk. No one ever went hungry in our house. My oldest and dear friend Ruth remembers mother as "Oreo cookies and chocolates."

I loved to shop with her for clothes—the one time I had her to myself and when she was cheerful. She took me to the theater. The first show I ever saw was Ethel Merman in *Red, Hot and Blue* in 1935. Mother also encouraged me to take ballet lessons, though I never made it up on my toes. I studied the piano too but not seriously.

Mother was not protective but overprotective of us. As for my father, I felt I didn't know him very well. He was out of the house so much when

I grew up. He spent most weekends on trips with the woman he later married, as he had been doing long before I was born. When I was nine, he moved out and after that he took me places for dinner Friday nights because he and mother fought so violently she withdrew her original offer to let him eat with the family once a week. We ate at exotic dining places, including the new La Guardia airport where I could see the planes fly in and out. Since then I have always loved flying.

I thought my father a vibrant, exciting person. He seemed as undepressed as my mother seemed depressed. At least on the surface. He occasionally took me out on his boat or asked me to lunch at the Williams Club in Manhattan.

As I look back, I don't think he really cared for me or any of his children very much. It wasn't that he left mother or had another woman but the way he flaunted the other woman in his family's face and used us children for his selfish ends. He didn't think of us as human beings. My analyst once said my father considered his children as little dolls he put up on a shelf and commanded to be quiet until he wanted to take us down when company came and show us off. God forbid we had a thought or a feeling or a need!

I both worshiped him and was terrified of him. Even when I was little, I thought he had a vicious streak. He would ask me to lie when Donna was along after promising mother she would not be. He would say, "Don't tell your mother." I obeyed but felt used and hated him for making me part of his deceit. I felt there was little integrity in him. I know he did this to the other children too.

I think what he did to Lucy was abusive. He took her on long trips with the other woman, made her part of the illicit conspiracy. She too had to lie to mother. Only Lucy knows what fantasies in her were aroused because she was so early in life drawn into the intimacy between my father and the other woman.

Like my brother, I married early, at nineteen, thinking the man would be my salvation. I left college in New London, Connecticut, over my father's strong objections. The marriage was shaky from the start. My husband had caught malaria while fighting with our troops in the South Pacific during World War II and that weakened him physically. Because of deep-seated emotional problems he was never able to hold a responsible, well-paying job.

But we had four children I brought up alone after thirteen years of marriage—if you can call it a marriage—when he left under the same circumstances my father left our house. I asked my husband to leave, as mother did my father. My husband soon married again, died at forty-nine from a heart attack.

When I became a mother my mother helped me out financially. I could not have made it without her support because my husband did not earn enough. Yet I was still angry at her in spite of her help. I felt she wasn't giving me what I really wanted, an understanding love and tenderness and respect. Somehow material gifts, while temporarily easing anger, do not make up for the underlying emotional deprivation.

I am thankful at least I had the ability to fight mother. Fight both her domination and later, through analysis, fight to change within. I never felt very happy as a child or adolescent, only in the last ten years. I think of happiness as the lack of psychic pain—my analysis certainly alleviated that pain.

Also thanks to the analysis, I finally made a happy marriage nine years ago to Warren Rosenberg, president of Warren Rosenberg Video Services, Inc. One night at a party (yes, it can happen), I met Warren, a widower. We were married a year and a half later. He never had children, loves mine, calls them his "family." We get along well in that we allow each other time to be separate. He enjoys golf and spends the sunny weekends (and sometimes the rainy ones) on courses with friends. That allows me to shop, go to movies he does not want to see, read, buy new flowers and plants for the terrace of our apartment. I work hard. I could never be idle all day as mother was.

My deep guilt about mother was somewhat eased when, in the last years of her life she came north and I found an apartment for her and her companion in the housing complex where I lived in White Plains. If she needed me, I was near at hand. My children constantly visited her, which I know she enjoyed.

Lucy says I also gave mother many more years to live because one day I discovered her in great pain and promptly called my doctor. He raced over, took a sample of her blood, then telephoned me from the hospital to say the test showed a dangerous high count of white corpuscles and she had to undergo at once an exploratory operation on her abdomen which, she had complained, hurt. Doctors discovered her gall bladder was filled with stones and severe peritonitis might have occurred shortly and killed her.

One day when I was tired of coping with the children, I said to mother in exasperation, "I wish my kids were grown up. Life would be much easier.''

Mother said thoughtfully, ''Don't wish the time away. They grow up so fast as is.''

I thought of her words many times over the years, especially after the four were out of the house and on their own. I realize now the childhood of children should be enjoyed by parents. Children should not be wished out of the way. Such a wish, incidentally, is transmitted to the child, who then feels he has no childhood, pushed prematurely into being an adult.

When mother died in Daytona I felt she had been dead for a long time. She had endured several years not aware of reality. She did not know who she was, where she was, who we were. When my father died I felt deep grief. I had adored him even though at times hated how he treated us.

Do I mourn mother? What does mourning mean? I feel guilty that I didn't do enough for her in the last years of her life. But Lucy and I did help her during the few years she returned to New York, as Sue did in the years mother lived with her. Lucy and I have remained close. We see each other often, shop together, share holiday dinners. She also loves my four children, never having had any of her own. We are there for each other if we feel in distress. I am also close to Eddie and his wife Dorothy, visit them once or twice a year.

All in all, we four probably did fairly well, given our unhappy parents. As Lucy points out, none of us became a delinquent, or a criminal, or ended up raving mad in a mental hospital or walks homeless on city streets—yet! So who has it perfect?

Thus my brother and two sisters hold vastly different feelings about our mother, as do I, mine are explored in this book. She was indeed a different mother to each. The emotional play between mother and child depended in part on what time in her life we were born, whether she was happy or depressed. Also her fears at the period of our birth, her relationship to Laurie at the time we were conceived, her wish to have or not to have that particular child. And her reaction to that child in terms of the fantasies, the wishes and the feelings the child aroused in her.

What she asked consciously and unconsciously of each of us differed. She asked me to be a substitute for the mother she lost so early in life. She asked Sally to hold her failing marriage together. Mother once told me she conceived Sally in a desperate attempt to keep our father, a mission no child could fulfill. Just as I could not serve as mother to my mother.

Parents ask children to live out their fantasies, carry out their desires, assign different ones to each child. One child may be asked to bring the parent the happiness he never knew with his parents. Another may be unconsciously and consciously asked to succeed in a career the parent had or did not have. A third may be the focus of the parent's sexual desires, never openly expressed but sensed in subtle ways. A fourth may become the object of the parent's violent feelings, expressed in sarcastic, cutting words or acts or both.

When our mother and father separated, then divorced, we differed on the reasons and which parent was to "blame." In one way or another we four have unconsciously repeated in our adult lives the marital breakup of our parents.

The fifth year of analysis was ending, I had started to accept my right to feel angry at injustice, the right to speak calmly when attacked unfairly in word or deed. To defend myself was not "hostile aggression." It was using assertion to protest against unwarranted psychic or bodily hurt.

I was allowed, nay encouraged on the couch, to feel murderous. To know I held and was entitled to hold fury in my heart and understand why becoming aware of it brought new freedom.

At long last some layers of my sugar sweetness were melting under the sensitive guidance of Dr. Aiken. He helped me understand the need to face the Vesuvius of vitriol I hid in my heart, perhaps from day one, if I wanted to feel less depressed, more in control of emotions.

That supersweetness held monumental anger, moments upon moments built up over the hypocritical years, then denied. As I slowly released it in his office I felt more humane, less a raging automaton. Now not quite so afraid of "hostile aggression."

What Freud called "aggression," if used wisely, did not lead to murder or mayhem. LaMarr Hoyt, pitcher for the National League in the All-Star game of July 15, 1984, once spoke of his pitching as "relaxed aggression." His words I now understood. Relaxation could reign when hostility was absent from the natural wish to win, not kill.

Dr. Aiken was willing to be the open target at whom I pitched words of sarcasm, self-pity and rage. He invited me to express all my thoughts, sacred and profane. Reach understanding of how much of my torment was caused by the fantasy I had to be a good little girl to win the love of parents who could never be pleased. My "cover" of sugary acceptance had stifled all rage.

Now I had to face something just as challenging as becoming aware of the unknown furies driving me. Ending analysis—all analysis—and going it on my own.

I thought of Dr. Emch's quotation from the Talmud, "If not now—when?"

12

The Courage
to Leave

One sparkling day in October 1981 I mustered the courage to mutter, "I suppose I should be thinking of ending analysis. It's almost the end of the fifth year."

I thought, It is time I stop leaning on someone else, I am tired of the complaining, depressed old me. I want to try steering my own psychic ship.

Silence. Which meant, Please speak on. Unlike the house in which I grew up where I sometimes heard the cruel "Shut up!"

I sighed, asked fearfully, "Do you think I can go it alone? Keep learning more about myself?"

Added hopefully, "Or do you believe I need more analysis?"

He uttered words that, ten months later, would give me the strength to leave the comfort of the couch. He said slowly, in that contained honest voice, "Some things you can only work out alone."

"I never thought of that." Wonder in my voice.

"You will not feel stronger if you remain in the analytic situation where the analyst represents the perpetual parent."

"I'll feel lonely." A complaint from the heart.

"We are all essentially alone," he said.

I had never thought of that, either. He was saying I would always have problems to solve, everyone does, but I could think effectively alone, no longer dependent on him or anyone else.

Each of us ends up essentially alone, even in marriage. Each of us in the long run has to depend on the self for answers. To depend on anyone else only crippled me.

"When do you think I should stop analysis?" I regressed to a whisper at this horrifying thought.

"How about when I go on vacation this summer?" he suggested.

I sighed again. This was the day of sighs, as though my very breath were leaving me. For the past year, because of temporary decrease in finances, I saw him only once a week. I now wondered if this were my way of slowly parting, a way unconsciously chosen so the final hours would not feel so disastrous.

I confessed, "The thought of leaving you, of no more analysis, makes me feel blue."

"You speak of the end of analysis and the end of seeing the analyst as the same thing," he said. "Analysis goes on within you even if you do not see an analyst."

I had never thought of being my own analyst. That was a heartening idea. Reach insights, become aware of buried feelings and fantasies, all by my own wits.

He went on, "You speak of analysis at times as though it were the Bible. As if anything valid in the Bible came from psychoanalysis. Freud took some important truths from the Bible as he devised the science of psychoanalysis."

Despite my panic at the thought of leaving Dr. Aiken, part of me felt challenged at the idea of making it on my own, imperfect and emotionally crippled though I might feel at times. Perhaps analysis was like weaning, you had to give up something you believed vital to your life to progress to thoughts and acts that gave you new power.

I comforted myself remembering the first day I lay down on the couch and dared feel fear of the unknown. But also strange excitement. As though about to embark on a sail to what Freud called "the far country." I hoped to emerge happier from the daring experience. I felt, too, a glimmer of courage in undertaking this perhaps perilous voyage to inner space.

Now the captain of the current ship was forsaking me and I felt stricken. Abandoned and alone in a hostile universe. I wrote a note to myself, headed "The Beloved Prison":

> I have gone from one prison to the next. First the prison where my mother was the jailor who fed me, clothed me, housed me but restricted freedom and independence of spirit. I could not wait to escape that prison, believing I had entered the haven of newspaper reporting. Only to discover another prison, one of daily deadlines and sometimes tyrannical editors. I escaped into what I believed the bliss of marriage, only to find the worst prison of all when it came to emotional torment. I just kept exchanging one prison for another.

The process of analysis would go on, Dr. Aiken assured me, even though he no longer was personally a part of my life. My analytic journey into the unconscious at regular weekly hours on the couch in his office would now take place at irregular hours in any position and on any piece of furniture I chose. Or on a train or high in a plane where I often allowed thoughts to flow.

I practiced "listening" to my thoughts as Dr. Aiken listened to my words, relating what I was thinking to a fantasy, wish or conflict of the past—all in preparation for the frightening future when I would have only myself to consult.

I was aware I owed much to analysis. When friends sneered, "How can you put all your money into lying on the couch?" I answered, "It's the best investment I could make."

We all endure lives of quiet desperation, according to Thoreau. Some lives are not so quiet, though they may appear serene on the surface. Mouths shape to emit screams of pain though the cries never coalesce. I am no longer amazed when a young man reported in the newspapers and on television as suddenly murdering his mother or father or even both is described by neighbors or relatives as "such a nice, obedient, quiet boy, always willing to help others."

Over the years on the couch I felt despair turn into anger, muted at first, then at times reaching a crescendo until it threatened to explode. I knew the release revealed part of the pain of childhood. If I remained choked by stifled cries, how could I know the peace that comes with knowledge of the inner self?

I learned to speak the unspeakable. Know the unknowable. Face the warfare within. The tormenting voices became whispers, then disappeared. The freeze of depression lost its capacity to lull me into catatonia. Doubt of the self no longer pulverized my spirit. As though I now urged, "Out, out damned thoughts," damned because my parents decreed them bad, obscene, evil.

At long last I knew that if I were not able to separate from the analyst, I would never emotionally separate from my parents, even though both were dead. I
had to go through the separation from Dr. Aiken and
accept the agony it brought as part of facing the truth
of my psychic bondage. Separation is hard when you
have not started it at the time you are supposed to, five
or six months of age. It is far more difficult decades
later.

With all the aplomb I could muster I would separate
from the analyst, something I had never been able to do
successfully from either parent. But at least a few
months lay ahead to prepare for the last grim hours.

During a November session I told him, "The
thought of leaving you makes me think of the day my
father was ordered out of the house and did not return.
I saw him after that almost until the day he died, seventeen years later. But it was never the same. He seemed
somewhat of a stranger."

A sigh, then, "The idea of separation from you
brings out the feelings of loss I felt the day Laurie left.
I was bereft but didn't know it."

"You also didn't know your anger," Dr. Aiken said.
"Both at your father for creating a situation that forced
your mother to ask him to leave and at your mother for
ejecting him."

I moaned, "And, oh my guilt!"

"You felt you were to blame because as a little girl
you wanted your father all to yourself, but another
woman now had him. You hated her, too."

"I adored her!" I protested. "She loved me. Shopped
with me. Treated me as a friend, her equal. Showed me
how to put on lipstick and rouge. Told me I was pretty.
I, the black sheep of the family, with a blond brother and
two red-headed sisters."

"You grew up too quickly, you had too much to cope

with," he said. "You missed part of your adolescence and are still living through it."

He was saying the child within took on responsibilities too early, the ability to enjoy adolescent play cut short by the war between parents. A dream that night proved him correct.

I dreamed a child protested, "I was rushed too much. I was always rushed." As though responding to Dr. Aiken.

I had been rushed into becoming an adult by a mother unable to cope with her husband and four children. I displayed this "rushedness" in newspaper work as I dashed out to cover a story, raced back to write it. I also rushed to eat, rushed to parties, rushed to leave them and rushed through sex, rushed into marriage and out of it. And now felt rushed again through this period of preparing to separate from the analyst. Not enough time to complete what had to be done, think what had to be thought that would enable me to go it alone.

Dr. Aiken said, "Life in your house as you grew up was a soap opera. The way you speak of the situation with your father, mother, the other woman and yourself is like an addiction to drama."

"Addiction to trauma." Sarcastically.

But I knew what he meant—I dramatized events beyond all reality, blamed the drama for my suffering. Drama was part of the psychic picture but far from the whole of it. And yet, I wondered, did I not dramatize because I saw it as the only escape from what I thought the often cruel reality of childhood?

Tennessee wrote in his *Journals*, as his official biographer, Lyle Leverich, reveals in his book *Tom: The Young Tennessee Williams*, that if he could no longer write, he wished to die. The drama of his plays told of the trauma of his life, kept him from suicide.

Dr. Aiken added, referring to my need for drama,

what I thought insult to injury. He said, "You needed similar drama in your later life. You would think it dull to be married and bring up children."

"Not dull. Drab," I snapped.

"You wouldn't want a stable, quiet man." He sounded as though he had a twinkle in his eye.

I said not a word, I felt he was right, even though it was a psychic stab to the heart. I *had* looked on life as both one long party and one long mourning, with me center stage.

Finally I said defensively, "I have always felt inferior and submissive. I feel I possess little sense of what analysts call 'the unified self.' Is that why I dramatized?"

"You copied your father, your hero. He was the one who dramatized."

"Both parents dramatized, each in his own way." Thoughtfully.

"And you use analysis to keep up the addiction of drama." His voice was not accusative but informative. He wanted to help me understand the reasons for my reluctance to give up the couch—I was dramatizing that, too.

I had never thought of being addicted to analysis, or to drama but I could no longer deny the truth. I had been addicted to both, wished to be. I had used analysis to keep dramatizing my soap-opera life as I unreeled episodes of it session by session.

I had taken in emotionally my father's dramatic life, romantically and professionally—his arguing of cases in the highest courts as well as his always exciting personal life, his becoming for a short moment legal champion of a gangster, Frank Costello.

As reporter, my existence had been as dramatic as a woman could hope to live. Racing forth every day to cover an exciting story, rushing back to the city room to write it in as many eloquent words as I could summon under pressure. Always in fear of the guillotine of the deadline. My books were dramas, the true story of the life of a murderer in Chicago. The trauma of a young woman seduced by her New York psychiatrist, which became a two-hour film on NBC. The biography of Bertha Pappenheim ("Anna O.," as Freud and Breuer called her), the twenty-one-year-old woman in Vienna in 1881 who was hysterical and hallucinatory as her father lay dying, later fantasied a pregnancy with Breuer as the father.

I grew up in a world that seemed a whirlwind, tossing me from one emotional tempest to the next as anxiety swept the house. When I entered the quiet of Bennington College, it was like putting into port. After graduation the whirlwind rose around me again and once more I felt a strange security. The calm was the torment.

Dr. Aiken helped me understand Mother's temper tantrums, which alternated with sweetness and generosity. This cacophony of contrasting emotions formed an unbeatable combination to create chaos in the mind of a child.

As the new year unfolded in January, a year that within six months would bring the end of analysis, I asked Dr. Aiken, "Is it true that good parents, those fairly at peace with themselves, who do not need to inflict verbal cruelty or violence or neglect on a child, give the child enough love and care so he can build a strong sense of self? Whereas 'bad' parents keep the child in emotional bondage?"

Silence. Then he deigned to say, "I don't know what you mean by 'good' and 'bad.' Some parents are very seductive and give the child the illusion they will always be there for him. This also prevents the child from separating."

I described a dream in which I searched for my mother, needing her desperately. "She had disappeared, did not even leave her telephone number," I said in a sad voice. "There was no way to reach her. I said to myself, Your mother is dead, you cannot find her, you are alone in the world and frightened out of your wits."

"It is as though if there is nobody to care about you, you cannot care about yourself," Dr. Aiken said.

Somehow that angered me. It hit too near the truth. As I marched out of the session I thought, I *don't* need him, I can get along fine without him, fuck him. Knowing the "fuck" meant anger. The day before, walking along the street, I heard one of two young white women in front of me say to the other, "So I told him 'What do you think I am, a super motherfucker?' " Now I wanted to say to Dr. Aiken "fuck you" when he pointed out I still needed my mother.

He was in a sense (speaking to my unconscious?) calling me a "motherfucker" because I was unable to separate emotionally from her, which meant my infantile sexual desire still focused on her. She was not an "appropriate sex object," as analysts say.

I began to realize I was learning the language of the unconscious. The words are not always pretty but they are right on the beam if you wish to explore the lower depths of your mind that have caused pain—the deepest psychic shit, you might say. But the deepest shit uncovers shining truth that will free you from the need to deny hidden impulses and wishes.

One of the most difficult tasks was to admit sexual feelings toward Dr. Aiken. Intellectually I accepted the Oedipal conflict, though the thought of wishing as a little girl to have sex with my father was anathema. Nice little girls do not hold such wishes. But during the natural development of the sexual drive, they do, loudly though we may deny this in adulthood.

Only as I could face and feel sexual wishes for Dr. Aiken could I understand they belonged originally to my yearning for my father. I knew, though I did not voice it at first, there were moments I felt like holding Dr. Aiken close, kissing him passionately on the lips, feeling his body close to mine. The way I felt to far lesser degree, since my sexual yearnings were not yet that intense, as a child with my father. And earlier, when the feelings were even less intense, with my mother.

The acceptance of the power of sexual, as well as aggressive feelings, occurs so slowly it is imperceptible at first to the conscious mind. As I now knew well, nothing proceeds at a fast pace in psychoanalysis. This is why it takes so long. You only accept dammed-up sexual desires and anger little by little, in minute doses.

This is true of all learning but particularly learning about the inner self because our defenses against awareness are so powerful. I understood an interpretation one minute, lost understanding the next. It took years to admit that as a little girl and adult I wanted my father sexually and wished my mother dead and gone. One reason it is difficult for those who have never been analyzed to accept the theory of the Oedipal conflict is the lack of time they have had to become acquainted with their feelings about this number one taboo. Though not so powerful a taboo, it would appear, judging by statistics in our country on the number of fathers who have sexually attacked small daughters and sons.

At first I scoffed at the preposterous notion I wanted to kill my mother and marry my father when I was a little girl of four. Or that when I was a baby the yearnings for my mother's breast held the stirring of a sexuality that would later lead to desire for a man. This is nature's way of trying to make sure we continue the human race.

But now no more mother. No more analyst. I would

be my own caretaker. I asked silently, Can I live without you, dear analyst, no one to listen to my traumatic, dramatic tales? If only I could stretch out in your exotic, erotic lair forever. And heard his reply, Ah, more of your drama.

All those "if only's"—if only this, if only that. I recalled Dr. Mack saying, "You cannot live by the 'if's.' "

I could accept my dependency on my mother and father only as I accepted my dependency on Dr. Aiken. Part of me had remained a yearning, screaming, angry baby wanting someone to take care of me. Jesus, I thought (little Jesus in the manger), this is hardly the road to self-esteem—if nobody listened, I did not exist, I *had to be heard.* When my mother refused to listen, this was the cruelest psychic cut of all. When I wanted her to see my point of view but she sang popular songs to drown out my pleading words, it nearly drove me crazy. As though she obliterated me from the universe.

I confessed to Dr. Aiken as one session drew to a close, "There will be no one to listen to me after I leave you. I feel emotionally destitute at the thought you won't be part of my life."

How can that be? I wondered. Me, the loner, who built her life believing she needed no one. A devastating denial. When my mother had asked, after my second marriage tottered, if I would move to Florida and live with her, I had replied, "I couldn't, Mother. It would end in matricide." Actually, I needed her desperately at that lonely moment in my life, about to divorce Tom and no steady job. But I feared if I lived that intimately with her, my unreal demands would explode. We would devour each other, psychic cannibals.

I now knew that whenever I felt rejected this fear was automatically followed by a burst of activity—the need to write, play tennis, golf, poker or bridge. Avoid at any cost the crippling depressions that were my mother's way of responding to humiliation and loss.

I knew now why men and women sometimes threaten, then murder the person about to abandon them. YOU WILL *NOT* LEAVE ME, I WILL KILL YOU RATHER THAN LET YOU GO. The baby's reaction as he screams his lungs out at the vanished mother he desperately needs or he will die. Starve to death or drown in urine.

I asked Dr. Aiken, "How will I know what to do when I have important decisions to make?"

"Decide for yourself, even if you are wrong," he said. "We learn from our mistakes."

This was a welcome new thought. It was not a deadly crime to make an error, something I never heard growing up. My parents not once admitted they were wrong or apologized if they were. They always had to be right and I always had to be right. Mistakes were not permitted, imperfections brought scorn, sarcasm, sometimes punishment. All my life I asked the opinion of others, not daring to venture the wrong one. As a reporter my daily life focused on questioning the famous, writing down their answers as though I had no mind of my own. My father and mother loved me when I was the submissive little girl.

I truly trusted no one. I asked Dr. Aiken one morning, "Can I trust you to know when I should end analysis?"

"Trust yourself," he said.

I started to learn to trust myself through trusting him. By accepting his many wise words relating to my distorted image of myself and my parents. The Bible says, "The wicked flee when no man pursueth," and I proved that statement. I had been fleeing fantasies from the moment I could fashion one.

I heard myself wail, the baby again, "How can I

trust you? You are ejecting and rejecting me." I felt he was saying, Out, out, damned patient.

"Separation is not rejection." Kindly tone.

"Will I be able to carry on by myself?"

"You may be so angry at me at first you will deny it."

I had recently read in a psychoanalytic article that one way patients show anger at analysts is by refusing to accept the analysis is successful. They do not want to grant the analyst the pleasure of knowing he has succeeded in the difficult task of helping them face the pain within.

Then he said the magic words: "You can return any time you wish a session."

"Thank you." Quietly. "I wanted to hear you say that. Even if I don't take you up on it. I didn't want to ask. To be once again the little girl beggar."

After a session I would often head, as I did this dismal day, for the solace of Sedutto butterscotch ice cream, my favorite, next to chocolate. I never chose a chicken or tuna sandwich but chocolate cake and ice cream because they acted so effectively as chemical antidotes to my psychic pain. In childhood, ice cream served to ease moments of loneliness or as reward for hard work. As an adult, I often treated myself to half a pint after eight hours of typing.

I thought of what one analyst wrote: "Separation starts with the first analytic hour." Separation is a ghost that haunts every moment of the analysis in an unconscious and sometimes conscious sense. It looms as an everpresent threat but when it occurs it is a sign of new courage and deeper understanding of the self if you accept its pain.

My analysis revived all the separations with which I never emotionally dealt—the early deaths of my two grandmothers, the later deaths of my father, mother,

Dr. Emch. Plus all the feelings of separation inherent in the loss of a friend and, in my case, the loss of working at the *Times*, where I enjoyed many friends.

"Oh, the sadness of it all!" I cried out to an empty room one warm May day, Virgil's tormented words, *Lacrimae rerum*, "the tears of things," from *The Aeneid*. Then in muffled tone, "And oh, the rage within."

I had a daring dream (time for the ending drawing near) in which I gave birth to a baby son by Dr. Aiken (*that* would keep him by my side). I wanted him to be everything—analyst, lover, husband, father, mother, brother and sister. Why a son? Was I afraid a daughter would face the same trauma I had experienced and by having a boy I could spare him that pain?

I told Dr. Aiken, "I feel like I did when my father died and I thought, What's the use of living? Who will love me now?"

He blew his nose. He rarely blew his nose unless he had a cold. I thought, My words have moved him, maybe he will miss me a little, or perhaps I reminded him of the death of someone he loved and he feels like crying, it is difficult for men to cry.

He said, "As you end analysis, remember you are still looking for the good mother."

"My mother will always be with me," I announced. "Dr. Joseph Sandler talks of the eternal 'dialogue with the ghost mother.' One that goes on in our minds until we die." Sandler, a famous British psychoanalyst, mentioned this in a paper he gave at the International Congress of Psycho-Analysis in New York in 1976. He referred to the phantom world within us all, a world we never leave as far as our mother is concerned, though a mother's voice grows fainter and fainter as we come to depend more on our own voice. I thought sadly of the homeless on our streets who often engage in loud angry arguments with the "ghost" mother hidden within.

Mourning streamed out of me during those last analytic days. First, for my mother, as I recalled all the times I believed I hurt her. Once when I apologized for defending my father so staunchly she said softly, "Your father charmed you as he did everyone. It was not your fault," and I loved her more deeply for understanding and forgiving.

I mourned the children I never had. I recalled a dream in which my niece Dale was taken from my arms as I protested, "But she belongs to me!" Unconsciously I felt she did. I loved her dearly from the moment I first held her on my lap at the age of eleven months under shady trees in Daytona. I now realized she was born at the time I suffered the agony of a second abortion. In my unconscious Dale became the daughter I never had. Sally was only surrogate mother.

The time with Dr. Aiken grew less and less—dear Freud, would I live through the lonely years ahead? I dreamed I was alone in a pitch-black apartment as bombs fell, the world about to end.

I told him, "I'd like to write the biography of Jack Nicholson. There has been no authorized one. I have a burning love for him. I also think he's a great actor. He portrayed a writer slowly going mad in *The Shining*, a brilliant book by Stephen King. Nicholson gave a sterling performance that chilled my heart. But when I wrote his agent, he never answered."

I thought, Nicholson's charm and openly sarcastic manner are much like Laurie's and he often portrays unfaithful men. Is it any wonder I love him?

Dr. Aiken was saying in that thoughtful voice, "And you, a writer, feel you are slowly going mad, burning with love for me and shortly to be rejected."

"Right on the nose." Sarcastically.

It had taken years to mention this "burning" love though I sometimes hinted obtusely at it, knowing, of course, he realized I was transferring my love for my father onto his staunch shoulders.

One night, watching the PBS film on the life of Lady Astor, I heard her son ask his father, who had remarried, "Did you love my mother?" This was exactly what I had asked my father a few years after he remarried. He had answered, "Yes, I did." I had not dared follow it up with my thought, Then why were you unfaithful?

Now I knew why he had been unfaithful. It had to do with both him and Mother and their unreal expectations of each other. It was also connected to his passion—before he became engaged to Mother—for the beautiful blond Lily his parents forbid him to marry because she was not Jewish. Donna was a beautiful blond and Catholic. He finally tasted revenge on his controlling mother and father.

I also wondered if my father had married my mother not only because she was young and beautiful but for the money he knew she would inherit from the Prince estate. If he did, he never received a penny. But he did not have to support her and us for long because after Grumpy and Granny died Mother lived on her inheritance, graciously accepted his plea that he could not afford to give her more money.

My dear aunt, Helen Prince, whom I have loved since a little girl, my only living relative in the older generation, recently said, alluding to her many ailments, "I accept." In her ninety-third year, she has accepted her life and limitations.

I asked myself, Do I accept the emotional turmoil in which I grew up and the later pain, physical and emotional, of the abortions, feeling I murdered two children? Work has always been my solace, replacement of all I have lost over the years. But will that now be enough without analysis?

I told Dr. Aiken, "I mourn the end of analysis as though it were the death of a parent."

"It is not the same," he said.

"Why not?" A demand.

"You didn't choose your parents."

"You mean I chose to end the analysis?"

"Didn't you?"

Grudgingly, "Yes. I brought it up."

It was only in *this* analysis that I came to grips with my mourning and rage at the loss of loved ones, though perhaps the others slowly prepared me to do so. I heard a speaker at one analytic meeting say the failure of children to "work through the necessary grief" associated with losses represents "a major predisposition to adult depression." Children are not allowed to grieve following a loss, be it a parent who leaves the house, the death of a beloved grandmother or a cherished dog. One of the curative acts in analysis, this speaker concluded, is "to do effective grief work. Analysts who cannot stand the tears of patients have not worked through their own grief and thus cannot help the patient face his."

I told Dr. Aiken of this paper. He said, "You are mourning me before I die."

"I am mourning as you toss me out," I retorted.

"You feel I'm throwing you out as if you were garbage."

"Garbage, garbage," I repeated mechanically.

Tears came to my eyes. "I feel like garbage at times. I remember Laurie calling me 'little stinker' when he was angry."

Over the years I kept a few of my childhood scribblings. I dug them out, found my first short story written in pencil at the age of ten. It described how a young daughter murdered her father's best friend, the mayor—obviously my father. I killed him not once but three times—shot him, poisoned him, strangled him—to make sure he was dead. This occurred when I first became aware he had fallen in love with Donna.

Yet I turned to my father as savior. I felt I survived because, in spite of occasional cruelty in words and deeds, he also gave what I believed love, affection and solace as well as excitement to life. Mother in contrast seemed cold. She rarely touched me, held me close, seemed afraid to show love.

When I refused to live with her I felt ashamed and guilty. I feared she would suffocate me emotionally, this mother who named me Saint Lucy, Santa Lucia, the virgin martyr and patron saint of light. I could not save my mother though I earnestly tried to find her a new husband.

At times I thought of my mother as a combination Lucretia Borgia, Medea and Medusa. One moment she engulfed me, the next, acted as though I were not there.

Now I thought, If only I were a more interesting patient—not so much like my mother, less depressed, anxious, unlovable—Dr. Aiken would not want to terminate analysis. He would insist I stay on and on, perhaps to the end of my life.

But he had been successful enough so I knew I was only rationalizing. He wanted me to gain the strength that arose only from going it alone.

13

The Final Hour

It was the darkest of days even as the late morning sun warmed my face. I sat dejectedly on the forest-green wooden bench backed against Central Park.

I was headed for the final hour. There was no escape.

Early as always, I stared across the street at the windows of the room in which he worked, the room in which I poured out my passions and hatreds. Parting is such sweet sorrow even when you know you will see a loved one tomorrow, I thought, but this is sour grief. At the end of this session I will be cut off from him forever.

The night before I hardly slept, thought of him alternately as the man I loved and that "bum." The sneering put-down my father hurled at men he did not like and boys with whom I fell in love.

At the previous session I spewed out, not knowing why, "Time wounds all heels," quoting the humor of a friend, Harold Masur, noted mystery writer.

Dr. Aiken had said, "I'm the heel in your life you now wish wounded."

I hated him and I loved him, that I knew. Hated him as I transferred to his handsome head childhood hatred of my mother and father. Loved him realistically for helping free me from much torment of the past. Loved him unrealistically as I transferred to him the love I felt for my father and mother.

I sighed. Aware reality drew near, the reality of my final hour. It was time to brave the saddest session.

My hour started at 11:00. It was now 10:50. I slowly stood up, thought, Goodbye, faithful bench, I may never sit on you again. For a moment I fantasied walking against the light on Central Park West. Perhaps a speeding car would strike and kill me, my blood splashing directly in front of his home, soon to be forbidden territory. But stalwartly I waited for the traffic light to turn green, grit my teeth, marched head high across the avenue.

Faithful Louis, who always greeted me with a warm smile, kept me up on the latest baseball news, reported, "The Mets are still out of first place, Miss Lucy." He was an ardent Dodgers fan, though the team had long forsaken Brooklyn for Los Angeles.

I shrugged my shoulders. "What does winning matter, Louis? They're playing good baseball." Knew I gave the pep talk to myself. I felt a loser, thrown out by my analyst but determined to play the analytic game as best I could without him, the star pitcher.

I walked into the waiting room as though to face a firing squad led by Freud. Who was kidding whom about wishing to be full of courage and gaining that amorphous sense of identity?

I slammed myself down on the chair I had occupied so long it seemed to belong to me. I thought of the recent hour in which I had wailed to Dr. Aiken, alluding to my two wretched marriages, "Why doesn't the passion of love last?" As though now all love would end, at least mine for him (because he was throwing me out). I did not know what he felt for me, probably relief I was leaving. Though I did think he cared that I continue by myself knowing the unconscious ever more deeply.

He had replied to my question as to why passionate love did not endure, one of the rare times he answered a theoretical query, "Because of ambivalence."

Ambivalence, that great despoiler of love. As you become more intimately involved with the one for whom you have felt that first passionate attachment, you also become more aware, in horror, of his weaknesses and frailties. Hate may overwhelm love if you do not accept ambivalence as natural, a feeling you cannot avoid. You have had it from the day you opened your mouth to take in those precious first breaths.

As I waited for the door to the sanctum for lost souls to open, I pulled out work from my tote bag, black, naturally. Something about Dr. Aiken's waiting room always inspired me to write away.

Instead, I looked sadly around as though to imprint everything forever in memory. The abstract painting of a woman's face, divided into two sections, one natural, the other, dark and disordered. The three Japanese prints. The posters of the Picasso and Degas art shows. The tall mirrored mahogany stand for coats and hats of winter. The table between chairs that held *The New Yorker* and a yachting magazine (did he own a boat?) among others.

Suddenly "the" door opened and the patient who now preceded me, a gray-haired, slim, never-smiling man sauntered out. Dr. Aiken stood on his side of the door. As usual, a welcoming smile on his bearded face, the expressive brown eyes, as always, reassuring.

Final session, final session. Like the beat of the jungle tom-toms as they played the last requiem. Jungle was the word for my unconscious. A part of the self both friend and foe, the latter, if you did not know what lay buried in it. The unconscious became more of a friend as you faced the unreal fears and distorted fantasies that thrived on your primitive impulses like leeches on the flesh of a naked body. The muck within, as I sometimes thought of it.

For my last session I wore black—silk pants drawn tight at the ankles in the new fashion and silk tunic—to honor this especially funereal moment. I lowered my dark-clad self, outer and inner, to my beloved brown leather couch, I would spend only fifty minutes before it, too, vanished forever from my life. Placed my head squarely on the white paper towel, feet gingerly on the small beige rug to protect the celestial couch from the dirt of Manhattan streets.

Silence. Usual for the start of my session.

I floundered for words. Suddenly there came to mind something I had said the day before in answer to a question asked by Dr. Jane Simon, a young psychiatrist and friend. She and I had attended a cocktail party held as part of the Annual Symposium of the New York Center for Psychoanalytic Training, founded by Reuben Fine, author of *A History of Psychoanalysis* and *The Intimate Hour* (often I wished mine had been more intimate).

I said to Dr. Aiken, after describing the cocktail party, "I told Jane, 'I am finally ending my analysis.' In both a victorious and defeated tone, if that is possible."

Drew a deep breath, continued, "She asked sympathetically, knowing well my plight, 'And now what will you do?' "

I fell silent, dare I tell him my answer? It might put him in a fury. I would not want my last hour to end in a display of rage by him. (Ah, hah, projection, I thought, always projection, watch it, Lucy.)

First I explained, as though in advance extenuation, "We were both on our second glass of wine."

No comment from behind the couch, there usually was not, this early in the session.

I wondered if I should go on, then thought, What can he do to me now? This is my final hour and he will not want my mutilated body found sprawled on his couch.

I swallowed fear, said, "I answered Jane, 'I'm going to kill the son of a bitch!' "

Silence, of course.

Suddenly I thought, Was this a deeply buried wish to kill my father when he abandoned us by leaving Mother?

I did not voice the thought but went on, "I was afraid Jane might be shocked but she roared in laughter. I laughed nervously."

Then I lay in silence and agony, thought, He is furious, I have never called him anything so obscene. But I had to take the risk, he was the one person in my life who encouraged me to speak of all emotions connected to him. He represented the childhood targets of my erotic love and flaming hatred, whose influence I was now trying to understand and accept rather than vehemently deny.

I awaited his next words, knowing ninety percent of the time they never came, he only wished me to speak on. So I added an apology, my mark in psychic trade, "I didn't mean what I said, of course! It was the two glasses of wine. Liquor always eases the way for obscenity."

I expected retaliation. Perhaps muted accusation of ingratitude for all he had done for me, as voices in my past would have proclaimed.

But instead, he said quietly, "As you near the end of your analysis you are able to express more of your rage at me. I thank you for this gift."

Tears came to my eyes. Instead of loathing me, he praised me for daring to reveal murderous wishes toward him. This gave me the courage to spew forth even more rage.

I announced, almost proudly, "I just wrote an article titled *Thirteen Ways to End Analysis.*" It took four rewrites—two day's work, time far better spent on something likely to sell, but a powerful force within drove me to dare it.

Silence. He was waiting, perhaps eagerly?

I plunged onward, down the trail of inner anger. "I started the article saying it was sent to me anonymously with a scribbled note that read: 'Am reluctantly concluding a long analysis. In desperation I have compiled thirteen ways to end analysis. I hope they may prove helpful to those who feel equally unhappy when they must give up a relationship that holds pain and yet brings a pleasure of the kind I never knew—acquaintance with the dimly sensed part of the self that has been causing misery.'"

I waited for his approval. There was only that cursed silence. He could at least have asked, "Why do you think you chose the number thirteen?" But he did not have to ask, thirteen was an unlucky number according to ancient sages, it was also the day of the month on which I was born, which I sometimes thought lucky, sometimes unlucky.

I shrugged my shoulders, as best one can on the couch. "I can't remember all the ways I described but one suggested murdering the analyst with a kitchen knife. I added that shooting was probably the easiest way but not a very practical one because you were bound to be caught when the noise of the gun was heard and prison was not conducive to increasing self-esteem, which is why you went into analysis."

I remembered a second way. "Commit suicide. This is a quick, decisive method of getting off the couch. You are telling him you were not ready to tackle the 'world of reality' as he unctuously put it. Unless you wish to consider a less self-destructive revenge, such as going to a behavioral therapist, which will make him gnash his beautiful white teeth to a pulp."

And a third: "Join a convent or monastery. That will tell him what you think of psychoanalysis. You can now transfer to God your feelings of idolatry, plus the hidden hatred that seethes beneath, which you bestowed on the analyst. And it won't cost a cent."

A fourth: "Display urethral and anal frustration. Go into the patient's bathroom, plug up the basin, turn on the water and start a small flood. Then scatter toilet paper all over the room, ditto the paper towels. Write in lipstick (borrow one, if you are a man) across the mirror, 'Fuck You.' This is called 'wet revenge' and he will toss you right out for regressing not in words but deeds, as too 'borderline' to treat." (Was I acting out the fantasy of the young Chicago murderer William Heirens when he scrawled in lipstick the desperate plea, "Catch me before I kill more"?)

A fifth: "Take notes. This will absolutely drive him crazy. He will have no alternative but to end it all. *He* may take notes occasionally but you are forbidden to do anything but lie there and suffer. Take down your every word and his. He will ask, 'What are you doing?' You will say, 'I am only identifying with you,' for which he will have no answer, for this is one of the purposes of analysis, to 'identify' with the good analyst and thus recover from the 'bad' parents of infancy."

I said, with a sigh, "I remember only one more. The last one. I titled it 'Walk Gently Out of That Dark Office.' Decide you have had enough of emotionally depending on someone else, no matter how wise and helpful, and that you want to make it on your own, imperfect and psychically crippled as you still may be. You have to give up the wish to merge with the strong, understanding, empathic analyst, as you once wished to merge with your mother and try to be somewhat independent at long last. *You* know you have changed for the better though he will give you no praise. Onward and upward into the realm of reality. With thanks to the sensitive, brilliant, understanding person who sat behind the couch lo these many years and tried his best to help you slowly enter that nonmagical stage of emotional development called maturity."

He spoke, words he uttered when I referred to him as a "son of a bitch." He said, reassuringly, "Again I am glad you are able to express your anger at me."

Even then I had to apologize. "You know I love you dearly. Even if it is 'transference' love."

Silence, which meant, carry on with the words. Over the years I described a number of dreams in which obviously I was trying to seduce him or he was seducing me. One recurring dream pictured us in the act of intercourse. I was aware I found him attractive, wished consciously he would take me in his arms, make love, kiss me passionately. The nearest to a touch I ever received was the friendly handshake when we parted for the summer—Freud said this was not a seductive act, though to me it was—it was all I had.

Once I said to him in a burst of insight, "I can wish to marry you and know this is totally unrealistic but still possess the wish. Is that right?"

"Yes," he said. "The reality is different from the fantasy."

In so many realms, I thought, chiefly those of love and hate.

I told him, in apology, "I know I regressed when I fantasied throwing toilet paper all over your bathroom and writing 'Fuck You!' on the mirror in lipstick."

He said approvingly, "But you didn't regress in deeds, just words."

"The only suggestion I *really* meant," lying a bit through my clenched teeth (aware he knew it), "was 'Walk Gently Out of That Dark Office.' " Added, in case he was ignorant of modern poetry, "It's a paraphrase of Dylan Thomas's 'Do not go gentle into that good night.' "

I mused, "As I recalled the line, at first I thought of it as 'Do not go gentle into that *dark* night." Telling him life without him looked black and bleak.

"You think of the end of analysis as death," he said.

I felt pleasure knowing I had arrived at this insight before he mentioned it. Needed that small victory to prepare for the lonely days ahead.

I sighed once again. "I am trying to accept, as seen in this last suggestion, that I cannot spend the rest of my life dependent on you. Or any other analyst. As I have done so many years. I must try life on my own." Sarcastically, "Imperfect and emotionally crippled as I still may be."

I had run out of breath and thoughts. He was quiet as a big gray mouse (sometimes in winter he wore gray tweeds). I winced, thought, Full speed ahead into the maze of reality with the best of grace I am able to muster in the face of imminent psychic disintegration.

There was now silence on both our parts. I knew he wished me to speak on.

I judged about ten minutes remained. "Time left for a dream?" Baitingly, "It's the last dream of mine you'll ever hear."

Knowing he would not answer, I pressed onward. "I dreamed last night that some strange woman ordered me to clean up a couch I had dirtied. She said I must wipe my lipstick off it.''

I embarked on thoughts needed to understand the deeper meaning of the dream. ''The couch must be this one, the one I am leaving forever, the one I feel I have dirtied with my head and feet and sordid thoughts. I feel I have to clean it up for the next patient. Get rid of the traces of my lipstick.''

''Like the end of an illicit affair,'' he said.

I joked, ''I feel more like your mother than an appropriate sex object, as they say in the analytic world.''

I knew he would not comment on this pseudo-attack on sex and his profession. Enough dalliance. On to more serious matters, given this special moment in my life.

I said thoughtfully, ''I don't want to go to my grave on the couch.''

Do I really mean this? I wondered. Did these brave words come from weak little me, does part of me want to try it alone?

I added hastily, wishing to keep his friendship, or whatever it was he felt for ex-patients, ''I'll never forget you.''

''Are you afraid I will forget you?''

I laughed, his words evoked a memory, one that confirmed what he said. ''About seven years ago at a party at an analyst's home, the wife of a well-known analyst told me she had once met her analyst at a party three years after she ended analysis. She greeted him warmly. He looked at her blankly, said, 'I'm sorry but I don't remember your name.' Not one to take rejection lightly, she snapped, 'I'll turn the back of my head to you, maybe that will help you remember,' and stalked off.''

I stopped. He waited.

''I felt furious at the analyst for forgetting her name.'' Indignantly. ''But even more disgusted when this woman told me she met his wife later in the powder room and confided that her husband did not recognize her as his patient. Whereupon the wife said, 'What do you expect of the old fart?' "

I was silent, then, "End of story."

"And if I don't recognize you at parties or analytic meetings you will think I am an old fart," he said.

"Not an old fart, a young one." I smiled.

Then dared say, "I have called you a son-of-a-bitch, told you to 'fuck off' and now describe you as an 'old fart.'" Laughed, "Not bad for a highly repressed patient."

I sighed once again, it was too near the end for humor. "I'm just not certain I can make it alone," I confessed.

Then the calm voice, reminding me, "Remember, if you feel the need, you can return for a session or two."

"I might want to come back sometime," I admitted. "Maybe to tell you how well I'm doing without you." Defiantly, "Or that I have finally made my first decent relationship with a man."

"That would be for revenge. To show you can get along without me. You can come back just because you feel angry at me."

I *was* angry at him. But I also felt analysis should be like weaning. Once off that substitute breast, stay off. There was a good chance I would never see him again. Unless we met at an analytic dinner dance. Or a meeting at the New York Psychoanalytic Institute. Or the annual convention of the American Psychoanalytic Association at the Waldorf, where I once heard him speak.

Two months before I told him I met a man I liked, who was living with a woman but confessed they were not getting along. There had been no sexual play between this man and me. We had only kissed lightly. I was determined to be careful about the next man with whom I became involved. If ever there might be one.

I threatened, in stiff upper-lip manner, "Maybe I'll get closer to this man." Defiantly, "He's been in analysis."

"What does that mean?" Slightly belligerent.

My mouth fell open. "You're saying someone can go to an inadequate therapist, a non-Freudian, and call it analysis?"

"I don't mean a non-Freudian but a Freudian. He could go five years to a reputable psychoanalyst and not be analyzed."

Is he crazy, I thought? Asked, "Why would an analyst keep a patient that long without analyzing him?"

"Because the analyst has hope the patient would break through his defenses and be analyzed."

"What *does* it mean to be successfully analyzed?" I demanded. "That's what I really want to know. Have I made enough progress to be on my own?"

"There you go again, wanting to depend on someone else. You are the one to decide."

Despairingly, giving up the analytic ghost for the moment, I said, "I am completely alone. There is no one out there who gives one shit about me."

He said gently, as he had once before, "Essentially we are all alone."

"Even in marriage?" My last hope.

"Even in marriage."

I thought about this devastating (to me) statement for a moment. Then, "Does that mean we can never ask someone else for comfort when we feel depressed or anguished?"

"We can ask—"

I interrupted, catching his thought in advance by the tone of his voice, "You have great humor."

He quietly finished his sentence, "but that doesn't mean we will receive comfort."

He certainly has given me a more realistic view of the human spirit, I thought. Maybe it *is* time I dropped down from Cloud Nine.

I heard from a friend, Dr. Henriette Klein, a psychoanalyst with whom I occasionally played bridge, that the younger analysts, of which he was one, had displaced several older analysts in honorary positions at the New York Psychoanalytic Institute. I told him I had learned this, added, "Congratulations."

Then I said quickly, "Don't interpret this for me. I'll do it myself. I'm sarcastically congratulating you on getting rid of a rigid older patient so a younger, more pliable, prettier one can take my place."

"Yes." He sounded as if he were proud of me.

I loved the way he said "yes," as though I now understood something important to my life—the way to the understanding of the unconscious wish or fear.

On that note we would part. "Termination," analysts called it. What a dreadful name for the ending of an analysis, only death was termination, I thought, sudden tears flowing. I grabbed a Kleenex from the table to the right of the couch. Over the years I had crumpled enough Kleenex to fill his mammoth office floor to ceiling.

I muttered, "I'm leaving not with sobs of grief but a few genuine tears of sorrow."

I stood up, the few remaining seconds of my final hour. He handed me the bill for July. I thought sadly, This is the last bill I will probably ever pay him. He shook my hand warmly, which he did when leaving for summer vacation, as he was now preparing to do.

He smiled, said, "Have a good summer. Goodbye and good luck."

What in hell has "luck" got to do with analysis, I wondered, probably his answer would be that luck was also a factor in reality. I remembered Bernard Baruch's words, "Luck belongs to the good card player." Perhaps on the couch the good patient was one who understood the way the analyst helped him reach his unconscious so he could continue by himself.

I muttered, "You have a nice summer, too, and thank you very much for everything."

I walked out clutching the blasted bill.

Louis opened the door of the elevator, my last ride downward from the blessed-accursed office in which I had gained a new emotional lease on life. Never again would I walk into the spacious room with the book-lined walls and the inspiring view eastward of a forest of trees. Unless, of course, for a visit to inform him how well I was doing without him.

I stepped into the downstairs lobby, said, "Goodbye, Louis, see you soon." Not wanting to tell him this *was* the darkest of days.

"Have a good vacation, Miss Lucy," Louis said.

Out of never-never land and into the grim reality strode Saint Lucy, I thought. Better late than never, this is late enough in life to start understanding the complexities of the hidden self.

That weekend at a dinner party I sat next to a psychoanalyst friend, Dr. Charles Fisher, worldwide authority on dreams, whose wife, Betty, is also a friend. I boasted to Charles, "At long last I have finished analysis."

He looked pleased, said, "Congratulations."

I confided, expecting praise for an amazing insight, "As I look back on my life I see how adolescent I have been."

Wise Charles, who reaches the heart of matters analytic with quiet but on the target humor, said, "Try infantile."

My first reaction was laughter, then I reeled. Muttered, "Charles, I don't know whether to kill or kiss you."

I leaned over, kissed him on the cheek.

He was saying until I more fully accepted the child within, there would be no giving up of the wish to be dependent on the "good" parent, the "good" analyst.

Infantile ties had hooked me to unhappiness. It would be infantile not to accept separation from the analyst, anguished though I felt. After all, as he had pointed out, no love is without ambivalence. Or as Freud put it, "No love is pure."

How could I expect to feel anything *but* ambivalent at giving up the fascinating, soul-searching moments on the psychoanalytic couch, painful and terrifying though they might have seemed at times. Those moments had yielded the strength I now possessed to go it alone.

I had walked away from the analyst's office feeling tearful, also a touch of terror. As I stood in the emboldening sunshine waiting for the number 10 bus southward, I thought, I must face the fact there is now only myself. I may never see him again, hear his calm voice help weld the puzzle pieces of my inner self to my outer self.

At that moment I put the odds against my doing it alone at thirty to one, the price of occasional long shots I bet at Belmont and Aqueduct.

I now would have to prove I could make it on my own.

Prove there was life after analysis. That in a very real sense I could be my own therapist.

14

The Elusive "Cure"

Often during the psychoanalytic journey I believed
I would be stretched out on the couch trying to
understand my unhappy self until the day I died.
I thought of the Greek mythological torturer, Pro-
crustes, a giant of Attica. We speak of a Procrustean
bed, named after him. He kidnapped travelers, tied them
to his bed after which he either stretched them or cut off
their legs until they fit the bed (was that where the word
"shrink" came from as applied to a psychoanalyst?).

At times on the couch I felt "shrunken," other times
forced to "stretch out," trying to reach awareness of
some threatening thought or wish. At first I wanted to
"know it all," now I realized such demand was unrealistic. I still sought mythical perfection, even in my wish
to dig psychically into the pain of the past.

Once I sent Sally a card that pictured a bag lady
sniffing a rose, a smile on her face as though in paradise.

The first page of the card read, "What you are expecting—" And the turn of the page, "—doesn't exist."

It helped to hear the ring of Dr. Aiken's reassuring words, "There are some things we can only work out by ourselves." The challenge of challenges. Easing the way to nebulous reality.

Was I like every person who dared lie on the couch I wondered as I asked myself, Am I cured?

Answered silently, What do I mean by "cure"?

What should a patient expect? Will a man change from Mr. Hyde to Dr. Jekyll permanently? Will a Lucretia Borgia blossom into a Florence Nightingale?

Will that elusive cure bring the ability to love and be loved? Will it take away fear, anger, depression, intense sexual desire or its opposite, a wall of stone that denies all desire?

I read all the psychoanalytic articles on "cure," tried to find out if I fit the picture of a cured patient. I knew the easing of emotional turmoil by a psychoanalyst is not comparable to cure in the world of physicians, who treat bodily ills, find the proper medicine for the flu or set a broken bone.

The subtle destruction of soul and spirit over the years is difficult to halt, then ease. Maze within maze of fantasies lie hidden from awareness. It takes time to gain the new strength that enables us to become more thoughtful about ourselves, thoughtful in a way that is not selfish but allows us to care far more about both ourselves and others.

I worked hard to understand what Dr. Vann Spruiell, noted psychoanalyst, described as the "frozen fantasies" from childhood that haunt us over the years. They became "unfrozen" as the analyst helped me reveal and confront them. The capacity to accept them and know their original purpose had been retarded until I reached the couch and tackled those fantasies "frozen" in time.

Psychoanalysis helps you think differently. It is not intellectual exploration but emotional, though reasoning becomes part of it. As you experience the process, you explore ever greater depths of your feelings, memories and fantasies.

I absorbed the process from the way my analyst thought, expressed himself, felt toward me, acted. And through my positive feelings for the analyst. The slow assimilation of his words and attitudes and a growing trust both in him and myself paved the way to the healing process.

Armed with that trust, I could then dare face my carefully guarded, tabooed wishes and fantasies of childhood, ones that became intensified in adolescence as the sexual drive took on power. I also understood that defenses arose to block awareness of feelings and fantasies, chiefly of an erotic or murderous nature. No simple process this, to grow up gracefully in an emotional sense.

What the "process" entails arose when my niece Dale, as usual, met me for my birthday luncheon at the Lincoln Square Coffee Shop on Broadway at Sixty-fifth Street. Dale is now a lawyer, executive director of the National Women and the Law Association. She was embarking once again on therapy after several unfortunate experiences.

She confessed over a vegetable plate, "I'm depressed. Treatment goes so slowly."

"If it goes fast, it probably isn't valid," I warned.

She half-glowered, half-smiled, then admitted, "I'm always in a hurry."

"Rushing runs in the family." I smiled back. "But if treatment is effective, you'll find yourself slowing down. Rushing is a defense. An attempt to escape dangerous thoughts and wishes as we try to leave in the lurch what we really feel." Added, "It takes time, dear, to feel comfortable with the inner self."

"It's a process, isn't it?" Thoughtful tone as she arrived at this conclusion by herself.

"That's right. A process. You slowly go deeper, level by level, until you feel safe enough to become aware of hidden thoughts and wishes that have ruled your life. The purest psychic water, so to speak."

Incidentally, her brother David was the only psychologist our family boasted when he practiced in the town of Bennington, Vermont. Then he decided to enter the business world and today is president of Finex, a computer consulting service for physicians in Manhattan. He is married to Rebecca Srole, whose father, Dr. Leo Srole, author of *Mental Health in the Metropolis*, represents an authority in our family wishing to improve the mental health of the nation.

I was now aware of how my identification with each analyst played a part in my ability to understand myself. It was not only the identification with a new way of thinking but also the analyst's understanding manner, empathic tone, degree of patience—what analysts call their "function as an analyst."

My analyst friend, Dr. Walter Stewart, former treasurer of the New York Psychoanalytic Institute and faculty member, titled his 1980 A. A. Brill Memorial Lecture "Building a Clinical Theory: The Science of Our Art." He spoke of one "unanalyzable given"—that the role of identification of the patient with the analyst played an important part in the scientific understanding of the process of therapy. He called this "given" the "science of our art, rather than the art of our science."

He also pointed out that in our very early life, "prolonged separations from the mother, her possible depression, impatience, rivalry and lack of empathy, create a bad relationship between the mother and infant." He continued, "The infant is poorly prepared to accept any frustration, including weaning. His character will be dominated for a lifetime by greed, mistrust, instability, chronic complaints, depression and paranoia."

I once asked Dr. Robert Langs, who writes extensively on the nature of "cure" in analysis, what that amorphous, intangible quality known as "inner change" meant and how it was achieved. He replied, "I think of cure as a visionary goal that permits the patient to feel more at ease with himself and others. It occurs not through intellectual insight but through the automatic, unconscious thought processes by which we become in large part what we are, from infancy on."

Among these processes "is the emotional taking in from the therapist anything he does that conveys his feelings, as we originally did from our parents through their words, attitudes, acts, facial expressions, unconscious and conscious wishes."

He concluded, "This is the *only* way we change— through sensing feelings in others and ourselves. How the therapist feels toward the patient—hostile or caring, loving or hating, unconsciously wishing to help or destroy—is the way the patient will feel about himself." He added that "cure" or change in the thinking about the self is achieved "perhaps in part from identification with an emotionally healthier figure than the mother and father of childhood—the analyst."

Langs also emphasizes the rule Freud laid down that there be absolutely no sexual involvement with a patient. This harms both patient and analyst. I knew of two instances where prominent analysts fell in love with a patient but promptly sent the patient to another analyst. In both instances they later married the patient. This, however, is very unusual. A disheartening thought to the many women patients who fall in love (immature love) with the analyst.

An internationally known psychoanalyst, Dr. Martin Grotjahn, warned analysts against using their profession as sublimation of erotic and aggressive feelings. An increasing number of analytic books emphasize the need for analysts to be aware of what Freud called "countertransference"—the analyst's emotional reactions to the patient's "transference": feelings, fantasies and desires he had as a child toward his father and mother.

In his book *Behind the Couch*, Dr. Herbert S. Strean, director of the New York Center for Psychoanalytic Training, points out that some therapists are frightened of their incestuous wishes, destructive fantasies, homosexual desires, dependency feelings. If they overlook these feelings in themselves and their patients, this hinders the patient's emotional development.

"If the analyst cannot relate to the child in his patient, he will not feel strong empathy as well as genuine understanding of the child within himself," Strean warned. "This means the patient will not understand the child in him."

There is also a way of "listening" in analysis that leads to the "royal road of the unconscious," in Freud's words. My new understanding of the words and feelings that emanated from me arose from how the analyst listened to me and how I listened to how he listened.

At first I did not really "hear" his interpretations because of strong defenses against both the pain of the past and the new pain he caused as I faced the threatening conflicts blocked by defenses. At times he had to repeat his words over and over and in different contexts before I could "hear" them in the marrow of my bones.

He listened to every word and the tone in which it was spoken—whether hurled in anger, muttered or said with passion. Each thought told of something vital to my life. Nothing I said was meaningless. Sometimes words and thoughts that seemed senseless to me spoke of fear and terror in shorthand clues he picked up.

Listening to the inner self, hearing and understanding the words you utter in analysis (and sometimes think but do not utter) is the new capacity you acquire when therapy is effective. You learn it by becoming aware of how the analyst listens to you. As you understand the way he listens and his interpretation of what you have told him, you listen and interpret in the same way.

It is difficult to convey in writing many things that take place in analysis. Not only is the process of analysis complex but inner changes often cannot be put into words. Suddenly you realize you feel more assured, more relaxed, more confident in yourself. You do not get upset easily. You take time to make up your mind.

The psychic potboilers the public so avidly buys in the hope of living more happily rarely offer the way to one iota of change, though they may momentarily reassure. The great unwashed—psychically speaking—public does not want more than a sniff of verbal snuff. Man accepts the idea he has an unconscious at about the same rate of speed he oozed his way out of the slime (learning of unconscious wishes and fantasies in a way is like oozing out of the slime of our thoughts).

Those who dare analysis feel they set off into uncharted dangerous territory to explore the tabooed. But they also hold as strong ballast the hope their torment will be eased, a hope needed by both patient and analyst. Dr. Karl Menninger has often said if the analyst lacks hope, the patient may as well give up.

Thus the word "cure," as applied to the development of our psyche, is like the word "perfection"—a magic goal, not achievable. No one, not even a psychoanalyst, can be "perfect" or "cured" of all emotional conflict. There will always be some conflict when our two most powerful instinctual wishes are frustrated: the desire to have sex with anyone we want and to act in a murderous way if we feel threatened physically or psychically.

I felt heartened by the words of Dr. Arnold Z. Pfeffer, psychoanalyst, in his follow-up studies of former patients. He explains, "Conflicts are not *shattered* by analysis, but rather reduced in their intensities and thus become more manageable. After analysis, such minimally experienced conflicts may be restimulated by life situations that have particular meaning for the individual. Distress and even symptoms may recur but are of short duration. The well-analyzed person is readily able to analyze, understand and resolve such brief and transient recurrences."

I acquired the readiness emotionally to separate from the analyst, recalcitrant though I felt in part. Roy Shafer, psychoanalyst, speaks of the final separation as a "tragic experience" both patient and analyst share. He says, "They lose each other in finding each other. . . . The end of the analysis combines fulfillment and deprivation."

"Cure" in analysis means you understand your forbidden feelings. Conflicts do not vanish but you are now capable of understanding and handling them so they no longer lead you down the dark alley of despair.

Instead of bemoaning what life and people had done to me, I could now ask, "What have I done to myself? Did I unconsciously set it up this way?"

I could also accept that when the formal analysis ended this did not mean all anxiety vanished like a puff of black smoke. At times I would feel anxiety over a real danger. But anxiety over unreal fantasies would disappear to a large degree. Conflict, which causes anxiety, is an inherent part of life. We are all forced at times to make difficult decisions, give up pleasures we covet, control childish impulses and rage.

Freud wrote words that critics, who claim he did not place enough emphasis on childhood suffering, would do well to remember: "This cannot be said among analysts too emphatically or repeated too often . . . anyone who neglects childhood analysis is bound to fall into the most disastrous errors. The emphasis which is laid here upon the importance of the earliest experiences does not imply any underestimation of the influence of the later ones. But later impressions of life speak loudly enough through the mouth of the patient, while it is the physician who has to raise his voice on behalf of the claims of childhood."

Do analysts miss patients after they leave? It depends on the relationship between the particular analyst and the particular patients, analysts say. "Some patients I miss very much, some I miss somewhat and a few, I must confess, I am glad leave," comments Strean, author of *Behind the Couch.*

I was surprised when Dr. Mack sent the note saying she missed me, hoped I would return. Perhaps I filled a need in her, perplexing patient though she thought me at times. I left because I felt dissatisfied with the analysis. After Dr. Emch became ill, I sent her roses on Valentine's Day, for I missed her acutely. Hilda told me Dr. Emch pressed one of the roses in a book, so I must have meant something to her.

Are there inept, unqualified analysts, as Freud suggested there might be, who neglect analyzing the patient's childhood? Or who perhaps do not know themselves deeply enough in other ways?

Just as there are inadequate lawyers, teachers, ministers, politicians, Presidents of the United States, so there are inadequate psychoanalysts. I finally had to accept this "awful truth." When I entered analysis I believed them all perfect.

Dr. Grotjahn once said, when I mentioned a certain analyst, "I wouldn't send my goldfish to him." As Freud advised, all analysts theoretically should return for more analysis every five years, though in his day training was exceedingly short, sometimes only ten months.

Analysts may prove ineffective because they have not sufficiently resolved their own conflicts. As with all other purchases, the watchword is "let the buyer beware." Even after we check the analyst's credentials, we have to trust our own feelings about the analyst. We may sense a particular analyst is not appropriate for us and seek another.

Some ask if there is a difference between men and women analysts. I had two men analysts and two women analysts and I would say it is not a question of gender but of the capacity of the man or woman to know the inner self and to possess a sense of hope for the self and the patient.

The analyst's life is not an easy one, physically or emotionally. The analyst is bound to a chair from early morning often to late at night, five days, perhaps six, a week, listening quietly, trying to relieve the pain of the patient. At times the analyst's own painful memories are revived. The analyst has to control anger but understand the patient's need to express it.

As I look back on my four analyses (one incomplete because of Dr. Emch's tragic death), each analyst differed. All helped propel me to some degree along the way to stronger self-esteem. Perhaps in the case of Dr. Mack, change was slightest but change it was.

Each analyst helped make conscious the feelings I had throttled over the years. Dr. Thurrott encouraged me not to deny buried fear and rage, both realistic and unrealistic, at my mother and father. He also enabled me to understand how closely mind and body were intertwined. And how, as he said, "we put our whole life into every act." I remembered well his quote from the Bible, "The wicked flee when no man pursueth." This alluded to my feeling like a "wicked witch" at times.

I cannot overestimate how much he helped at a crucial era in my life. Physical illnesses, including severe sinusitis, mysterious stomach aches, constant colds, and intense menstrual cramps, disappeared. During the last year of analysis he helped me weather the death of my father. He also helped me gain the courage to write my first book, about the analysis with him. I remarked in it, "I realize I have come a long way but still have a long way to go."

When I first started analysis I spoke of my feelings about Dr. Thurrott in a letter to Margaret Parton, then covering news in India for *The Herald Tribune:*

> Dearest Margaret,
>
> I wanted to let you know about my becoming a guinea pig. I decided, after much confusion, about four months ago, to take on psychoanalysis. The time for just talk was over. I found, through the help of a relative [Dr. Kubie], an analyst just out of the Army, who had worked with both children and adults. I have seen him three times a week at nine in the morning and the hardest thing I have ever done is to drag myself out of bed at 7:30 A.M. since I never get to bed before midnight.
>
> Margaret, this is almost like a miracle. I think that the analyst you go to is the factor that counts the most. Analysis is supposed to be painful—it is, it has to be in part because you face painful memories. But the analyst can make it easier and this man is gentle and sweet and philosophical and makes me feel as

though I have a right to live and think through
things for myself. I have changed my whole attitude
toward myself and, what is important, toward others.
Paradoxically, as you start understanding what
makes you tick, you become more aware of the world
you live in. You accept other people rather than fear
them. I always thought it "wrong" to think about my
own problems but, as the analyst says, if you can't
think through your own life, how can you expect to
help anyone else?

According to this analyst, the underlying cause of
neurosis is anxiety. It is caused by a feeling of not
being wanted or loved more fully during childhood.
Oh, parents love you as best they know how, but the
tragic thing is that they, in turn, were little loved.
Love is giving, without expecting a return—and how
many parents live up to that definition?

It's fascinating and I could go on and on but I
don't want to run the risk of boring you. I only
wanted you to know that already work seems less of
a compulsion. I am even enjoying horse races without
feeling guilty. It isn't wrong to have fun certain
moments in life that are a relief from work. I have
found new joy in sunbathing or a pint of ice cream
savored. Chocolate, of course.

Accept my love, all my wishes for happiness, and
don't work too hard.

Lovingly,
Lucy

My second analyst, Dr. Emch, helped me become
aware of the power of the unconscious and how it affected daily behavior. She opened new emotional vistas
by helping me understand my crippling dependence on
my parents and masochistic attitude with men. Her
words, "Let it percolate," rather than indulge in a hasty

act, would echo in my mind, cause me to postpone a decision until my conscious had a chance to think it over.

With her I started to feel truly civilized, more in control of my acts. I also could speak more freely with a woman about my sexual fears. When she died I felt a devastation I had never known because I had denied awareness of her impending death. My father had been ill two years, my mother seven, there had been far more time to mourn in advance.

Dr. Mack helped me delve into the unconscious wish to be a boy, carry out my girlhood fantasy to be the first woman baseball player in the National League. I also lost some of my fear of aging as I saw her grow old gracefully. She looked glamorous on opening night at Tennessee's *Slapstick Comedies.*

I also was able for the first time to feel (though not daring to express) angry emotions for an analyst—dislike, contempt, mistrust. None of which I voiced but consciously knew. Truly a step in the direction of knowledge about hidden reactions and thoughts.

Dr. Mack may have been more at ease, more successful with men patients, I thought, after talking to several she had analyzed as part of their training at the New York Psychoanalytic Institute. My amateur analysis of her is that perhaps she feared her own promiscuity when she attacked me unfairly as promiscuous. A leading analyst told me recently that one prominent male analyst was not effective with creative writers because he envied them. I worked with this analyst on a book and he had not accepted one idea I offered. I thought this strange but, masochist me, accepted his decisions in true peon fashion.

Analysts may feel more empathy for certain patients, depending on the analyst's likes and dislikes. Most analysts help most patients though it may vary in degree. Strean believes "the finest analyst may occasionally fail with a patient who consistently is unable to assume some responsibility for delving into his inner self. Some men and women possess such self-hatred, a hatred they project on the analyst, that they are unable to reach out for help even though they go to the analyst for months, perhaps years." He adds, "I cannot be totally hopeful about every patient. One may be very receptive, another will fight me all the way, keep threatening to leave and eventually carry out the threat."

Analysts try to do their best to relieve the pain of the patient, at the same time recognizing they are human. Ghislaine Boulanger, clinical psychologist, and a friend, who was my editor on *The Story of Anna O.*, recently wrote: "One of the things I have learned as a therapist is that I am fallible, not just as a therapist but also as a person, but that it is all right to be fallible, in fact it is human. I believe it is our job as therapists to pass this understanding on to our patients, not just that we are fallible, they are going to find that out soon enough, but that we accept this fallibility in ourselves and that we expect and welcome this same fallibility in our patients. If, in their turn, our patients can accept this very human quality in themselves, then our job is done."

Dr. Aiken enabled me finally to give up analysis, gain the feeling of trust in my unknown (but becoming less so) self. He helped me realize analysts were not gods, nor were my sometimes terrifying parents of childhood. He also suggested I be more skeptical of others, less submissive, not accept everyone as "right," indict myself as "wrong."

He helped me face the pain of the Oedipal conflict. When I complained that Dr. Mack wrongfully accused me of sleeping with many men, he said sympathetically, "The many stand for the one." He meant it was difficult to give up my passion for my father.

Most important, he helped me express anger at him, leading to awareness of the depth of rage at my parents. Slowly I was able to reach those "depths beyond depths" of which Ralph Waldo Emerson wrote.

True, each analyst broke one or more of the sacred rules of the profession outlined by Freud. Dr. Thurrott occasionally allowed his manservant to bring in breakfast, always offered me coffee. He also divulged details of his personal life.

All the analysts saw me in their home, rather than the separate office Freud advised. Though his was in the same building as his home, it was located one floor below, which gave it a certain separateness. Today analysts disagree as to whether it makes much difference whether office is separate from living quarters. Since all my analysts saw me in their homes, I cannot judge.

Perhaps it is the quality of the analysis that counts, not the locale. Maybe an analysis could be conducted on a desert island, if need be (my tantalizing sexual fantasy that I could have Dr. Aiken all to myself, the only interference the roar of the ocean?).

As a patient treated in the analyst's home, I felt a sense of intrigue. This proved a plus, it brought out the familiar feeling, as I told Dr. Aiken, that "I have always lived a life of intrigue. My mother and father continuously involved me in intrigue of one sort or another." Added, "No wonder I write of terror, suspense, murder, lying and artifice."

Dr. Mack broke a number of rules. She often ate supper in my presence, answered the phone. Sometimes all I heard was the click of knitting needles as I tried to muster thoughts, speak freely without swearing at her.

Other times she scratched away on notepaper, told me about her personal life, twice forgot my appointment. These acts were all *verboten.* The "psychic straw" that broke all trust occurred when she called me a "liar" after I described lying in a hospital bed following an abortion.

I once asked an analyst friend, "What was wrong with Dr. Mack?" He said, as though in apology, "We knew she was getting a bit senile." I complained, "Why didn't you tell me?" He said, "We had no real proof. And besides, we do not talk about analysts to their patients." I could understand but still resent.

All four analysts helped me in some way to face the part that had to be explored if I were to feel a more unified self. It is difficult for many of the psychoanalytically uninitiated to accept the terrifying, to them, idea that they possess a powerful part of the mind that remains hidden over the unhappy years, waiting to be brought to consciousness.

The idea that we hold back memories, fantasies, feelings unknown to us may seem unbelievable. But Freud's theory that the brain is our storehouse of memories has been proved valid by a famous neurosurgeon, Dr. Wilder Penfield, and his associates at the Montreal Neurological Institute. His pioneer discoveries, described in *Speech and Brain Mechanisms,* written with Dr. Lamar Roberts, are now widely accepted by science.

Penfield proved the unity of mind and body as he revealed how memory operates in our brain. While performing brain operations, he discovered as he used electrodes to mildly stimulate certain sections of the brain that his patients started to talk freely about past experiences. This happened only when he applied the electrodes to particular places on the cortex just above the two temporal lobes. These sections of the brain, lying under the temple on each side of our head, are the locations of our thought processes and memory.

Electrical stimulation thus caused a flow of memories. Penfield believed that since this did not occur when he stimulated other lobes in the brain, it seemed justifiable to conclude those specific areas of the cortex "have a particular relationship to the record of experience" and the reawakening of memories tied to those experiences.

He compared the part of the brain that stores memory to a continuous filmstrip with a sound track. At any point in the strip a person could remember and talk about whatever he had experienced and felt.

During such electrode experiments one man recalled hearing a piano and a voice singing "Oh, Marie." A woman described how she felt giving birth. Another woman heard her son calling to her when he was small and standing in the yard outside her kitchen. Some described feelings about the past as "familiar." Others claimed they were distant and unfamiliar. But all agreed the memory was more vivid than any they could voluntarily recall.

The discovery of these reactions showed the existence of a permanent recording of memories by the ganglia, masses of nerve cells serving as a center from which nerve impulses are transmitted. Penfield said it seemed likely we use part of this record in our current life when challenged by new experiences. His patients did not regard their memories as a "remembering" but rather as a "hearing-again and seeing-again—a living-through moments of the past time." In a sense they experienced a double consciousness.

Each patient, Penfield stated, "enters the stream of the past and it is the same as it was in the past, but when he looks at the banks of the stream, he is aware of the present as well. . . . The thread of time remains with us

in the form of a succession of 'abiding' facilitations
... it runs through the waking hours of each man, from
childhood to the grave."

This "thread of time," psychoanalysts believe, is
molded in its pattern by wishes that stem chiefly from
erotic and aggressive impulses and their frustrations.
Earliest man, according to anthropologists, gave in to
all his instinctual impulses. He slaughtered anyone who
angered him, had sex with anyone he desired, be it his
mother or daughter. But as man grew civilized, he
learned to repress such abhorrent wishes, though occasionally they would erupt and overwhelm his "better
judgment."

Penfield's patients seemed to speak of lost feelings.
We all carry feelings of loss within us. The psychoanalysis of adults shows the unconscious contains endless
memories of earlier losses and deprivations. They appear with special clarity in dreams, which often reveal
wishes to restore lost loved ones.

When we feel hurt, this stirs memories of past
hurts that caused us to feel unloved, arouses feelings
that come under the label of "unfinished business." It is
as though in our mind-computer we punch a button labeled "hurt" and out fly all the cards telling of times we
felt psychically wounded. Every feeling we have is registered somehow, somewhere, in our mind and body. It
forms our state of inner being. Feelings in large part
dictate our choices of how to act, if we do not know what
we feel we may act unwisely.

Intertwined fantasies and memories spin through
our unconscious in haphazard disregard of time. The
unconscious has no sense of time. Yesterday is as today.

Buried most deeply are wishes and fantasies connected to the earliest losses and hurts. Fantasied or
threatened loss of genitals in the Oedipal-phallic period.
Loss of feces in the anal period. Loss of the mother's

breast or the warmth of her body in the oral period. And, perhaps the earliest loss of all, felt as we are born, loss of her breathing for us when we were in the womb.

We can never regain what has been lost in spite of our wishes, wishes still so strong that if we have not made peace with them, they may find expression in physical illness, destructive acts toward the self or others or deep depression.

That I had in many ways, with the help of analysts, accepted the existence of the buried self proved profitable to me emotionally. The analysts provided ways I could never have known to explore my inner life on my own.

It was a new feeling, at first an unsteady feeling. But I started on the way—the lonely way—of exploring the unconscious by myself. I was no longer entrapped by the fantasy I would one day be completely "cured." I settled for feeling secure in the knowledge I could live a far happier life if slowly I understood more and more the reasons for my unhappiness.

It was a challenge—the challenge of challenges. One that led me further out of the realm of fantasy and down the now more comfortable road of reality.

15

The Beloved
Prison Vanishes

The truth about the self never corrupts—only denial of it. But the truth is often difficult to face, so painful at times that many prefer to endure life continuing to inflict duplicity on the self and others. They fail to sense the savagery that may lie beneath the veneer of so-called civilized speech and deeds.

"Life is difficult." These are the three courageous words Dr. M. Scott Peck dares use to open *The Road Less Traveled.* We do not wish to admit life is difficult but it is—for each of us. "Baseball is a constant game of adjustment," remarked an announcer during the World Series of 1988 in Los Angeles. So is life, I thought grimly.

I learned much in analysis—a learning different from that of book or classroom. Analysis brings not intellectual knowledge but how to live more peacefully. The goal of analysis is to ease "neurotic suffering" so "normal misery" can be endured, in the words of Freud. You leave the couch with a more realistic view of yourself. A greater wisdom about the world at large and what a dangerous place it can be. Knowing you need all your wits and wisdom to survive gracefully.

You learn of a new kind of murder, what analysts call "soul murder," the crimes committed on you by parents when you were a child. Analysts may be thought of as detectives who track down killers of the mind. Clues to the inner villains (including at times yourself) appear as you pursue the psychic traumas of the past that shape the present.

There are two kinds of terror, I learned: the terror felt when someone threatened me physically or psychologically and the terror that arose when my own destructive impulses and fantasies threatened to overwhelm me. As I became aware of the latter I lived more peacefully with myself and others.

It would be an ideal world if reason ruled us. But reason cannot rule if we are too controlled by the unconscious. For the unconscious does not know of reason. Only our conscious mind can reason.

The power of reason grew as I probed hidden feelings and fantasies. My unconscious held labyrinth upon labyrinth of intricate thoughts and wishes waiting to be explored. I thought of it as a great psychic cobweb, layers deep and interlaced.

My analysis was not as long as it appears. The Freudian analysis ideally requires five days a week, usually between five to ten or more years. From day one I did not have the money for such an intensive schedule and Dr. Thurrott permitted me to come only three times a week. I sometimes missed days when sent on out-of-town assignments. I managed the four times a week Dr. Emch and Dr. Mack requested, on royalties from my first book. I told Dr. Aiken I could afford only three times a week and this dwindled to once a week the last year.

For many, one analysis may suffice. The length of time varies with the person and the analyst he chooses. An analyst may see one patient for fifteen years, another for six. It depends on the nature and depth of the early emotional trauma, not the same for everyone. And, as Dr. Ernest Jones warned, the more the theories of psychoanalysis develop, the longer treatment takes.

Every emotion we possess exists to be used at one moment or another—"there is a time." The phrase *human being* gives equal weight to both "human" and "being." We all hold the right to love, to hate, to feel fear, jealousy and greed. But we also need the wisdom not to act destructively because of intense feelings. Analysis restores an equilibrium in feelings that may be distorted. It leads to what we call "common sense"—the use of "sense" in humane fashion toward ourselves and others.

My mother once gave me a decorative silver spoon, two inches wide at the thickest part, seven inches long. I stored it in a closet for years, one day took it out, black with age. I started to polish it with silver cleaner. There emerged as handle a two-masted schooner flying three flags. Beside the ship four men sat in a rowboat, the fifth climbed aboard. A woman's face emerged as figurehead.

The process of psychoanalysis may be compared to the polishing of silver on which the dirt of years has accumulated, similar to the cleaning of the Augean stables. With each successive shine, the silver slowly emerges (at perhaps the same slow pace as insights), gleams brighter and brighter. Layers of darkness removed.

Psychoanalysis is the only true game in town, if you want to understand the deepest self, I thought, after a friend remarked, "It costs a lot to stand alone." He did not mean money but the ability to admit you may be controlled at times by what you do not know in yourself. The heart of the psychoanalytic process lies in the fact that after a revelation arises you become able to "suppress" rather than "repress" it. You now possess the ability to repudiate a wish knowingly rather than bury it blindly, denying it. This is control over emotions.

As you slowly gain understanding of the hidden self you find new strengths. A friend, Liz Otto, who never had a day of analysis, once remarked, "If you don't feel a sense of identity it's like looking in a mirror and seeing no reflection." During analysis your face, as it slowly appears in that formerly void mirror, is distorted in fear, rage and frustration. But slowly it assumes a look of peacefulness, acceptance of your conflicts, knowing you can solve them with greater wisdom.

Many understand psychoanalytic concepts even though they have never been on the couch. I once said to my friend Flora Rheta Schreiber, author of *Sybil* and *The Shoemaker*, "You must have undergone years in analysis to write so eloquently about the early trauma in the life of a multiple personality, then of a murderer." She replied, "I haven't been on the couch one second." But Flora spent years interviewing leading psychoanalysts and psychiatrists for articles she wrote as contributing psychiatry editor of *Science Digest*.

I received new awareness of the traumas a parent may unknowingly inflict on a child and/or the emotional conflicts that develop within the child, from the work of Kerstin Kupfermann, M.A. and D.E.S.. She is a friend, and co-author of *The Power of Fantasy*. She studied with Dr. Margaret Mahler, Dr. Bruno Bettelheim and Dr. Marianne Kris, who all emphasized the importance of the relationship between parents and child in the first years of life. Kerstin treats children and adults, sometimes children with their parents present, for, she points out, it is important the parent be involved in the process of achieving a healthy functioning of the child.

When I left Dr. Aiken I did not know whether I would ever again enter that hallowed apartment on Central Park West. But after a year's absence (the mourning period) I took up his invitation to return for a session. I did so, I thought, not because I felt angry at him, as he suggested for the reason to return (or was I still "unreally" furious at parting?) but because I wanted to report I was alive and well in spite of mourning the sudden death of Dr. Stewart. Dr. Aiken knew Walter as a fellow member of the New York Psychoanalytic Institute.

He signaled me to a chair rather than the couch for which I swiftly headed. The couch evidently was reserved for the regular patient. I was not there to resume analysis but to discuss one or two feelings that upset me. I sat down gingerly, a bit uncomfortable, knowing part of me wished ardently to be once again the patient.

To offset this sudden weak streak I promptly announced to reassure him (really myself), "I'm doing fine. I keep getting new insights. Dreams help a lot. So do memories that suddenly come to mind and lead to new thoughts and feelings."

Added, "Sometimes I shed a few tears as I did here. Especially when I think of my mother. This is my one great guilt. I never realized how terrified she felt when she lived with a companion in the Barclay after Sue asked me to take her north."

I sighed, went on as in the old times, "I didn't understand why she called me the minute her companion took the day off, leaving her alone in the hotel room. I did not know the depth of her agony. That she felt in a panic, like an abandoned child."

"You did all you could to comfort her," he said.

I felt the tears arise. "The death of Dr. Stewart

reminded me of her death. Though I felt bereft at losing him, too.''

Dr. Aiken's brown eyes looked at me with the empathy I well remembered. I summoned the courage to repeat what I had said before on the couch, "I think I could go to an analyst my whole life and keep discovering new truths more easily than going it alone." This obviously was what I had come to tell him, tied to my anger at his dismissal of me.

"Isn't this still making gods of analysts?" That warm voice.

"Remember? I believe they *are* gods." Bitterly.

"Have you ever thought that some analysts may not have received the help they needed?"

I assumed he meant their analysis was not deep enough, thought of Dr. Mack, wondered to whom she went. But I was not there to sympathize with analysts deprived of an adequate analysis, brought the subject back to my losses.

"I think I now understand how desperately I depended on my parents all my life."

"They made you feel they were indispensable," he said.

This meant it was difficult for me to break free. They wanted me to remain a part of their lives, unable to help me make it on my own.

The precious time was soon gone, I thanked him, paid for the session. We parted with a handshake. He seemed glad I had come. I returned to life without him.

One year later I called, once again headed for his apartment and the chair. After assuring him I was indeed making progress alone, I told him the real reason I phoned. A woman psychoanalyst informed me in gossipy fashion Dr. Aiken was leaving his wife because he had fallen in love with a younger woman. At first I was aghast, thought, He could not possibly do this, it is not part of his nature (the wish my father had stayed faithful to wife and children). Within a week I learned my informant had mistaken him for another analyst. I felt relieved, Dr. Aiken had remained faithful to his wife (and me?).

I told him this, then added, "You will like my initial reaction the moment I learned of this misguided gossip."

The all too familiar wait.

I sat up straight in the chair, announced proudly, "My first thought on hearing you were in love with another woman was, I wish it had been me."

I smiled in triumph, I had been able, face-to-face, like a mature ex-patient, to confess my "transference" love, difficult to admit during couch life. This illicit passion for him mirrored my feelings for my father, the cheerful Casanova of my youth (though it often felt like current passion).

Dr. Aiken half-smiled.

Another thought came to mind. "I was shocked recently when Sally told me she felt she could exist only if she was married and had children. I felt just the opposite. I could not exist unless I had a career and didn't marry. I did not want crying children at my feet."

"Sally never saw crying children at her feet as she grew up," he commented.

He meant Sally had Mother all to herself, no younger rivals screaming to be the one and only. Her brother and sisters welcomed her into the world except perhaps Sue, only six years older.

When I left his sacrosanct office I wondered if I would ever return. A small part of me felt ashamed I still wanted to see him. But I knew my self-esteem had risen in the two years I had been on my own. Perhaps I did possess the courage to truly go it alone, to understand the "human condition" of which Freud spoke.

I discovered moments I felt tranquil, a word I had never used about myself. I began to accept past behavior without deep guilt or shame—the two abortions, the occasional sexual fling and the two marriages that held misery. I realized at the time, given my unhappiness, I could act no differently.

New awareness arose after analyzing a dream. Though it may seem fragile and fragmented a dream reveals the hidden wishes and mournings in your heart if you can decipher its deeper messages via thoughts that flow from various scenes. The cause of your torment can be spun from a dream, perhaps even much of your life if you give enough time to your thoughts.

The average person has 1,460 dreams a year, according to a recent television report. If I understood only one dream a week I would add to the awareness of my inner conflicts.

One dream with a powerful impetus occurred the night after I watched the television program. I woke feeling plunged in the dream's nostalgic aftermath. I saw myself sitting proudly in the front seat of my father's elegant Cadillac as he drove along a highway. This was often a real situation until I was relegated to the rear when Donna took my place.

Suddenly the car stopped for a red light. Acting on impulse I opened the door, fled. I did not wish to ride with my two-timing father. Suddenly I stopped running, thought, I cannot lose my father, he is my whole world. Feeling desperate, fearing abandonment, I ran back to find him. The car had vanished.

I walked around in a panic, asked, "Has anyone seen my father?" Men and women looked at me curiously, went their way.

I wandered onto a street where a large wedding was taking place on top of a hill. I joined the fashionably dressed guests. A tall, bearded, handsome man, who told me he was married, tried to comfort me, make love to me.

Then I woke. The first question I asked: Who was the stranger who gave me comfort? Immediately thought of Dr. Aiken—tall, bearded, handsome and married.

The dream offered a partial outlet for feelings of loss of both my father and analyst as I brought them back in fantasy. The dream played out my anguished wish my father had never deserted his family, much less died (in the dream he vanished forever). And the wish my analyst had not deserted me but would always be on hand, as in the days of the couch. The dream also showed how I was trained to return to those who at times seemed cruel but whom I loved and depended on for my survival.

What during the day before, called by Freud the "day residue," sparked the dream? Something I saw or heard or read about or felt had touched off long-buried memories. My first thought was of the bridge game that evening and the words of my partner during a quiet interlude. She mentioned a married man who slept with many women, saying, "I don't know how his wife stands it."

In the dream I fled the car in desperation, identifying with my mother, feeling I could no longer bear my father's infidelity. I thought of Mother and how she bore her agony for years. Recalled the guilt I felt the night she asked, "Lucy, what will I do? . . . about your father," and I had replied, "Mother, how can you stay with a man who doesn't love you?" (And yet as he died, he was calling out my mother's and Sally's names, though not mine, Alice told me.)

The dream showed my guilt at the belief that I had persuaded my mother to throw him out of the house (shades of the Oedipal wish she would, so I could then have him). It was a burden I still bore, a mourning I still suffered.

The remark of my bridge partner stirred the buried feelings, set off the dream. It served to release some of my pain and anger at my father's betrayal of wife and children as I grew up. And as my analyst appeared in the dream, what I felt his betrayal of me by abandonment.

I thought again of Freud's words, that awareness of *feelings* releases hurt and pain. Not memories or thoughts, not fantasies, but feelings associated with them. I always felt relief after crying over some heartache of the past I had never mourned.

There were dreams I could not interpret fully or at all because my internal resistance was too strong. But as a rule parts of the dream aroused emotions, usually of aggressive or sexual nature or the mourning of a loss.

I discovered music might arouse memories, bring a truth to consciousness. Tears suddenly flowed one evening as I listened to a television ad that featured strains from an old song, "Irresistible." The last line ran, "I'm in love with irresistible you." I thought first of the loss of Dr. Aiken, then the loss of my father, my whole world as a girl.

I now realized more and more how I consciously and unconsciously had taken in attitudes, beliefs and acts of my mother and father, along with their fantasies and wishes. I agonized over the years, Who is really *me?* I became more fully aware of the parts of my parents I had unconsciously "incorporated," taken in emotionally—who else was there to copy? As Dr. Thurrott once said facetiously, "Who did you expect to be like— Mahatma Gandhi?" selecting someone who lived halfway across the world.

It was natural for me when what Dr. Reuben Fine calls the "honeymoon" with the analyst ended after several months, to resent some of Dr. Aiken's (and the other three analysts') interpretations as criticism, wanting only praise and love—what I wished desperately from my parents. But slowly I started to appreciate the psychic perceptiveness inherent in Dr. Aiken's interpretation of a wish, feeling or fantasy.

I had sought analysis believing it would bring an end to life's torments. But, as Dr. Aiken said, "Psychoanalysis is not magic." The process worked slowly and it could not solve problems that stemmed from reality, only "unreality," though it enabled you to solve the real problems far more easily. As I unearthed more of the buried self, reality did not loom so terrifying.

I saw the truth in the words of George Santayana, philosopher and poet, "Those who cannot remember the past are doomed to repeat it." "Remember" not in the conscious sense but delving into the unconscious.

This new "remembering" brought a higher self-esteem (more "ego"), a less punitive conscience ("superego") and a less powerful compulsiveness ("id"). Such achievement took much effort and hard work on the analyst's part—he was not a magician though I wished he were—to help me reach even one small but valuable insight.

I felt rewarded as I was able to speak the unspeakable. Know the unknowable. Then make a modicum of peace with the war within.

Most important, I became aware how difficult it is to be a parent. I prevented myself from becoming one, gripped by fallacious fantasies. I could at last admit my parents were entitled to be human, too. I placed myself as best I could in their shoes, understood their suffering. They did all they could, given their emotionally deprived childhoods. My mother was afraid to speak of love. As a child she probably never heard the word *love* from her cruel stepmother or Granny.

Neither my mother nor father felt free enough to

go into analysis and understand their terrifying thoughts and feelings. They were too frightened to tackle their inner world. Doomed to remain controlled by the hidden self, fated to project their fantasies on their children.

Nor could they mourn their losses, not only of those near and dear but losses within themselves. I owe them more than I can say for not standing in the way of my seeking analysis. Though at the start my father muttered, "You don't need analysis, you're not crazy." Mother never said a word and at times I needed small financial help gave it willingly.

Before *Fight Against Fears* was published I asked my mother to read the manuscript, let me know if there were anything she wished to change or delete, for I had taken a few psychic potshots at her. She handed it back in a few days, said everything looked fine (perhaps she never read it?). When the book came out she bought me the most beautiful gift of my life, a lovely gray fox stole that fell to the knees. She also held a party in her hotel room on the day of publication.

She was proud of her children even though she screamed at them as they grew up. Taking care of four precocious children must have been difficult, given her severe vulnerability. But even though wounded emotionally so early in life, she gave us enough strength so we could seek psychoanalytic help (except Sue, who says she never felt the need for it).

After Mother's death we found a letter among the hundreds she kept, which must have been her most treasured possession. Valued far more than the sapphire and diamond bracelet Laurie gave her along with it on their tenth wedding anniversary a year before Sally was born. The letter addressed Mother as "My Sweetheart."

He went on to say that after ten years of life together "isn't it wonderful that the same old feelings still live and that, with a full realization of what it means to share everything, we have drawn closer and continue to do so. The old love mellowed by time has not suffered but improved, and to it has been added a feeling of dependency—a need real and constant. And the children and the house! Isn't life wonderful? First the two of us and now the five and each addition weaving all of us more tightly together until we have the family, an inseparable unit.

"After all what do outsiders count for? The two of us and ours—we have grown together and now with old love is the understanding and a new love—a stronger love—a lasting love and one that outlives good and bad—good times and bad times! That is what counts and we have it. You are my darling of the honeymoon days—the mother of our oldest and of the two others—in health and sickness—all times faithful and kind and loving. Still my darling, and still, your Laurie."

I was stunned by his words, amazed he could express himself so lovingly and eloquently since I had seen chiefly legal briefs as examples of his writing. Stunned, too, by the new knowledge that though involved with Donna two years, he did not want to desert mother or us. He wanted both his family and his new love (as I imagine many men in this situation feel). Had I known this I never would have advised mother that night in the kitchen to give him up. Though Dr. Aiken assured me she made the decision because she wanted to, not through any words of mine.

I knew my father thirty-five years and my mother, fifty-five. But I really did not know them until I left Dr. Aiken. Only then did I understand the depth of their fear, terror, heartbreak. I realized mother screamed at us as she unconsciously copied her stepmother's way of control. At least she did not chase us with a carving knife as she had been chased. Mother's father remarried to obtain a mother for his three forlorn children but his new wife hated them, wanted only her children.

I now understood why my father pretended to be the carefree playboy. He hid his depression and anger by overwork and compulsive weekend "gallivanting," as he called it. I saw his parents as difficult, his mother used sarcasm as a verbal whip. His father discouraged him from becoming an engineer, the profession he coveted, insisted he become a lawyer. Both parents forbid him to marry the woman he originally chose.

One day I suddenly reached another new awareness about my father as I asked the question: Why did Laurie, somewhat of a Don Juan before he met Donna, decide to love her and her alone the rest of his life, unable to give her up? He was thirty-two, she, eighteen, she told me, when they met.

I now became aware not only was she beautiful, sweet and fun to be with but she gave him a sense of being his caretaker, mothered him. She knit him sweaters, cut out and sewed jackets (she was studying fashion design, intending to make a career of it). She cooked delicious meals, including chocolate cakes from scratch. She made the little boy part of him feel nurtured and loved, whereas Mother had all she could do to take care of four young children. She expected Laurie to nurture himself, perhaps also be the nurturer she never had.

I felt grateful for the strengths my mother and father gave me. They spent much of their free time with me as I grew up. Dr. Robert A. Solow, a psychiatrist, suggests, "Parents should listen more to what their children say, try to understand and help the child with his conflicts. It is this communication between parent and child that helps the child mature wisely."

My parents also encouraged me to embark on a career. When I refused to become the lawyer my father wished me to be, wanting instead to write exciting fiction and nonfiction rather than dry legal briefs, he did not object but encouraged me. He called Mr. Sulzberger, asked if there was an opening on the *Times,* as a result of which I became a reporter.

The question of questions: How does analysis change you? I can only describe the ways I believe it changed me. And is still changing me. I accepted Dr. Aiken's belief I could not depend on the analyst the rest of my life without continuing to cripple myself.

Perhaps the most important change is that I act more out of "choice" than "compulsion." I am no longer driven so obsessively by the unconscious—we are always somewhat under its power but far less as we know ourselves. Now I weigh the consequences of an act. Then decide whether to act—"to be" or "not to be" in control of my feelings.

Primitive man and the child act on impulse. The mature adult accepts his impulses as natural but controls outwardly destructive and self-destructive ones. If the murderer could do this he would not kill, nor would the incestuous parent seduce his child.

The ability to use choice over compulsion is a measure of maturity. It brings a pleasurable, calming feeling. Several months after analysis ended I had the chance to sell my apartment and make a profit of fifty thousand dollars when the building suddenly went cooperative. I decided to remain as a renter, for there was a noneviction plan. I will move when I *choose* to move, I thought. I wrote four lines to express my new feeling of calm in the face of this important decision:

> Down with rigidity
> On a par with frigidity
>
> Up with relaxing
> Compulsion is taxing

There is a wild, momentary, world-be-damned pleasure in carrying through on an impulse every so often. But holding back on a destructive act may save your life. The unprecedented demand for cocaine and other drugs brings a temporary sense of euphoria to the addict but often also death. Life requires most of us work and live using our good sense, not seek a way out of what seems a hopeless stupor. The false emotional "pickup" of drugs and alcohol only promotes violence on the self and others.

I no longer confuse joy with indulgence. Joy holds a certain elation yet there is freedom in it. Not wild freedom but a controlled freedom that does not hurt others. Indulgence is letting go for selfish pleasure alone.

Another important change is that I no longer feel the helpless innocent victim as I did before analysis. I now accept I am the cause of my suffering. I refuse to automatically blame others. I feel empathy for them rather than anger.

I value highly two qualities I have achieved in greater depth. Patience and persistence. They developed imperceptibly. I did not set out to acquire them. Change does not occur by conscious edict but by working for awareness of hidden fantasies and wishes.

My motto had been "Damn the unconscious, full speed ahead." When I first started on the couch, the moments I moved with ease and assurance were rare as a rainbow—how seldom we take time to delight in the beauty of a rainbow's subtle colors. I feel more patient with myself and others now.

I had possessed more of a super-id than super-ego. I lived in synthetic drama. I drove a car fast, walked fast, worked at hurricane speed. I hurtled to wherever I headed, only to race away once I arrived.

All my life the hardest thing in the world to do

was—nothing. My father complained, "You've got ants in your pants, can't you ever sit still?" The combination of "ants" and "pants" infuriated me. I loathed the little black scurrying creatures (my brother and sisters?) and I associated "pants" with his assaulting my rear when I wet the bed at the age of two. My father also rebuked, "Haste makes waste," which I vaguely believed but could not honor, driven by inner demons.

Now I could drive a car more slowly, work more slowly, walk the street more slowly. I could stroll rather than race. Life no longer was a splash and a dash but enjoyment of the moment. I found a new sense of leisure in reading, writing, shopping for food or clothes, dancing, theater, bridge, poker and dining out. I no longer feared the unconscious hostile and sexual impulses that might break loose if there was time on my hands.

Hours pass, sometimes days, even weeks and I do not write a word yet feel no guilt because I have thrown away the day. I had used writing to escape feelings of abandonment, grief, anger, depression.

Buddy Hackett told Cindy Adams, as she reported in her column in *The New York Post* on November 23, 1987, he wanted to retire. She asked, "What do you want to do?" He answered, "I've done it all and I don't need the money. I don't want to *do* anything. I want *not* to do. I want to think." I knew what he meant. I wanted time to think and be, all pressure removed.

Recently over lunch at her office I asked my friend Harriet Pilpel, one of the hardest working lawyers I know, "Have you ever thought of retiring and just doing nothing?" Harriet is counsel for the Planned Parenthood Federation of America. She is also a former board member and now a vice-chairman of the national advisory council of the American Civil Liberties Union—in addition to her busy life at Weil, Gotshal and Manges.

Harriet gave my question a few moments thought,

then said, "I don't think I could ever do nothing. If I don't have anything for my mind to bite on, I'm afraid it will bite on itself." Then asked, "Could you do nothing?"

"I'd like to try but don't really believe I could," I said. "At least not for long. Maybe a week or two."

While I may dream of living in a small house in Montauk, surrounded by the sea, I know in my heart I could stand the isolation only a few months, then feel driven to dash for the plane to Manhattan.

At times I enjoy the fantasy I will leave New York City and the writer's world of gambling. Writers spend years producing books and gamble they will pay off. Publishers take a gamble on the books, though they cannot guarantee a best-seller except in rare instances. Literary agents gamble they can sell authors to the publishing world. But then many businesses are also gambles, as is the world of art, movies, plays.

I still enjoy the races though I am far from an addict. Dr. Edmund Bergler, psychoanalyst, in his book on gambling, describes the gambler as a masochist. He maintains all gamblers unconsciously seek to lose in order to punish themselves for what they believe wicked thoughts and deeds.

When I worked at the *Times* I started to go occasionally to Belmont and Aqueduct with John Willig, a writer in the Sunday department. In Chicago I went to the track several times with Nelson Algren, once took my twelve-year-old niece Jan, visiting from Florida. She put me to shame, picked a winner in every race, has never gone since. Instead of using her talent at the track, she is a social worker with a master's degree and lives outside Albany in Delmar, with her thirteen-year-old son, Atman.

Today I bet perhaps once a month, usually in the company of my friend Marjorie Krimsley. To make life easier The Inside Track on Second Avenue and Fifty-fourth Street has come to Manhattan. You walk upstairs, pay five dollars admission, sit at a table where you may order lunch when ready, watch the odds change, study *The Racing Forum*, bet at a window that resembles those at the outdoor track, then watch the race on television screens.

We make sensible two-dollar bets, occasionally take a chance on a long shot. Each rarely spends more than sixty dollars, which covers entrance fee, food and the horses. Occasionally we earn a small profit if a long shot comes in or our daily double or "box" succeeds. On the whole we lose but consider it equal to paying for a Broadway play.

I have not approached a horse nearer than the rail at Belmont or Aqueduct since my memorable experience at Estes Park aboard Cocoa. I am content to use my energy cheering my choice, knowing though my purse may be at stake, my life is not.

I was asked recently by Ruth Cavin, a prominent editor of mystery books, "Do you enjoy the races if you do not bet on a horse?"

I thought for a moment, said, "No, I don't. I have never not bet. Except when I watch the big races on television."

I need to be part of the action by placing a bet on the horse. What does this mean psychologically? For one thing, that I identify with the horse I have chosen as the winner. This is an aggressive feeling, I want to beat the system, expect my horse to vanquish all other horses. If he loses I have somehow lost to the system, berate myself for failing to win. Who wants to be a loser? Perhaps horse players are driven by the echo of parental voices cheering us on to win at school, win at the playground, win at life and, when we lose at the track, feel rejected by those we love. Bergler may be right about the masochism of bettors, they lose far more often than they win.

One very strong unconscious drive is also present at the track (where is it not?). There is a subliminal erotic quality to the sport of racing. Rider "mounts" horse. Horse "shoots out of" the gate. "Charges" down the track. Gains speed toward the "finish." Winds up "sweaty" and "spent."

There is also the hidden fear of danger and violence, a vicarious thrill felt throughout the running of the race. One horse may crash into another or jump the fence. Both horse and rider are sometimes severely injured in a spill, the jockey may wind up in a hospital, even die in rare instances on the track. Jockeys may "accidentally on purpose" cut each other off, slam into each other. A jockey may whip a horse mercilessly, one jockey blinded a horse striking his eye with a whip.

Sometimes a horse destroys itself. Marjorie and I had tears in our eyes July 7, 1975, when Ruffian, who had won ten races in a row, ridden by Jacinto Vasquez, went down during a two-horse race called "The Great Match." Foolish Pleasure, the other contender, was ridden by Braulio Baeza. The champion filly hit her foot on the steel gate as she broke out of it but then appeared to regain footing. Midway down the back stretch she tried to overtake Foolish Pleasure, stumbled and broke her foreleg. An ambulance took her away, veterinarians tried but could not save her, the damage too severe.

Foolish Pleasure trotted the rest of the way home almost halfheartedly, as though Baeza did not know whether to finish the race. I reluctantly cashed my two-dollar winning ticket, said to Marjorie, "I'll buy flowers for Ruffian." She was buried, as a tombstone verifies, in the grass directly behind the winning post at Belmont.

In the train returning home we sat in silence, stunned by the equine tragedy. Marjorie's eyes every so often filled with tears. She feels more deeply for horses than I do, photographs and paintings of them adorn her apartment in mid-Manhattan. She even wears necklaces with silver horses dangling from them.

I discovered in my new thoughtfulness away from the couch that I mistook rebellion for courage, danger for excitement. I courted perilous missions. Flew low in a plane over Texas City during explosions erupting from the two burning ships that might have blown our plane to pieces. Rode a risky elevator to the top of the Empire State Building the day after a plane crashed into it, demolishing a whole floor. This was not courage but daredevil act. Real courage entails facing the unconscious wishes that "make cowards" of us all.

As a result of analysis I understand that every one of us lives as we wish and can deeply influence only the self. I cannot live for anyone else. It is all I can do to live for myself. I tried to live for two husbands, give them all my energy, attention, love, please them in every respect. But I could satisfy only the self, control only the self.

I do not wish to control others (having suffered so deeply at the control of parents). I never, *never* tell people how to lead their lives. They will only hate me. Each person must decide how he wishes to exist, think, feel.

I accept our differences—differences in the way we think, taste in art, clothing, furniture, paintings on the wall, pleasures. No one has to be my clone, as perhaps my parents wished me to be for them.

I try to keep my mouth shut even when someone asks for advice (as my psychoanalyst did with me). I listen with far more interest to what others say, at times understanding what they "unreally" mean underneath the spoken word.

I will make observations if I feel strongly about a

subject, such as psychoanalysis or a Presidential election or the merits of the Mets. I no longer get upset when someone disagrees with me even in violent fashion. I do not need the approval of others to feel self-worth. It is my own approval that matters.

I called Dr. Aiken to ask if he wished to read in advance what I wrote about my analysis with him for this book. He replied, in a reassuring voice, "No. I don't have to read it." I said in amazement, "But suppose I've written something you would like taken out?" He said, "It's your book." I told him, gratitude in my voice, "Thank you for your trust." He trusted me and my trust in myself rose. This is how children learn to trust themselves.

I wish to be needed but not possessed. At long last I do not accede to every demand as a wish I must fulfill. I am able to say "no" to those who try to take advantage of me, demean, exploit or control me. I can also bear someone else's quiet "no" without feeling pulverized.

As I feel less despair, anger, guilt, I demand less of myself and others. I am no longer so driven by the inner fantasy world, I understand how it arose and its irrational demands at times.

I have stopped judging myself so harshly, which means I have stopped judging others so harshly. If there is one thing of which I am sure, it is that the more understanding we are of ourselves, the more understanding we are of others. In large part we acquire the need to be critical from our parents. One friend angrily spouts unkind words about everyone. As I listen to her mother slash verbally into her, I understand why my friend obsessively carries out the same attack on others. Her defense tells of how she has been treated.

My energy has increased threefold. I can write twelve hours a day if need be without feeling tired and work with far more pleasure. I no longer require energy to hold back fantasies and wishes believed dangerous, ready to burst out of control.

At long last I am aware of the drastic difference between romantic love and mature love. Romantic love centers on childish fantasies that whirl within. It keeps us from caring tenderly and unselfishly for someone else, insists our needs be taken care of first. Mature love does not demand possession of the other person, possessive love is the feeling of a child for the parent upon whom he depends for his very life. Mature love contains the realization neither the self nor the loved one can be perfect, accepts imperfections in both. Mature love also recognizes each has the right to privacy at times.

Did I feel "dis-illusioned" as a result of analysis? Hopefully I did, recognizing the high price paid for illusions. As you become aware of illusions, know childish wishes cannot be fulfilled, you feel far more in control of your life. Becoming aware of reality gives you the true power.

Analysis also helped me acknowledge jealousy as a natural feeling. I now handle it more comfortably, know it arises out of childish needs for love and attention, know also that jealousy, when extreme, can cause endless suffering.

I try to be aware of the "repetition compulsion," avoid it as though it were the psychic plague. You perpetuate your suffering when you remain trapped by a fantasy or fear that drives you to repeat an act that brings only despair. The more I faced what I fantasied or feared, the less desperate I felt and the easier it became to give up destructive acts such as eating the wrong food or allowing others to control me.

I discovered a body change as a result of analysis. I stood straighter, my shoulders thrown back. I laughed, remembering Granny's concern about my posture when she bought an iron contraption for me to wear under my dress in high school, so large and ugly that, sensing my distress, Mother soon threw it in the garbage. I also now treat my body less roughly, using a tender touch seldom shown by Mother. Formerly, in the shower I scrubbed hard—out, out, damned dirt, as Mother instructed. Now I slowly and gently soap my skin, let the warm water soothingly carry soap and dirt down the drain. I take time to use a sweet-smelling powder, then perfume.

Remembering my mother I try not to be seduced by suffering. This was one of her unconscious ploys to persuade us to do what she wished. Suffering may be used in a warped, distorted way by those in emotional pain to extort love from others. As Bel Kaufman, author of *Up the Down Staircase,* once put it, "Pain is not enobling. It's debasing, like poverty. Happiness is ennobling."

At long last I feel I am permitted to be wrong at times. Dr. Emch started to free me from such guilt when she apologized after I accused her of sounding sarcastic like my father. I realized she was entitled to imperfections and I, too, did not have to be that perfect little girl who never uttered a curse or dirty word, never upset the laundry pile. I no longer feel so consumed by unreal guilt. As I became aware of its roots in fantasy it vanished like a psychic cloud of smoke. To quote Browning: "Oh, fancies that might be, oh facts that are!" This does not mean I do not feel guilt when I deserve it, if I hurt someone unfairly or speak thoughtlessly. Guilt is needed to keep us honest and from hurting others.

Formerly I lost my temper at what I call the "emotional illiterates." Those who unfairly attack psychoanalysis or those who never question why they feel angry but inflict their rage on others. I now feel sorry for them, know I cannot change them or lessen their anger—it is all I can do to slowly change myself, lessen my anger. I possess faith in analysis as a strong science of the psyche that will survive on its own and grow even stronger over the years, as it has in the past. It is part of our culture—the law, the medical profession, colleges and universities, high schools, even the stock market, influenced by psychological swings of customers and brokers.

More and more men and women accept the words of Freud as he wrote in a letter to the young writer Bruno Goetz: "My purpose is to help as well as I can the many people who today live internally in hell. My scientific findings, my theories and methods, aim at making them conscious of this hell so that they will be able to free themselves from it."

Nothing is simple when it comes to human behavior. There is no one answer. The accumulated traumas in every life and the unique way each of us responds makes Einstein's theory of relativity seem easy to understand. We all possess many levels of awareness. We "internalize" different parts of our parents. We hold hundreds of fantasies, undercover thoughts and feelings.

I formerly wailed, "Who am I, apart from my parents' patchwork parts of me?" I referred particularly to my "identification with the aggressor," a phrase Anna Freud coined (who wants to be a victim?) The aggressor may be either or both parents. I had never openly dared be the aggressor except when tackling a story for the *Times*.

Via the analysis with Dr. Aiken I realized the world was not the wonderland of childhood but quite a dangerous place. As it has been since man emerged from the cave. And in the Middle Ages when the cry of religion during the Crusades sanctioned the murder of millions. And in America when the first settlers stepped on the shores of Plymouth and faced Indians. Danger today stirs the very air we breathe, tainted by chemical wastes from nuclear plants and automobiles and trucks as well as destruction of the ozone layer.

There are those who believe greed too strong in human nature to allow man to change. But if enough statesmen throughout the world understood the price paid by mankind as a result of greed and the wish to dominate, perhaps we might reduce warfare. Lloyd De-Mause, psychohistorian and founder of the International Psychohistorical Society, says, "War is a great fantasy that gives people the opportunity to act out their private fantasies of murder and sex."

When I first lay down on the couch I felt a strange exhilaration. I believed I embarked on a journey into the unknown from which I hoped to emerge far happier. I never wanted that journey to end. I felt stricken with grief when I started to go it alone. It was difficult to separate emotionally from the analyst, who listened to my every word. Helped me face with greater psychic valor the darkness I believed lay ahead without his constant wisdom.

I departed uttering the silent scream. I did not want to leave yet knew it was time. In contrast to the separation from my mother when I fled to Manhattan and *The New York Times*, deserting her. Now I was the one deserted—at last I knew how Mother felt. Knew also the power of the ties of childhood. You can flee to the opposite ends of the earth but the ties—either in affirmation or rebellion—remain.

Then I enjoyed a new vital discovery: Analysis within never ends. I could explore memories and fantasies until I died, experiencing them in ever greater depth. As I have done so, I have become more independent. I function far more effectively on my own without the need of a mothering person.

Do I miss Chicago? I will always miss Dr. Emch, she is now a part of my thoughtfulness. I have kept up my friendship with the Paleys, who gave me the fare-well party, with Deborah and Robert Cunningham, who became my Chicago family, and with Rhoda Pritzker, wife of the late Jack Pritzker. Rhoda, a former member of the board of directors of the Chicago Institute for Psychoanalysis, describes analysis as "a maturing pro-cess that helps one find inner peace, brings an aware-ness of the self, no matter what the age—six or sixty."

I take pleasure in the apartment where I have lived for thirteen years. The view of Central Park offers con-stant beauty. It is like living in the country if I shut my eyes to skyscrapers on three sides that frame an always shifting scene. There is the quiet of the early morning except for the chirp of birds before their swift flight from rooftops to trees. Maples and ginkgos line the southern strip of the park outside my windows. In win-ter the snow falls lightly on skeleton trees and huge rocks hidden in summer by bushes, transforming the park into white fragility.

During July and August the high winds of a sudden storm toss the sea of trees around like ballet dancers spinning on a carpet of grass. Each summer the trees become fuller, taller, forest-thick. In autumn the park blazes with fall's fiery pyre of leaves that slowly drift to earth. During each season fog occasionally rolls in, settles in waves between the trees, which then resemble rows of miniature mountains.

The sun rises in red glory to the right, the sunset unfolds to the west. A new painting stretches across the sky almost every evening. There seems a palette in the heavens out of which flows clouds of deep purple to mauve, fiery red to pale pink, mixed with green, yellow and orange. No two clouds are ever shaped the same.

Strange sounds occasionally reach my ears on the nineteenth floor. The trumpet of an elephant in the zoo, the bark of a seal, the neigh of a dilapidated horse in the park as it pulls a carriage weighted down with tourists around winding curves. This symphony of city sounds has become part of what is now a comfortable home for a former rebel who moved every two years. An analyst once remarked that those who have difficulty facing deep feelings may often move frequently, as though a new place will magically change their lives.

I accept at last the painful fact my fantasies kept me from achieving a solid lasting relationship with a man. My relationships were always based on passionate persiflage. Today, acceptance of realistic conflicts has supplanted useless self-pity because of fruitless attempts to relate to a man.

I could never be a child again nor could I, as a result of analysis, grow up "right" the second time around. But I could learn from the past so I could influence my future.

I still have far to go but only I know how far I have come. I have learned of hope, not the false hope of the past that blinded the mind's eyes but a new kind of hope. Based not on the fulfillment of forbidden wishes of the past (that forever press for fulfillment, Freud said) but wishes of a more mature nature that do not unconsciously call forth guilt.

I have tried to come to terms with feelings that disturbed me at the ages of two, four, six and every other year of my life. As I developed physically, sexually and intellectually, my fantasies and desires became increasingly more complex. One feeling might negate another. There was inconsistency in how I met difficult moments. Not just one fantasy but a "constellation" of fantasies, as noted psychoanalyst Dr. Jacob Arlow describes it, were connected to each experience, each memory. There was a raft of reasons for any one act.

The severity of our scars from what Freud described as "inner bleeding" depends on what aroused the wrath of a parent and the type of punishment. Parents have the privilege of power and control. The two dictators in my life were more than I could handle at times. I early learned to seduce them with sweetness and sadness, as if to beg, Don't hurt me, with your hands or words or the tone of your voice. I idolized them but unfortunately idolatry holds deep fear.

Children are asked to accept as reality what the parent sees as reality. If the parent lives in unreality to a large degree, so will the child (how murderous wishes start when violence stirs the air). If a parent calls a child "idiot," the child will feel like an idiot, act like an idiot.

I now possess more money, no longer needing to invest it in analysis (I told those who criticized me for the money I spent on analysis, "It is the best investment I could have made"). Freud said, "Happiness is the deferred fulfillment of a prehistoric wish. This is why wealth brings so little happiness; money is not an infantile wish." But money may be an aphrodisiac. The "sweet smell of money" is seductive, money can buy anything you covet. You feel more secure when you possess money. It gives the temporary gloss of self-esteem.

Money can bring everything but surcease from tormenting fears, furies and frustrated sexual desires. Though as one seer said, it is better to possess money and feel frustrated than to be poor and frustrated.

I have tried to tell troubled people, "You don't have to suffer. There *is* help out there." Recently I received a heartening letter from a man in Kansas, who wrote he had read my first book *Fight Against Fears:*

> Everyone thinks farmers are simple men who live contented lives. But, at least in my case, this is not the truth. I grew up on a farm, the son of a fairly prosperous farmer, and decided, after mar-

rying a young girl whom I had known since grammar school, to stay on my father's farm and carry
on.

Dad died a few years ago (mother died many
years ago) and my wife, our two children and I
have been making a go of the farm but not of our
lives. I don't know what happened but after a few
years of marriage, we started quarreling. I didn't
know what to do, so I would take long walks up and
down the hills, stroll the paths, look at the night
sky fiery with bright stars and wonder if people in
the city went through such misery, too.

Then I picked up some books about how emotional troubles could make people unhappy no matter where they lived or how much money they had.
It advised seeing a psychiatrist if one felt deeply
upset.

Luckily, there is a new, large general hospital
not far from us and I went there to see a psychiatrist who is in charge of the clinic. He has been
helping me now for several months and I think I
am beginning to feel a change in myself. My wife,
too, wants to go to him but he is not sure he should
take two members of the same family and he says
another psychiatrist is about to move to town and
she should wait and go to him.

Anyhow, I thought I'd let you know that psychiatry is coming even to the farms of America!

A second letter from an entirely different locale, a
prison in Texas, arrived another day.

I am writing you this letter out of gratitude
for the books you have written telling people there
is help when they feel troubled. Without them I
don't believe I would ever have been able to stop

THE BELOVED PRISON VANISHES

and start looking inside myself to see what was really wrong with me.

At the present time I am in a mental institution for criminal prisoners. They send here prisoners who can't be controlled in a regular prison or reformatory, either because of violence, not being able to conform, or similar reasons. I was sent here because I was excessively violent and depressed at the time of my incarceration. The reasons for this I now know are that I thought that everyone hated me, so I in turn hated myself and everyone around and in order to keep them from knowing how I felt I would attack first to protect myself. I was taught very young that the best defense was the best offense and the one who attacked first had the best offensive and always won.

At least this is what I believed but I know now that I was very wrong. I still have many problems to overcome and hope that with the right kind of help and enough understanding on my part that eventually I will be able to make a good life for myself and live on better terms with the world and myself and if I don't, then I know there will be no one else to blame except myself for I'm not a child anymore as I'm 25 years of age.

I wish to say thank you for your book *Fight Against Fears* for at the time I read it I was at the rock bottom of despair and depression. I had tried to kill myself several times and was still contemplating doing so, but when I started reading your book it caused me to stop and start thinking, and I said to myself, "What's wrong with you, boy? Don't you know that what you have been trying to do and what you are still about to do isn't what you really want? That all you are doing is running, running away from yourself and what's inside of you, and the reason you are doing this is because you are more afraid of what's inside you than you are of anything else."

Because your books have helped me to stop running away from myself and start looking for the truth of what I really am, I wish to thank you with all my heart, because I don't believe that I would be alive today if it hadn't of been for your books and I wouldn't be having another chance at life.

I felt deep gratitude at receiving this honest letter. At least I helped one person wish to keep living. I hope he is far happier, that somehow he reached an empathic therapist.

Looking back, I realize the truth of the old saying, "I have met the enemy and he is me." I can no longer blame my mother or father for my unhappiness. I know they loved me as best they could. Dr. Helene Deutsch, noted psychoanalyst, wrote that when we understand ourselves, we understand our parents, forgive both ourselves and our parents, then realize there is nothing to forgive.

As I could free feelings and fantasies of the past that led to destructive and/or seductive liaisons that proved dangerous (Tom might have killed me in a drunken moment, I might have died during the first abortion), I became aware I had unconsciously sought such danger. I acted out childhood experiences that had both terrorized and fascinated. I had sought rescue from their everlasting torment only to suffer a double dose.

At times I played my mother's role, victim of cruelties inflicted by a man. Other times I played the temptress, my father's second wife, as I seesawed between unconsciously copying the two women of my early life.

I dared my first marriage, which gave me a modicum of increased femininity, one year after starting with Dr. Thurrott, when there came a lessening of the fear that a man would treat me as my mother had been treated.

I thought of my books as babies—no coincidence each took about nine months to finish. When I handed in a book to an editor I felt it was dead and gone. I rushed on to another, as Mother rushed to produce babies, abandoning the previous one or ones as she had abandoned me.

I had tried to please my mother and father, be a devoted daughter-warrior. When I finally felt desperate enough, no one left to please, I sought analysts to rescue me.

I wound up knowing I had to rescue myself. Though I had failed in life's toughest assignment—to raise a child—I could salvage valuable knowledge gained in analysis, leave behind the partial shipwreck of my life.

The benefits of my analyses far outweighed a few destructive acts primarily by one analyst. I do not think I was an easy patient—are there any easy patients? I, of course, wanted to be the perfect patient, to win the analyst's love as I had tried so desperately over the years to win the love of my parents.

I am delighted to discover there *is* life after analysis. A life in which a certain peace with the past is achieved. I have faith the process of psychoanalysis will go on and on. I possess confidence in the more constructive aspects of my life as opposed to the destructive ones of former years. Changes appear small but the small changes create the larger ones.

Onward and upward into reason's light. As James Russell Lowell wrote: "They must upward still, and onward, who would keep abreast of Truth." The elusive truth that leads to fuller understanding of the hidden self.

I do not regret one second of my view from the couch. A view that enabled me to become my own therapist and thus escape the beloved prison of the past.

First the prison of childhood where my parents seemed the jailers. Then the prison of adulthood I imposed on myself, chained by fear and fantasy, locked in unconscious reign. Lastly, the prison of the couch, had I remained on it all my life.

To become free I had to understand the earlier torment, know life held both joy and sorrow, frustration and fulfillment. And that only love of and trust in the self could lead to love of and trust in others.

I finally believed, as Freud put it, "To be completely honest with the self is the best effort a human can make."

The best, and the most rewarding.